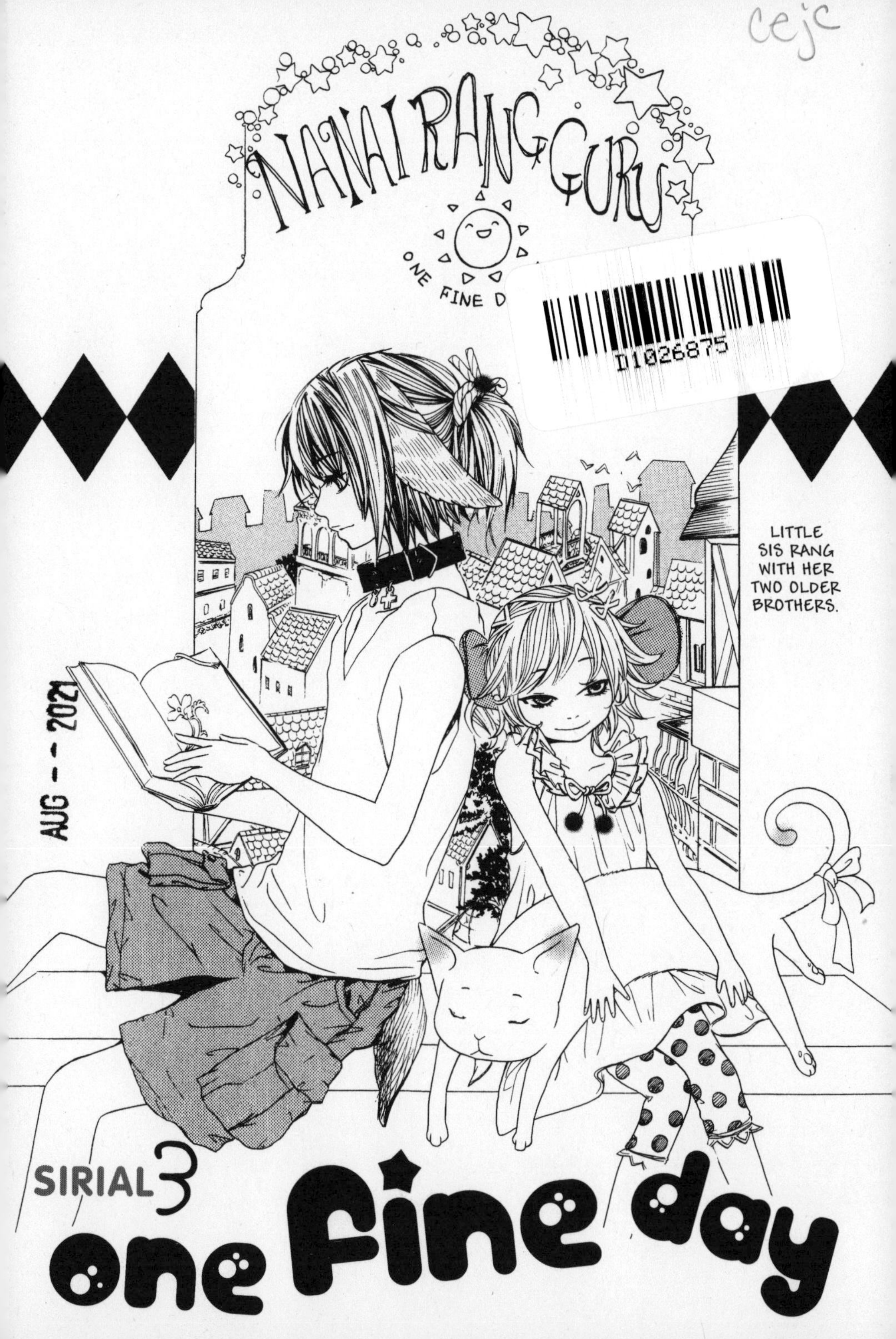
NANAI RANG GURU
ONE FINE D
LITTLE SIS RANG WITH HER TWO OLDER BROTHERS.
SIRIAL 3
one fine day

CONTENTS

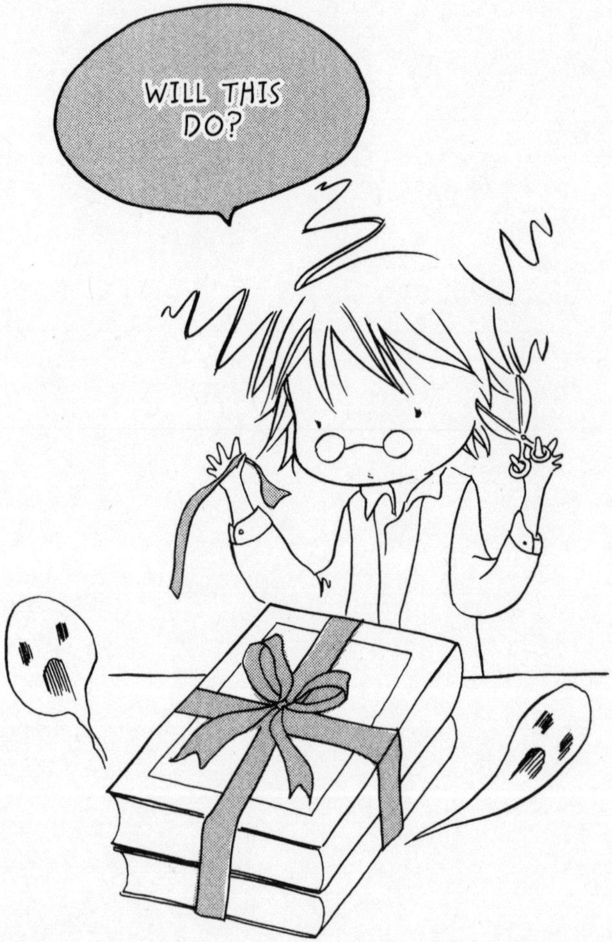
WILL THIS DO?

DAY 23.
INVITATION FROM SNOWLAND

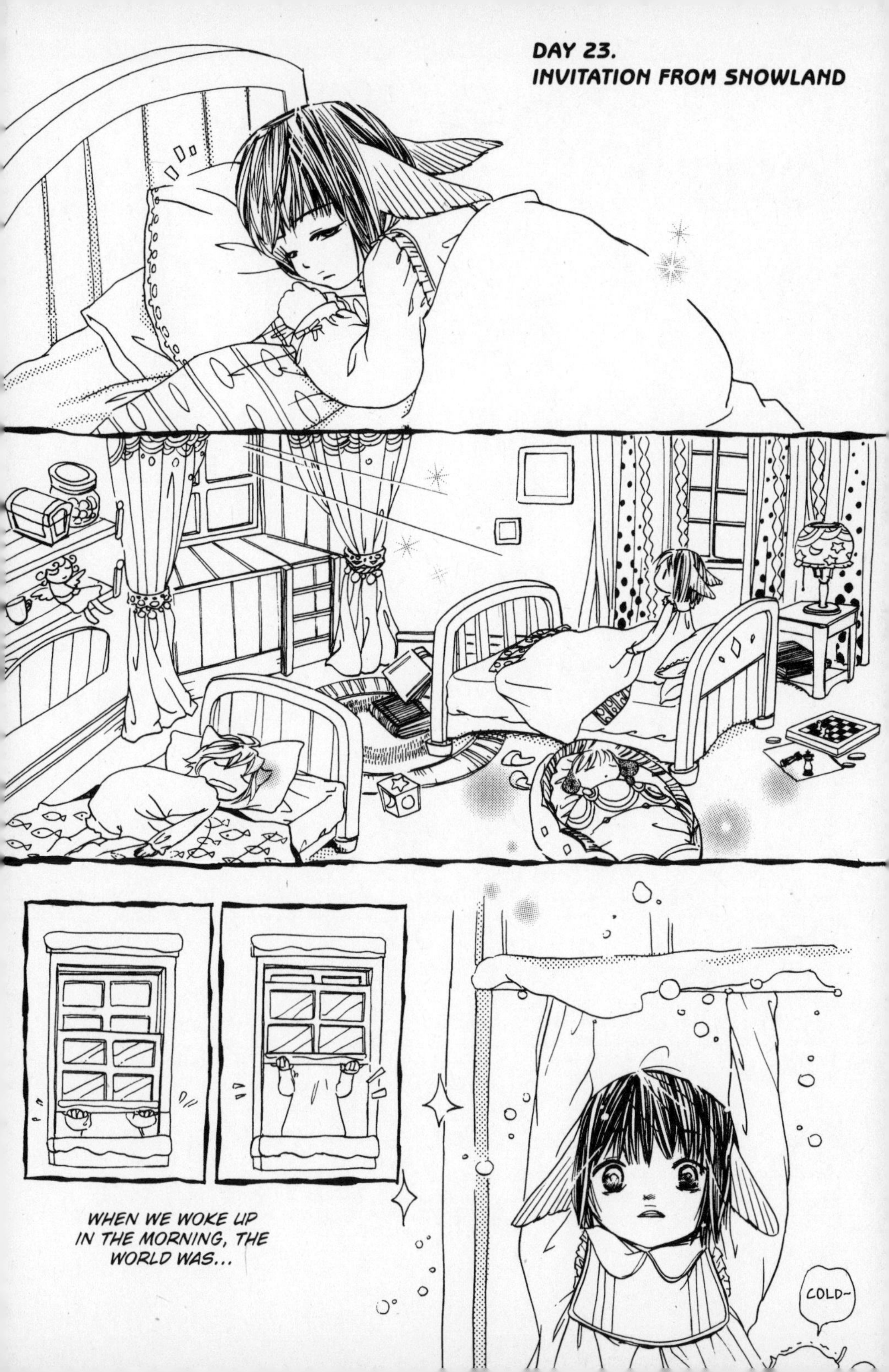
WHEN WE WOKE UP
IN THE MORNING, THE
WORLD WAS...
COLD~

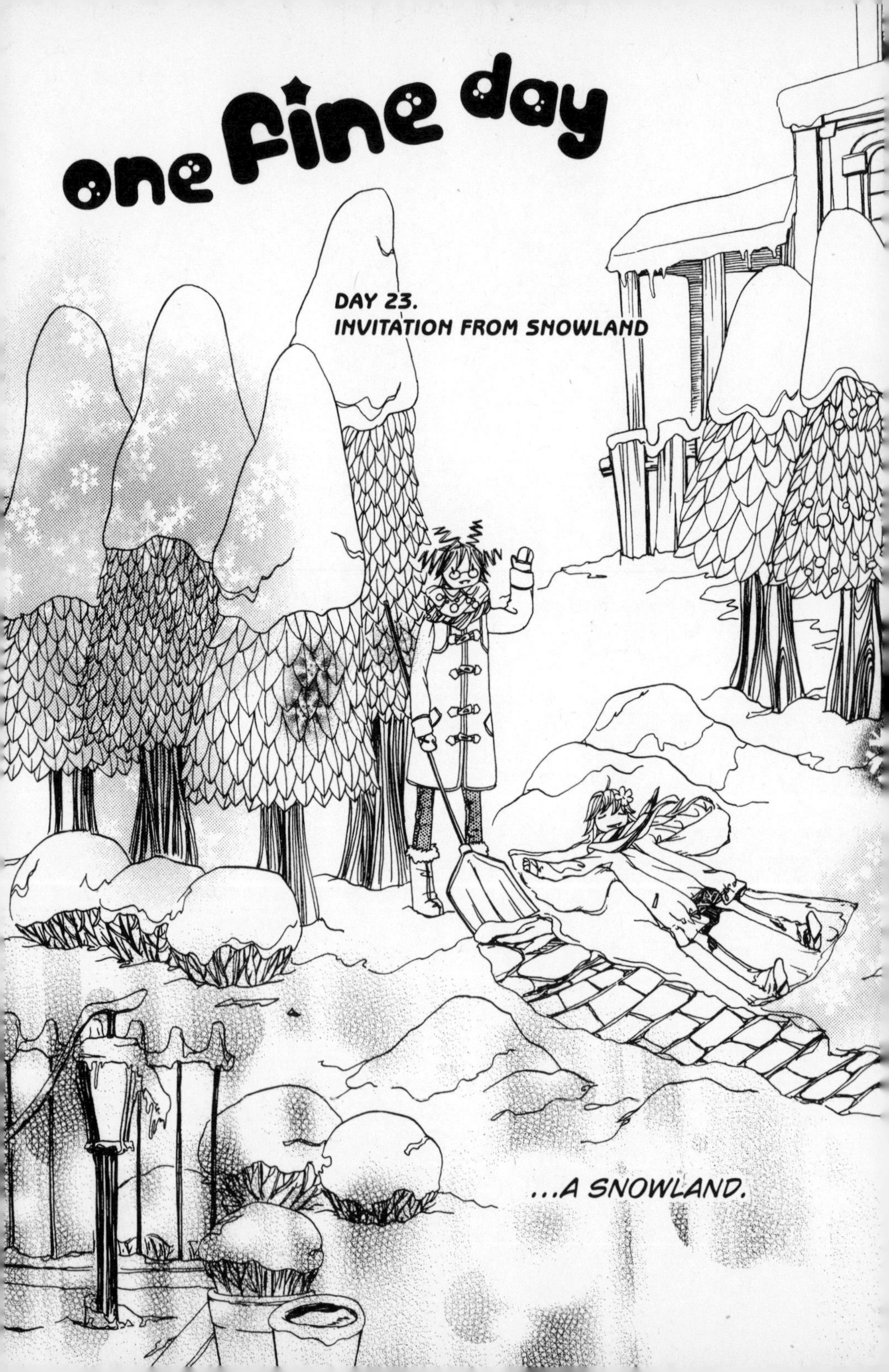
one Fine day
DAY 23.
INVITATION FROM SNOWLAND
...A SNOWLAND.

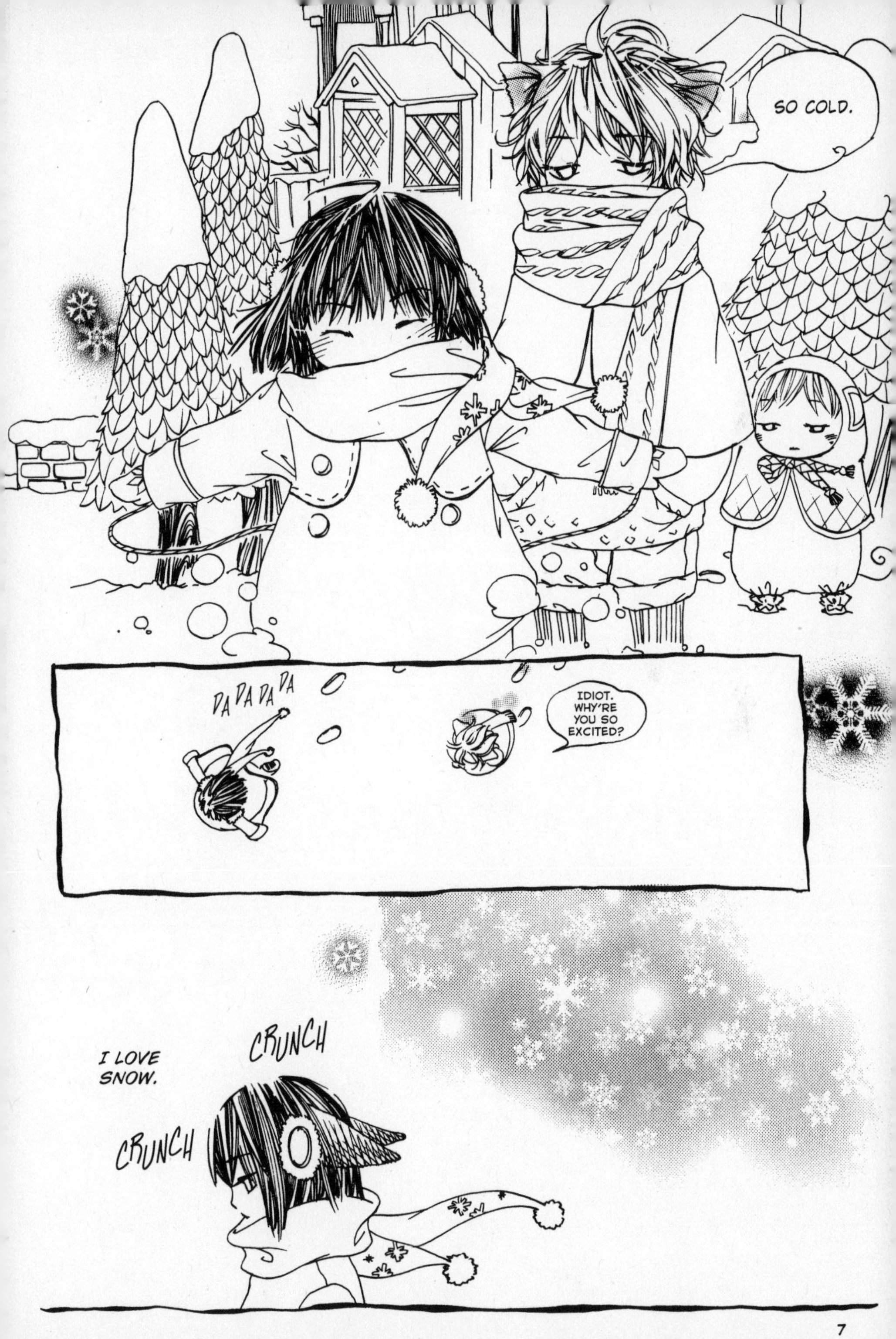
SO COLD.
DA DA DA DA
IDIOT. WHY'RE YOU SO EXCITED?
I LOVE SNOW.
CRUNCH
CRUNCH

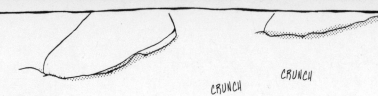

CRUNCH   CRUNCH

BUT WHEN
YOU WALK THROUGH
THE SNOW...

...EVEN WHEN
YOU'RE NOT ALONE,
IT FEELS LIKE
THERE'S ONLY YOU
IN THAT PLACE.

IT'S DIFFERENT
FROM LONELINESS...

...MORE LIKE
ANTICIPATION.

POW

HEH
HEH
HEH
        HEH

KYAAA!

KYAAA!

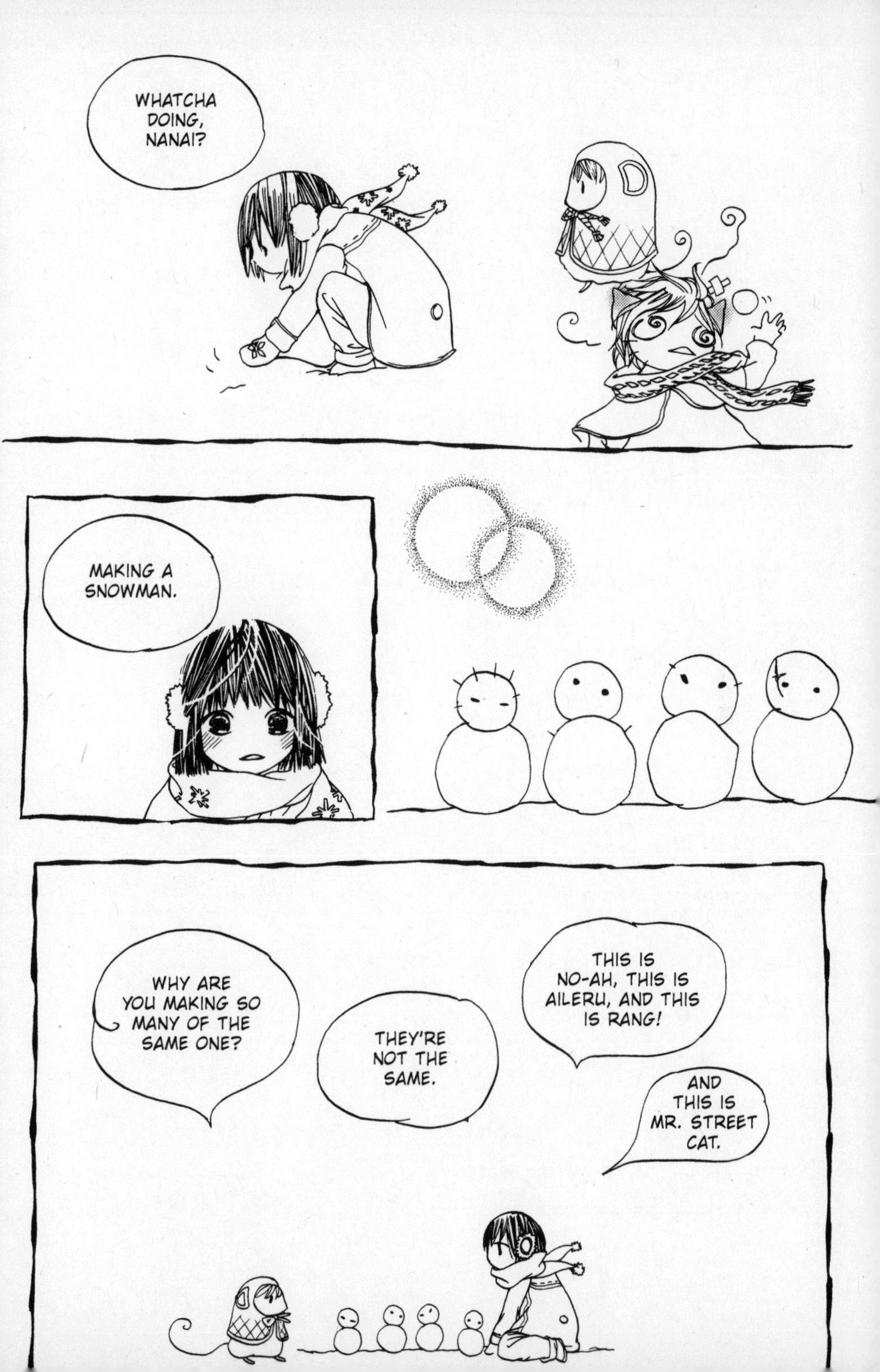
WHATCHA DOING, NANAI?
MAKING A SNOWMAN.
WHY ARE YOU MAKING SO MANY OF THE SAME ONE?
THEY'RE NOT THE SAME.
THIS IS NO-AH, THIS IS AILERU, AND THIS IS RANG!
AND THIS IS MR. STREET CAT.

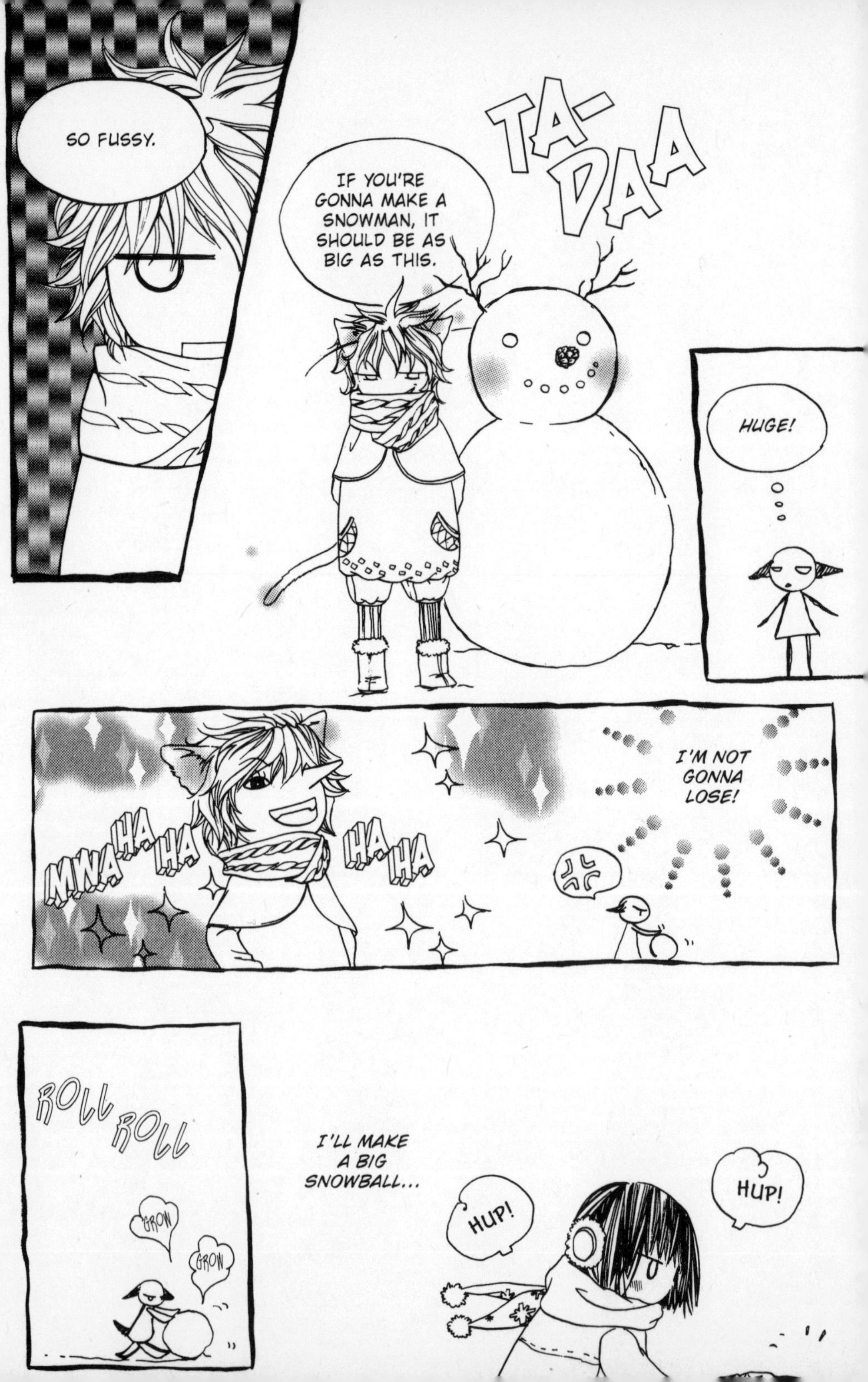
SO FUSSY.
TA-DAA
IF YOU'RE GONNA MAKE A SNOWMAN, IT SHOULD BE AS BIG AS THIS.
HUGE!
MWAHAHAHAHA
I'M NOT GONNA LOSE!
ROLL ROLL
GROW
GROW
I'LL MAKE A BIG SNOWBALL...
HUP!
HUP!

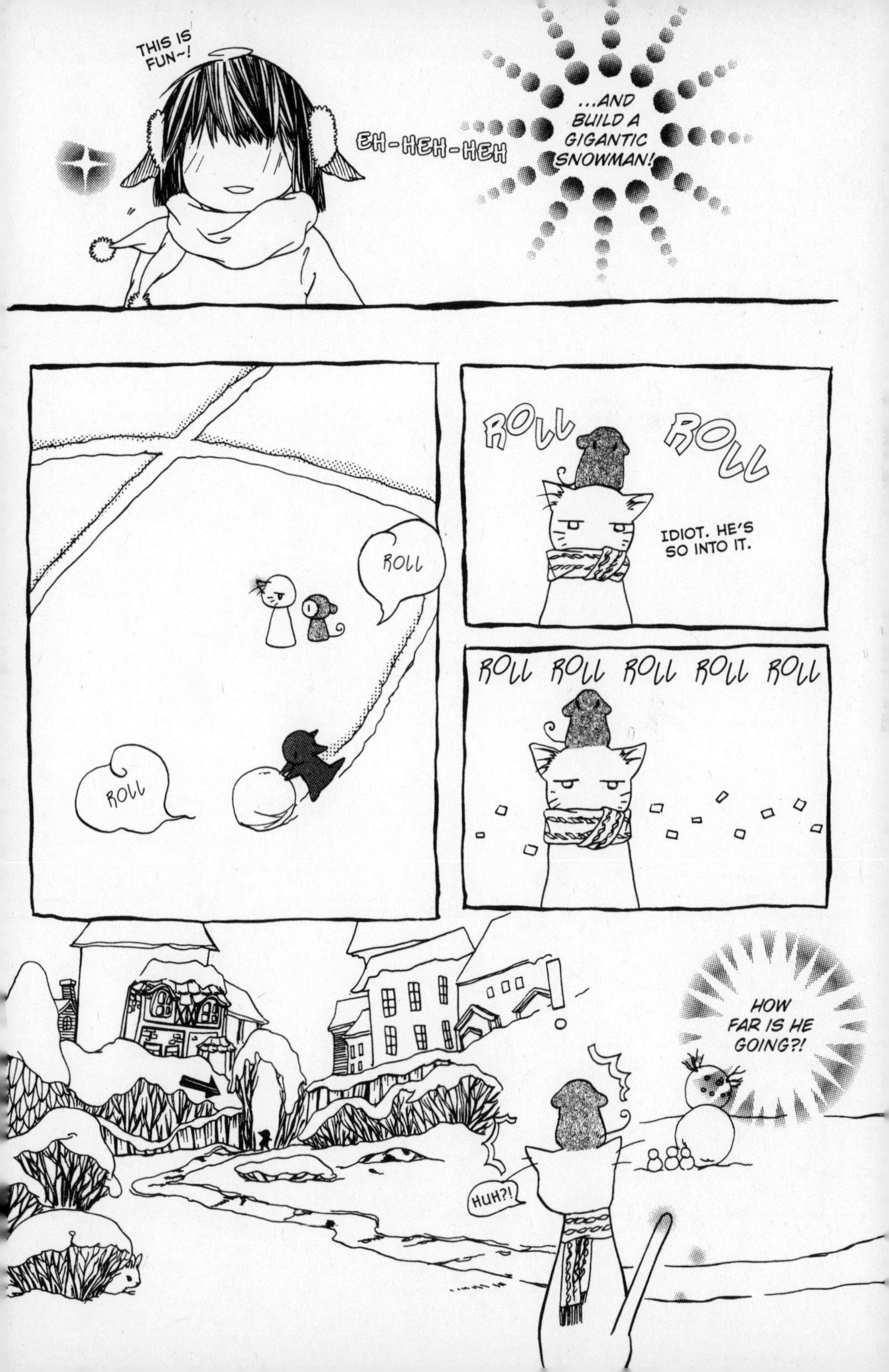
THIS IS FUN~!
EH-HEH-HEH
...AND BUILD A GIGANTIC SNOWMAN!
ROLL
ROLL
ROLL ROLL
IDIOT. HE'S SO INTO IT.
ROLL ROLL ROLL ROLL ROLL
HOW FAR IS HE GOING?!
HUH?!

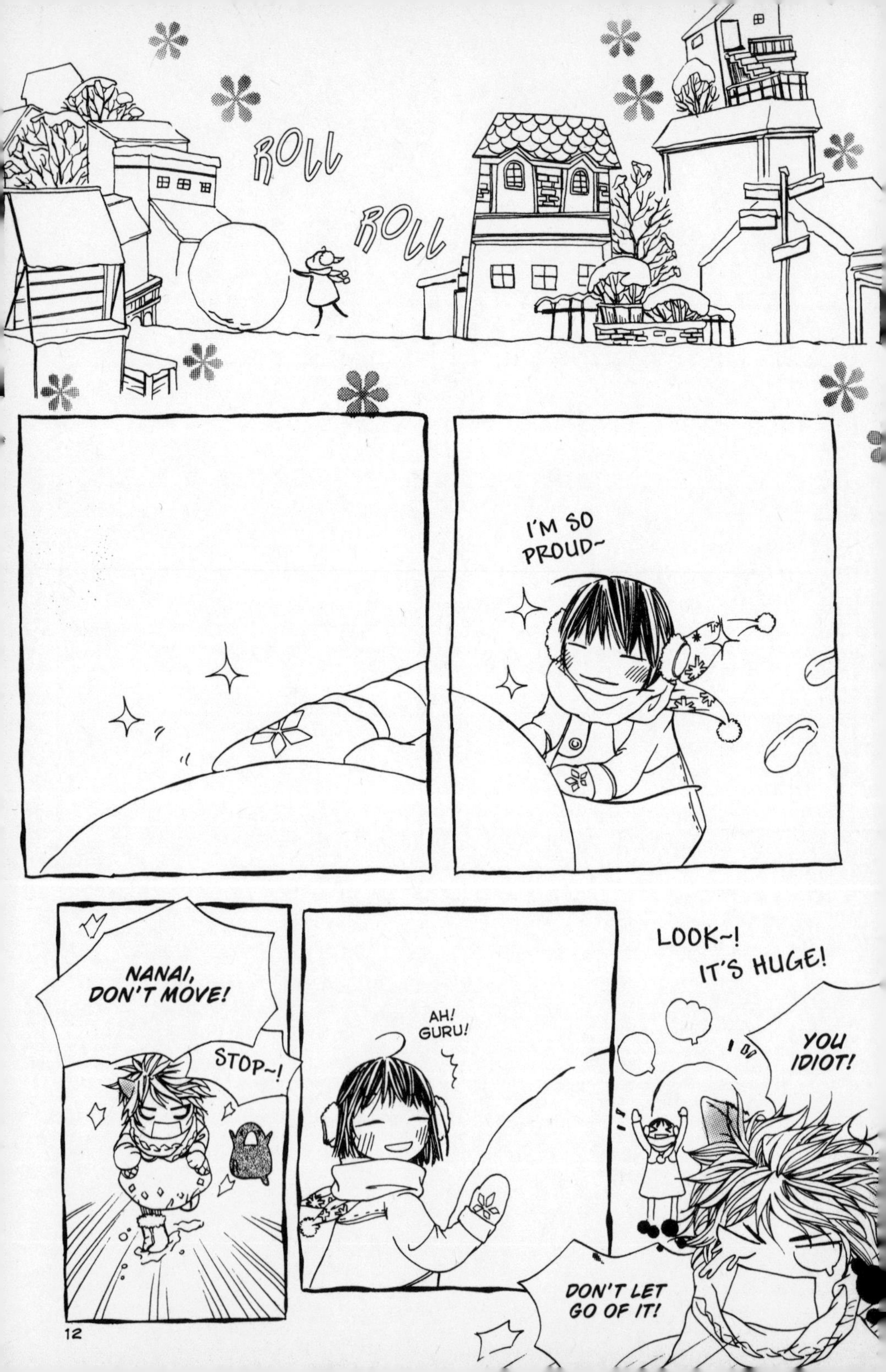
ROLL
ROLL
I'M SO PROUD~
LOOK~! IT'S HUGE!
YOU IDIOT!
DON'T LET GO OF IT!
AH! GURU!
NANAI, DON'T MOVE!
STOP~!

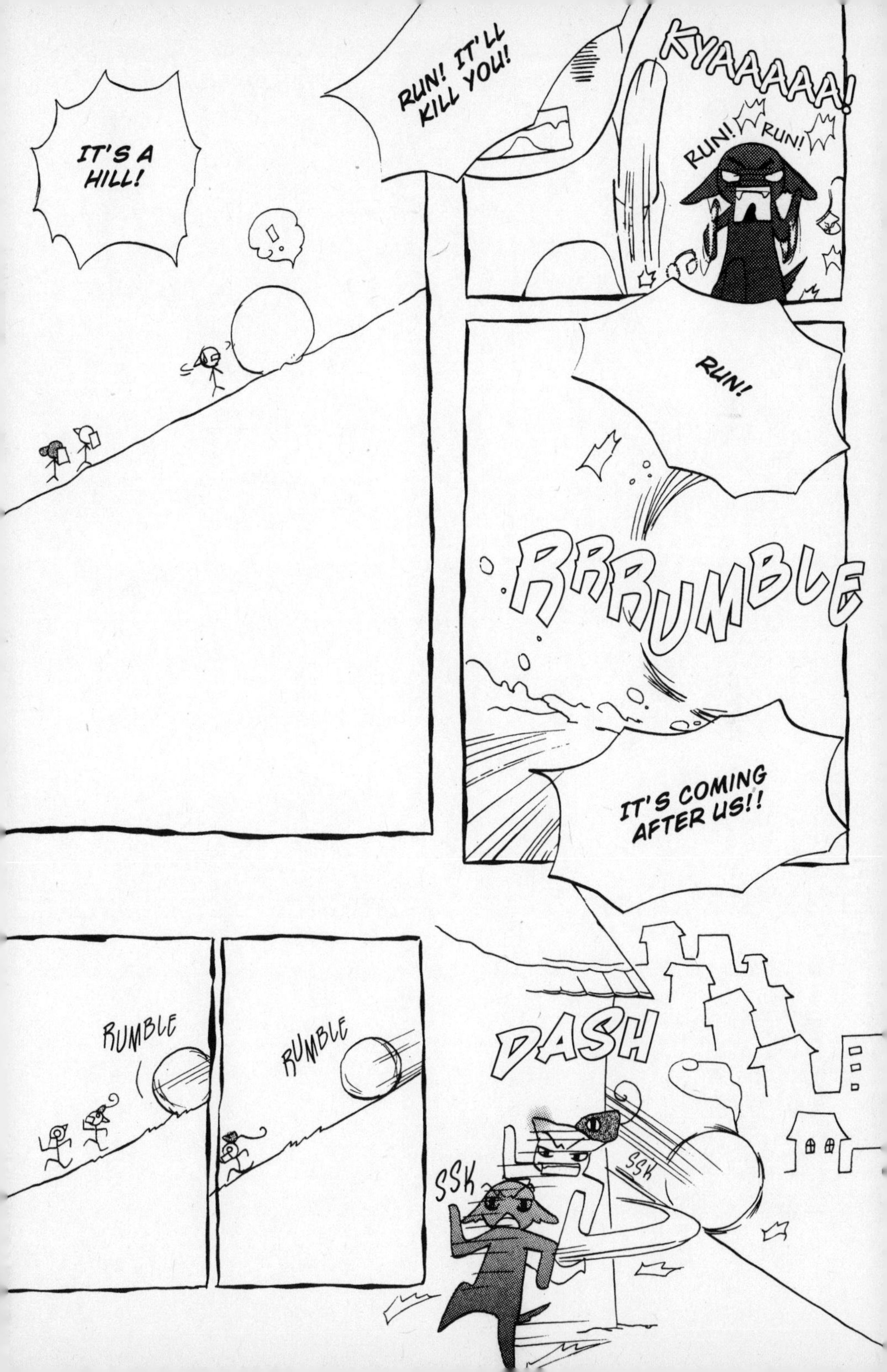

KYAAAAAA!
RUN! RUN!
RUN! IT'LL KILL YOU!
IT'S A HILL!
!
RUN!
RRRUMBLE
IT'S COMING AFTER US!!
DASH
SSK
SSK
RUMBLE
RUMBLE

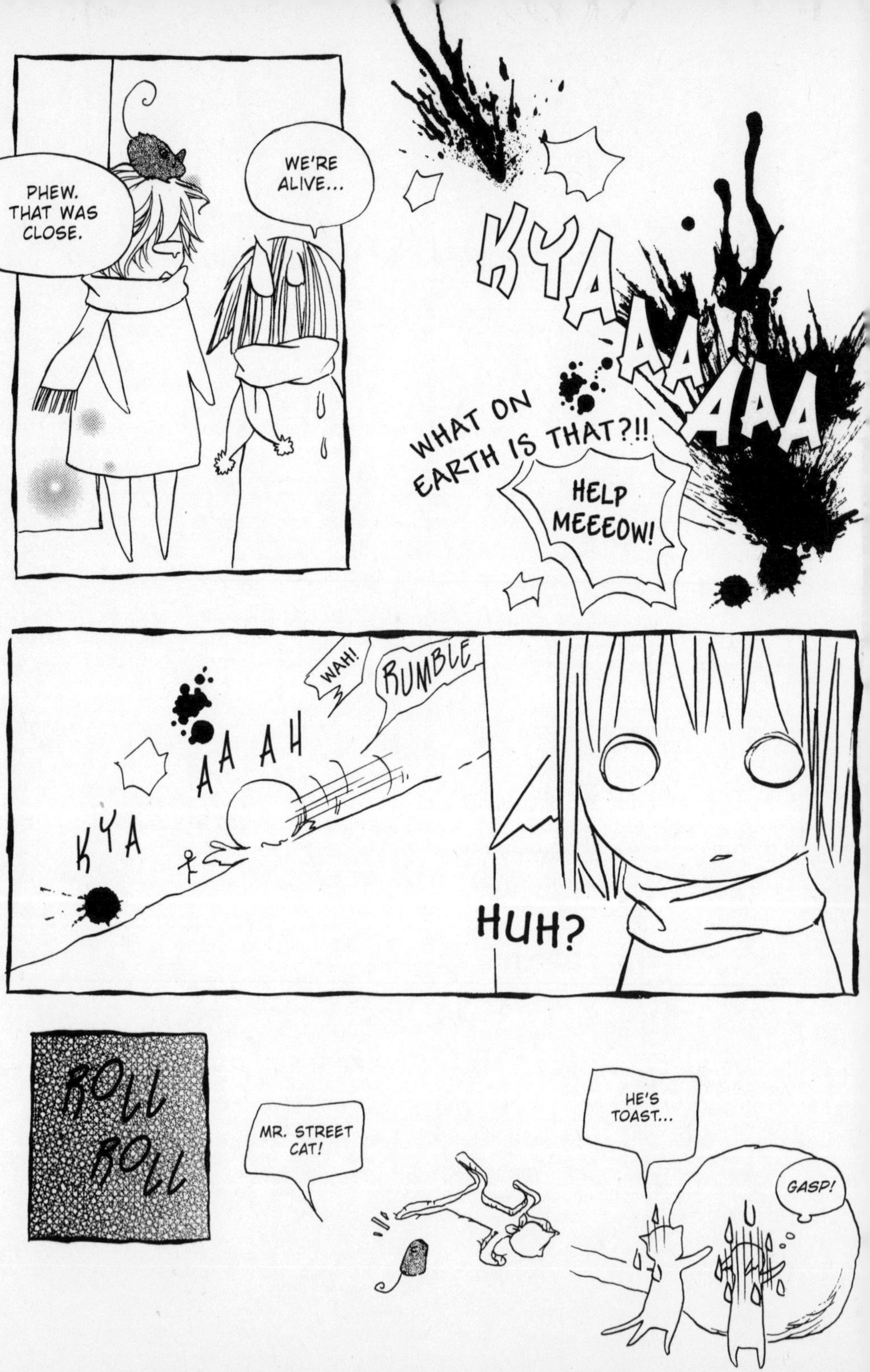
PHEW. THAT WAS CLOSE.
WE'RE ALIVE...
KYAAAAAAA
WHAT ON EARTH IS THAT?!!
HELP MEEEOW!
KYA AA AH
WAH!
RUMBLE
HUH?
ROLL ROLL
MR. STREET CAT!
HE'S TOAST...
GASP!

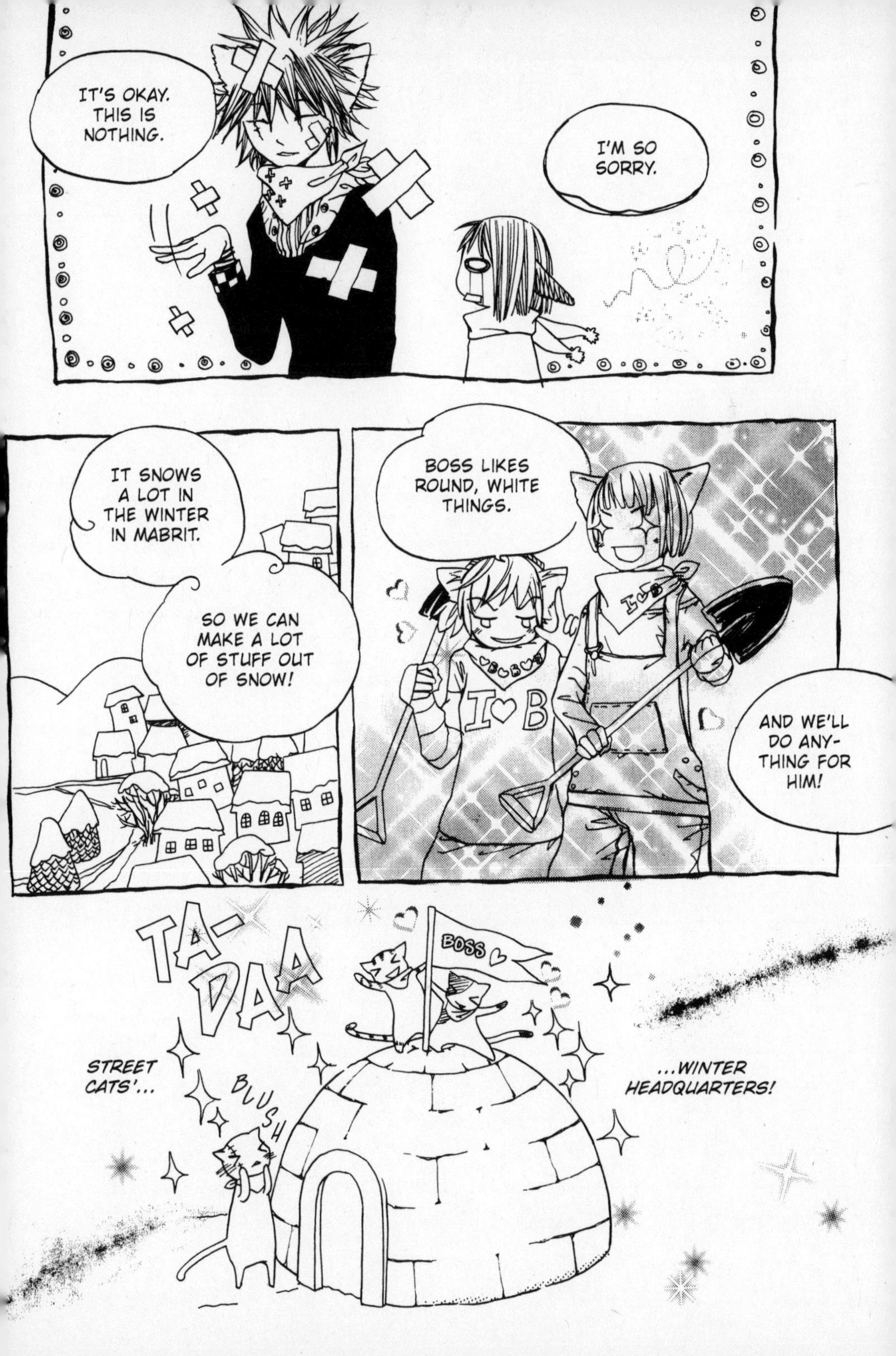
IT'S OKAY. THIS IS NOTHING.
I'M SO SORRY.
IT SNOWS A LOT IN THE WINTER IN MABRIT.
SO WE CAN MAKE A LOT OF STUFF OUT OF SNOW!
BOSS LIKES ROUND, WHITE THINGS.
AND WE'LL DO ANY-THING FOR HIM!
TA-DAA
BOSS
STREET CATS'...
...WINTER HEADQUARTERS!
BLUSH

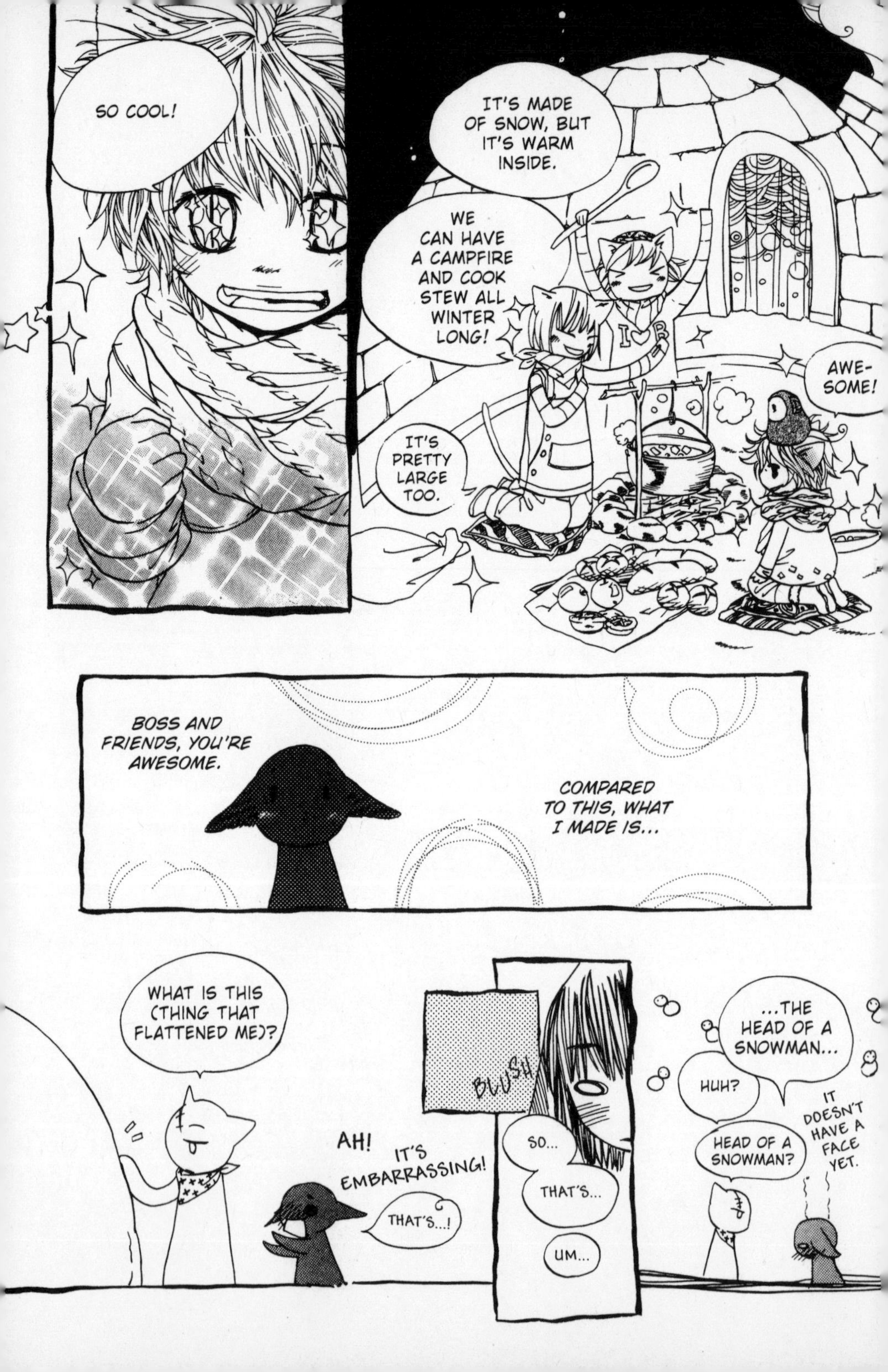

IT'S MADE OF SNOW, BUT IT'S WARM INSIDE.
WE CAN HAVE A CAMPFIRE AND COOK STEW ALL WINTER LONG!
AWE-SOME!
IT'S PRETTY LARGE TOO.
SO COOL!
BOSS AND FRIENDS, YOU'RE AWESOME.
COMPARED TO THIS, WHAT I MADE IS...
...THE HEAD OF A SNOWMAN...
HUH?
HEAD OF A SNOWMAN?
IT DOESN'T HAVE A FACE YET.
BLUSH
SO...
THAT'S...
UM...
WHAT IS THIS (THING THAT FLATTENED ME)?
AH!
IT'S EMBARRASSING!
THAT'S...!

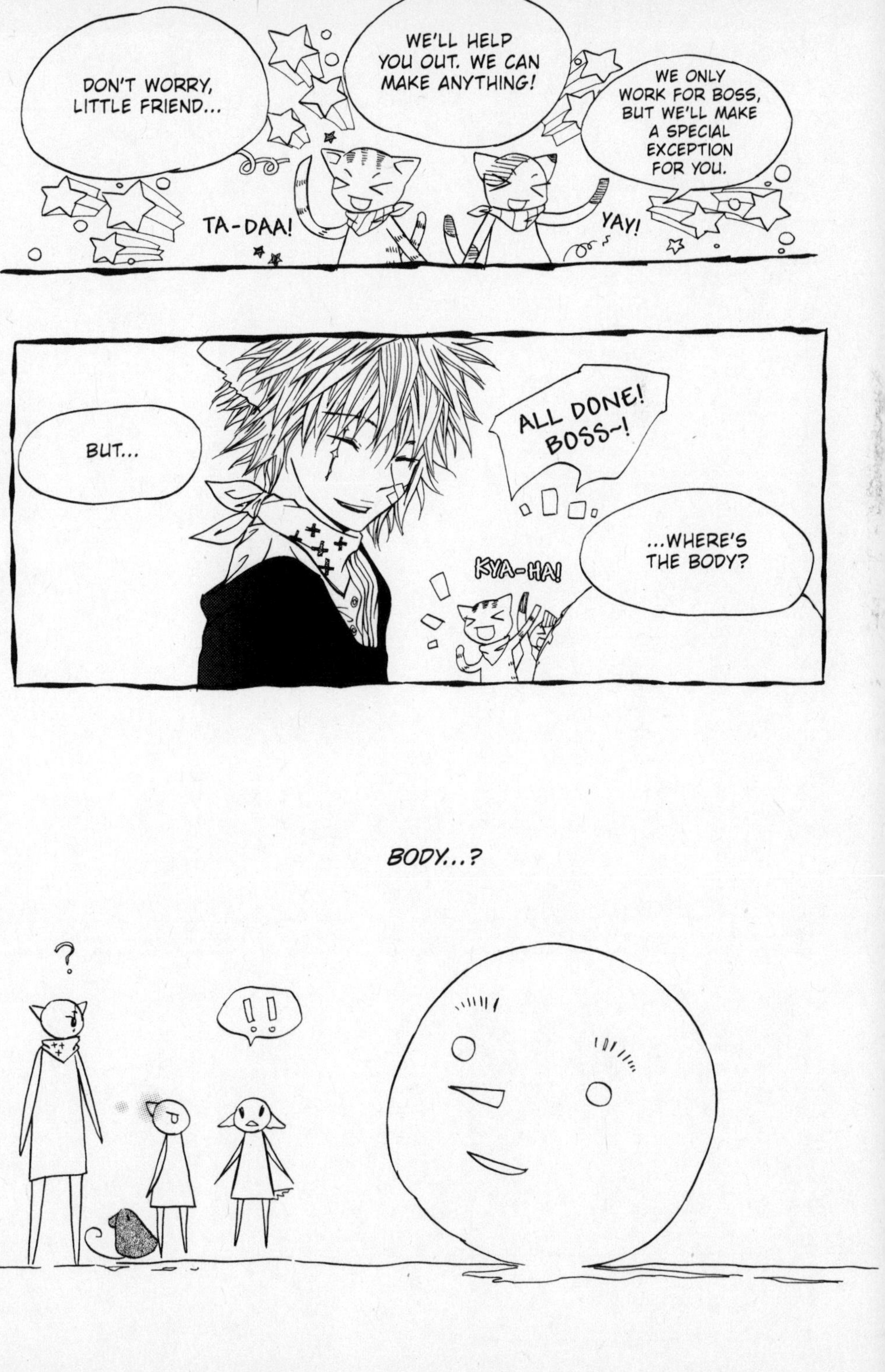
DON'T WORRY, LITTLE FRIEND...
WE'LL HELP YOU OUT. WE CAN MAKE ANYTHING!
WE ONLY WORK FOR BOSS, BUT WE'LL MAKE A SPECIAL EXCEPTION FOR YOU.
TA-DAA!
YAY!
BUT...
ALL DONE! BOSS~!
KYA-HA!
...WHERE'S THE BODY?
BODY...?
?
!!

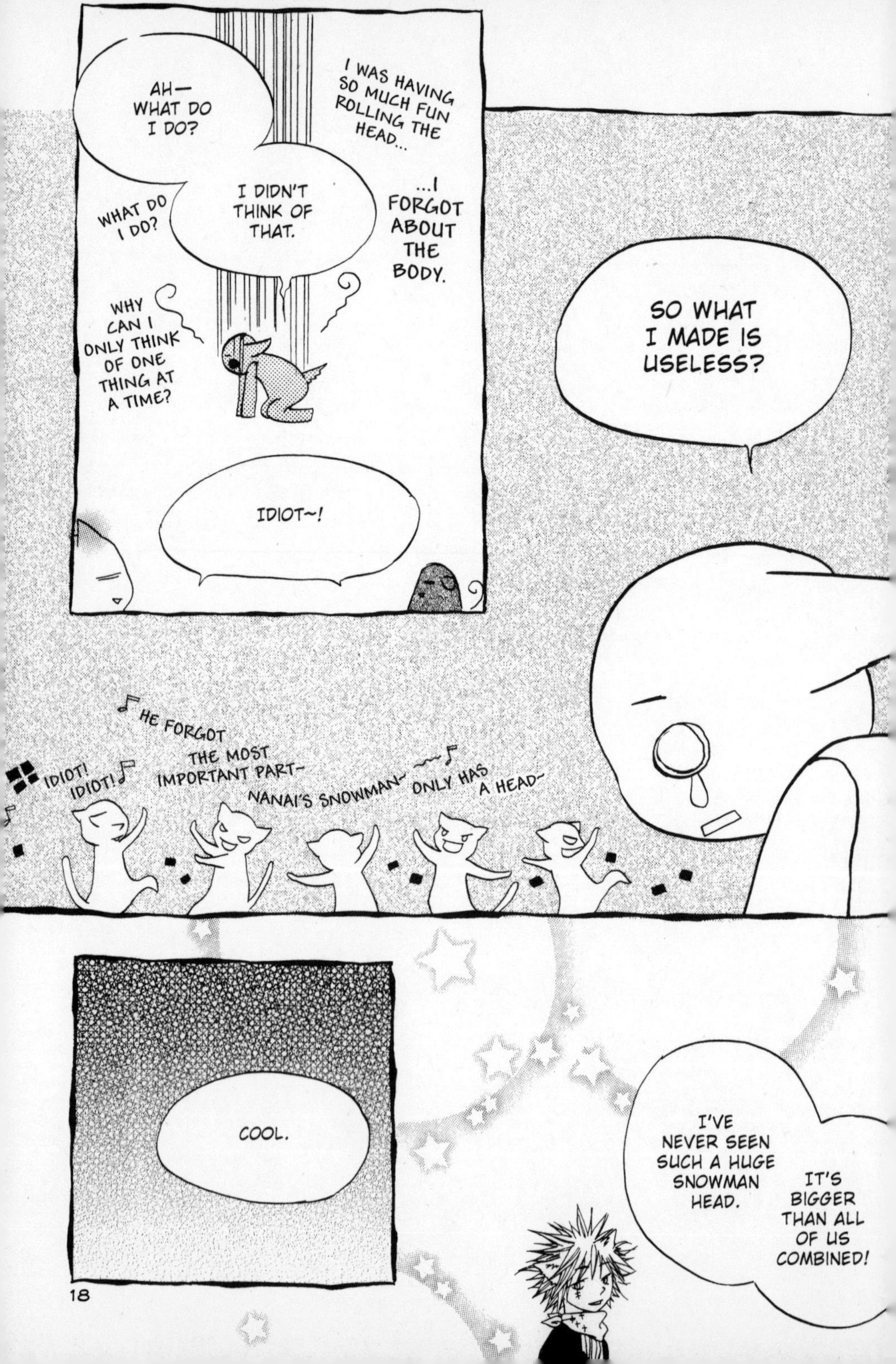
AH— WHAT DO I DO?
I WAS HAVING SO MUCH FUN ROLLING THE HEAD...
I DIDN'T THINK OF THAT.
WHAT DO I DO?
...I FORGOT ABOUT THE BODY.
WHY CAN I ONLY THINK OF ONE THING AT A TIME?
IDIOT~!
SO WHAT I MADE IS USELESS?
HE FORGOT THE MOST IMPORTANT PART~
IDIOT! IDIOT!
NANAI'S SNOWMAN~ ~~ ONLY HAS A HEAD~
COOL.
I'VE NEVER SEEN SUCH A HUGE SNOWMAN HEAD.
IT'S BIGGER THAN ALL OF US COMBINED!

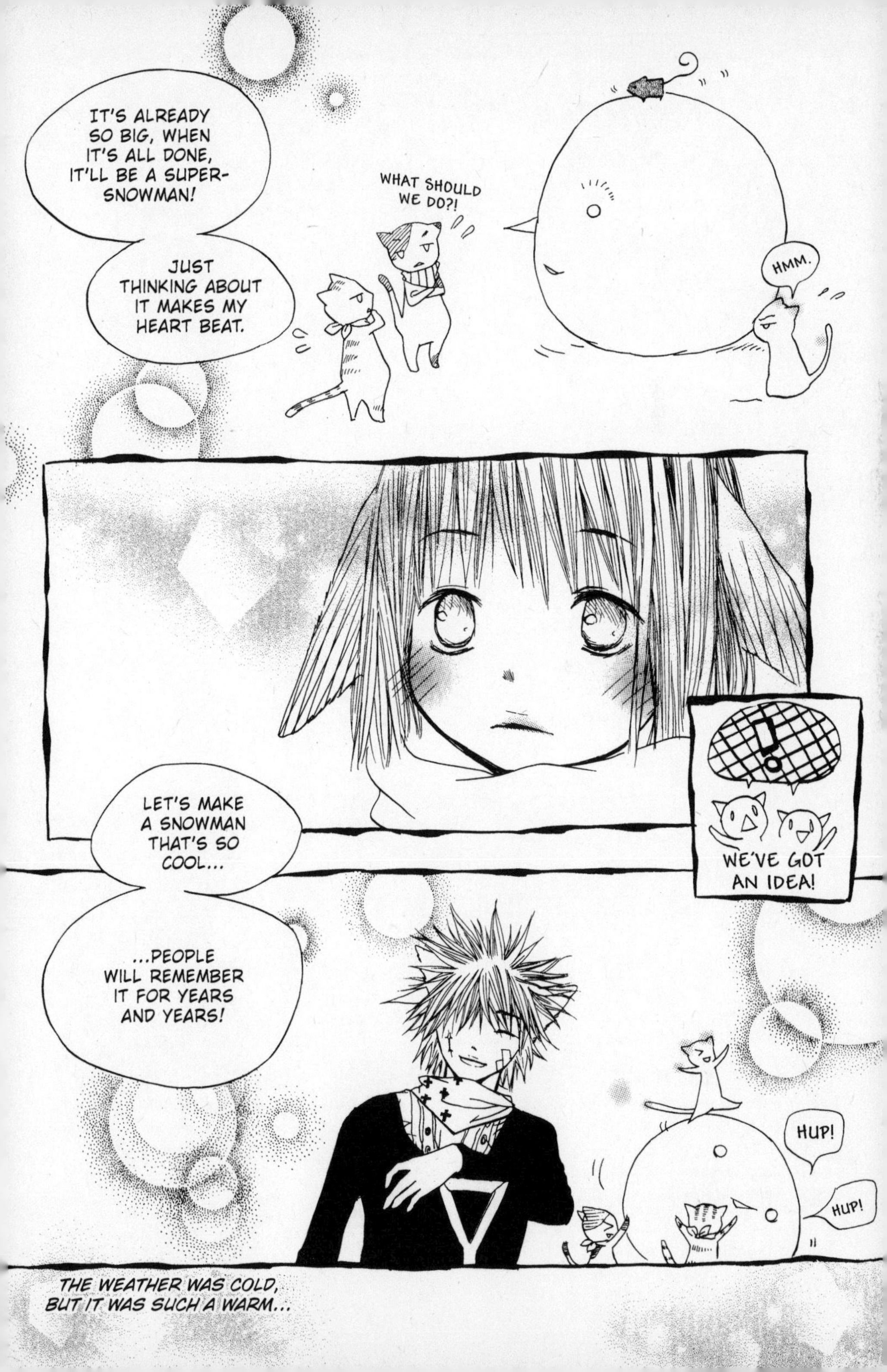

IT'S ALREADY SO BIG, WHEN IT'S ALL DONE, IT'LL BE A SUPER-SNOWMAN!
JUST THINKING ABOUT IT MAKES MY HEART BEAT.
WHAT SHOULD WE DO?!
HMM.
!
WE'VE GOT AN IDEA!
LET'S MAKE A SNOWMAN THAT'S SO COOL...
...PEOPLE WILL REMEMBER IT FOR YEARS AND YEARS!
HUP!
HUP!
THE WEATHER WAS COLD, BUT IT WAS SUCH A WARM...

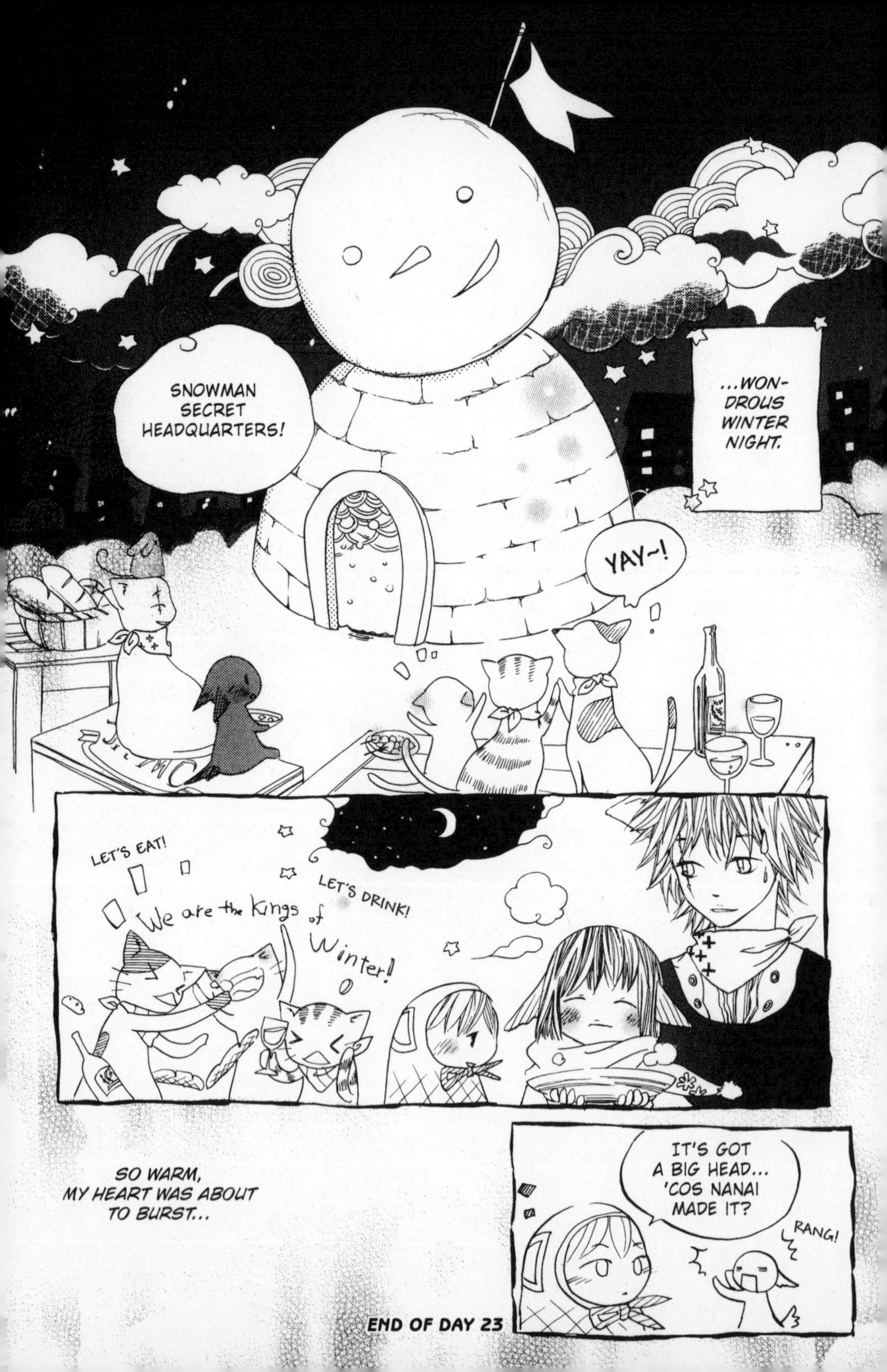
SNOWMAN SECRET HEADQUARTERS!
...WON-DROUS WINTER NIGHT.
YAY~!
LET'S EAT!
LET'S DRINK!
We are the Kings of Winter!
SO WARM, MY HEART WAS ABOUT TO BURST...
IT'S GOT A BIG HEAD... 'COS NANAI MADE IT?
RANG!
END OF DAY 23

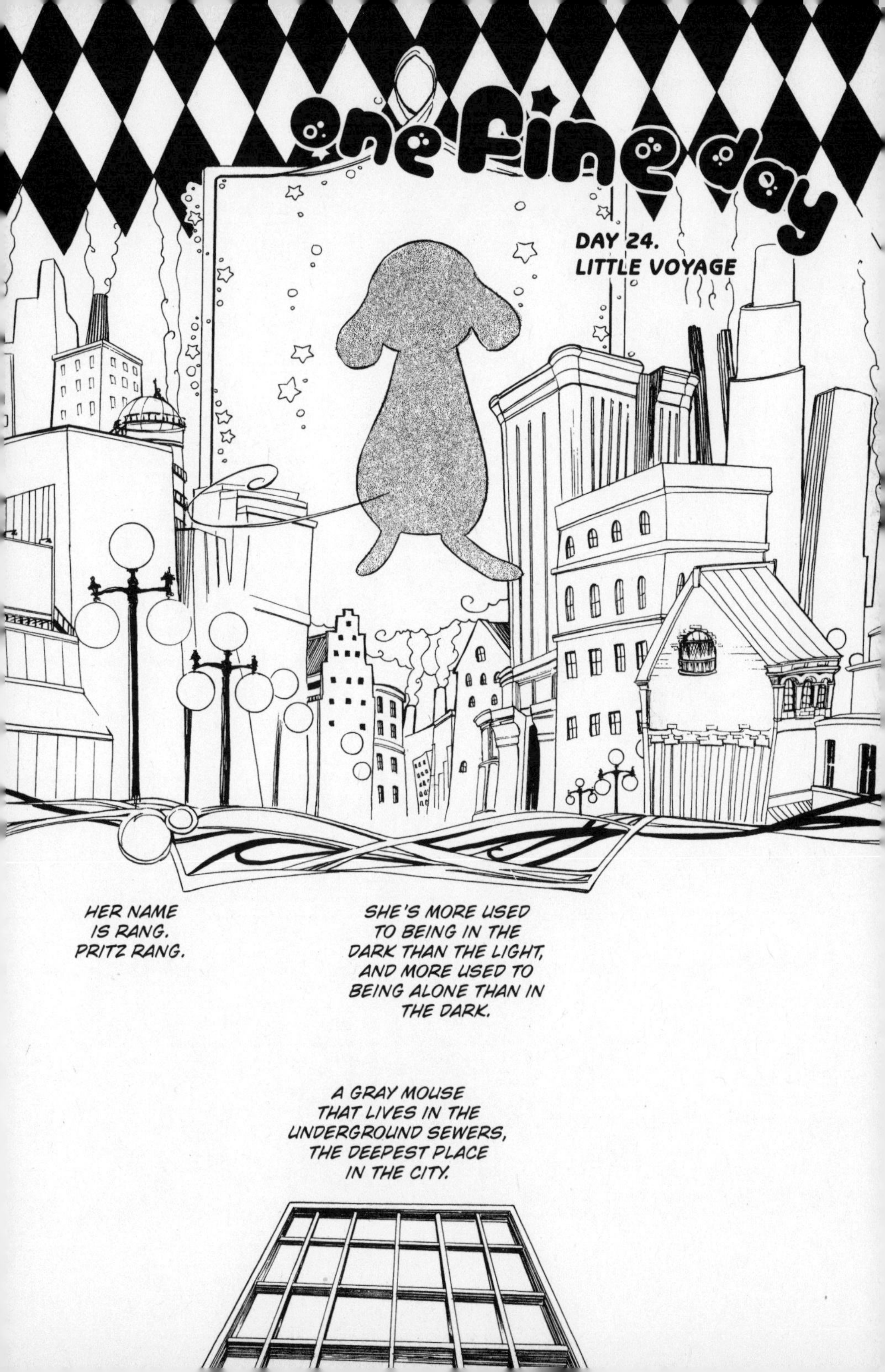
one fine day
DAY 24.
LITTLE VOYAGE
HER NAME IS RANG. PRITZ RANG.
SHE'S MORE USED TO BEING IN THE DARK THAN THE LIGHT, AND MORE USED TO BEING ALONE THAN IN THE DARK.
A GRAY MOUSE THAT LIVES IN THE UNDERGROUND SEWERS, THE DEEPEST PLACE IN THE CITY.

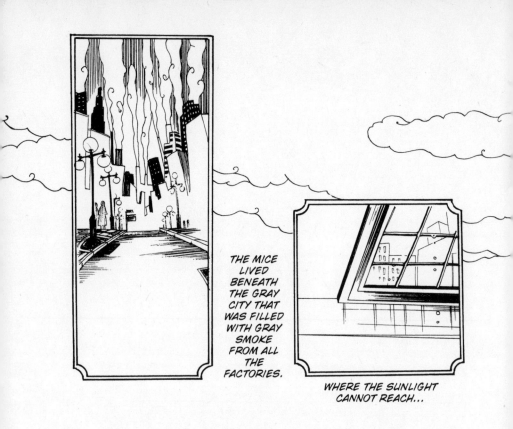

THE MICE LIVED BENEATH THE GRAY CITY THAT WAS FILLED WITH GRAY SMOKE FROM ALL THE FACTORIES.

WHERE THE SUNLIGHT CANNOT REACH...

...THE MICE LIVED BY GATHERING JUNK.

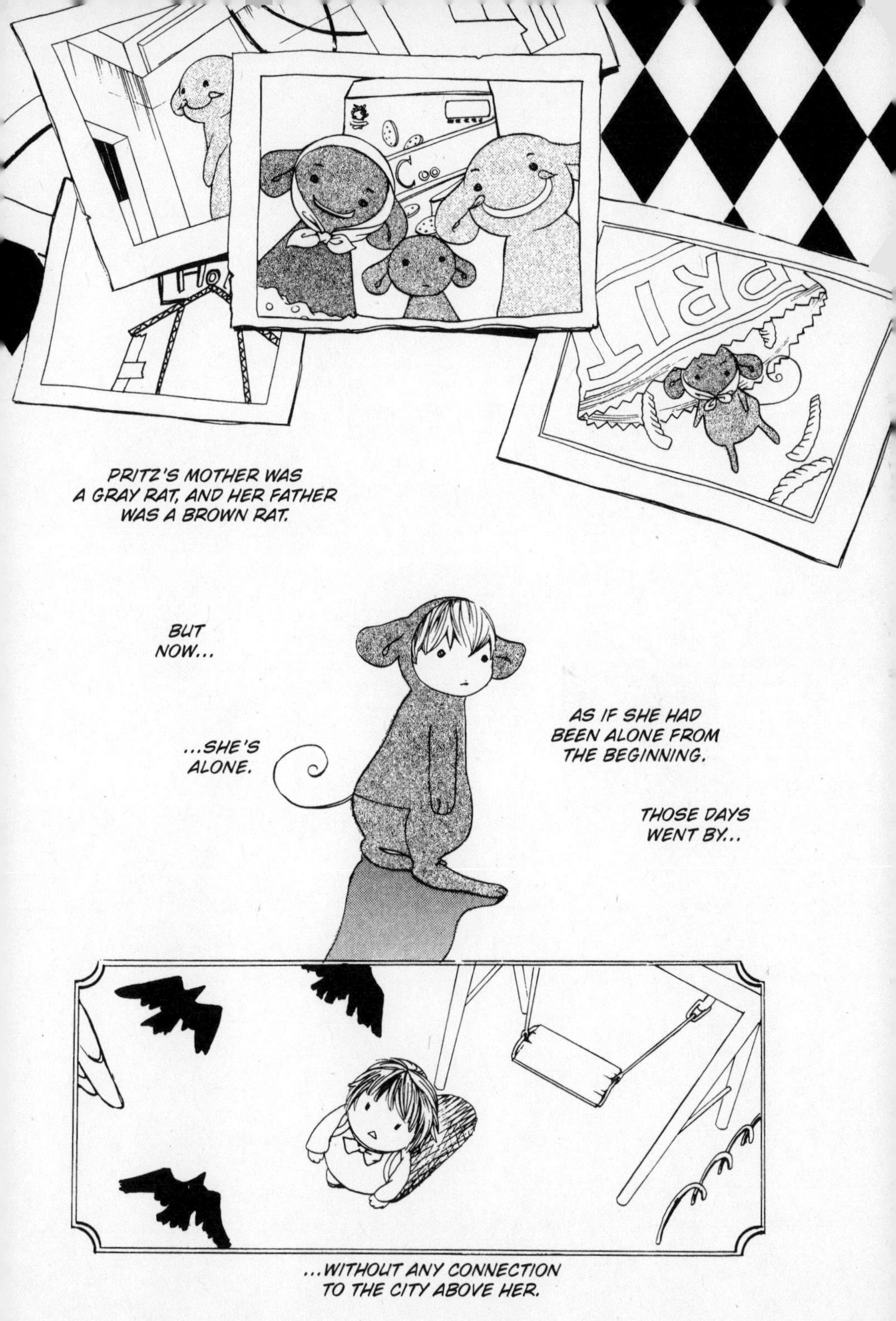
PRITZ'S MOTHER WAS A GRAY RAT, AND HER FATHER WAS A BROWN RAT.
BUT NOW...
...SHE'S ALONE.
AS IF SHE HAD BEEN ALONE FROM THE BEGINNING.
THOSE DAYS WENT BY...
...WITHOUT ANY CONNECTION TO THE CITY ABOVE HER.

THERE
WERE SO MANY
PIGEONS IN
THE GRAY CITY.

MAYOR SHARLIE
BELIEVED THE SNOW-WHITE
PIGEONS WOULD COVER THE
GRIME OF THE GRAY CITY
FILLED WITH GRAY SMOKE.

SO AT EVERY
FESTIVAL, HE
RELEASED HUNDREDS
OF PIGEONS PAINTED
WHITE INTO THE SKY.
THE PEOPLE WERE
HAPPY AND THE MAYOR
WAS PROUD.

BUT! AS SOON
AS THE WHITE
PIGEONS LANDED,
THEY TURNED
GRAY, JUST LIKE
THE CITY.

STILL, SHARLIE
WOULD HAVE IGNORED
THAT FACT AND
CONTINUED TO RELEASE
PAINTED PIGEONS YEAR
AFTER YEAR...

...IF HIS GRANDSON HADN'T GOTTEN
COVERED IN PIGEON POO.

THE MAYOR
WAS FURIOUS, AND
WITH A FACE AS RED
AS A TOMATO...

...HE GATHERED HUNTERS TO
GET RID OF THE PIGEONS.

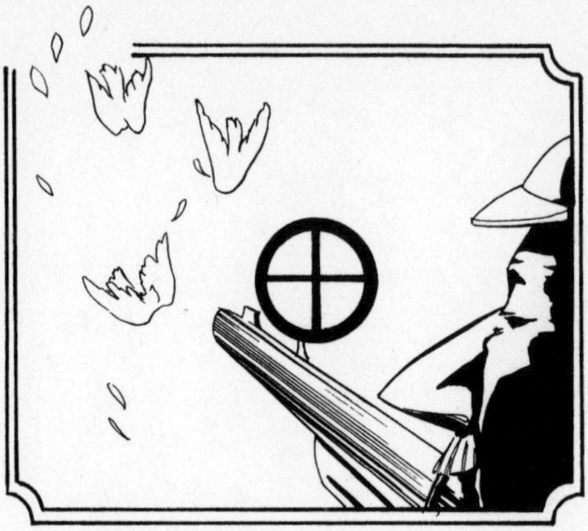

THE HUNTERS BEGAN TO HUNT.

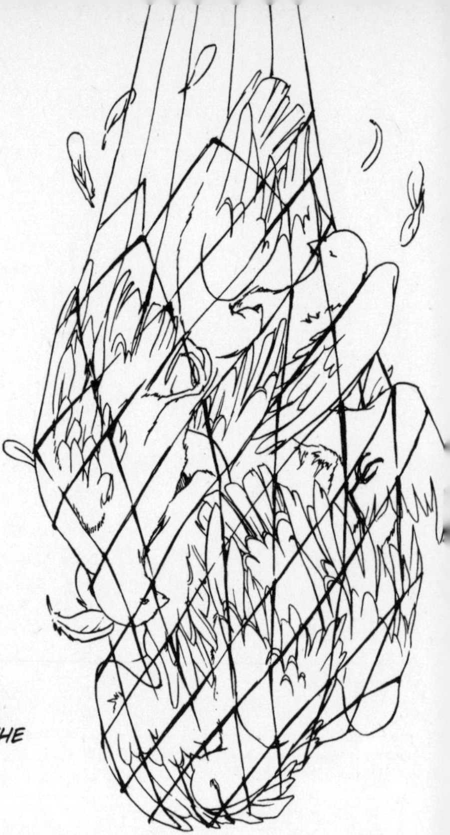

SOME PIGEONS WERE
STRUCK AND FELL INTO THE
HUNTERS' NETS...

...AND SOME WERE
HIT IN THE WING, NEVER
TO FLY AGAIN.

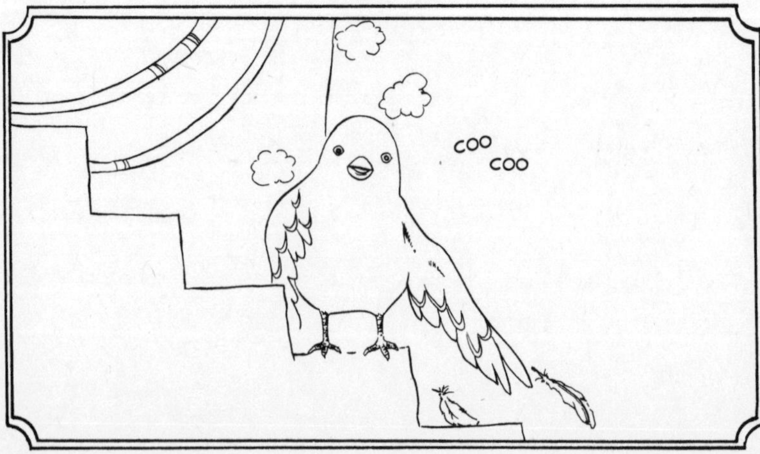
COO
COO

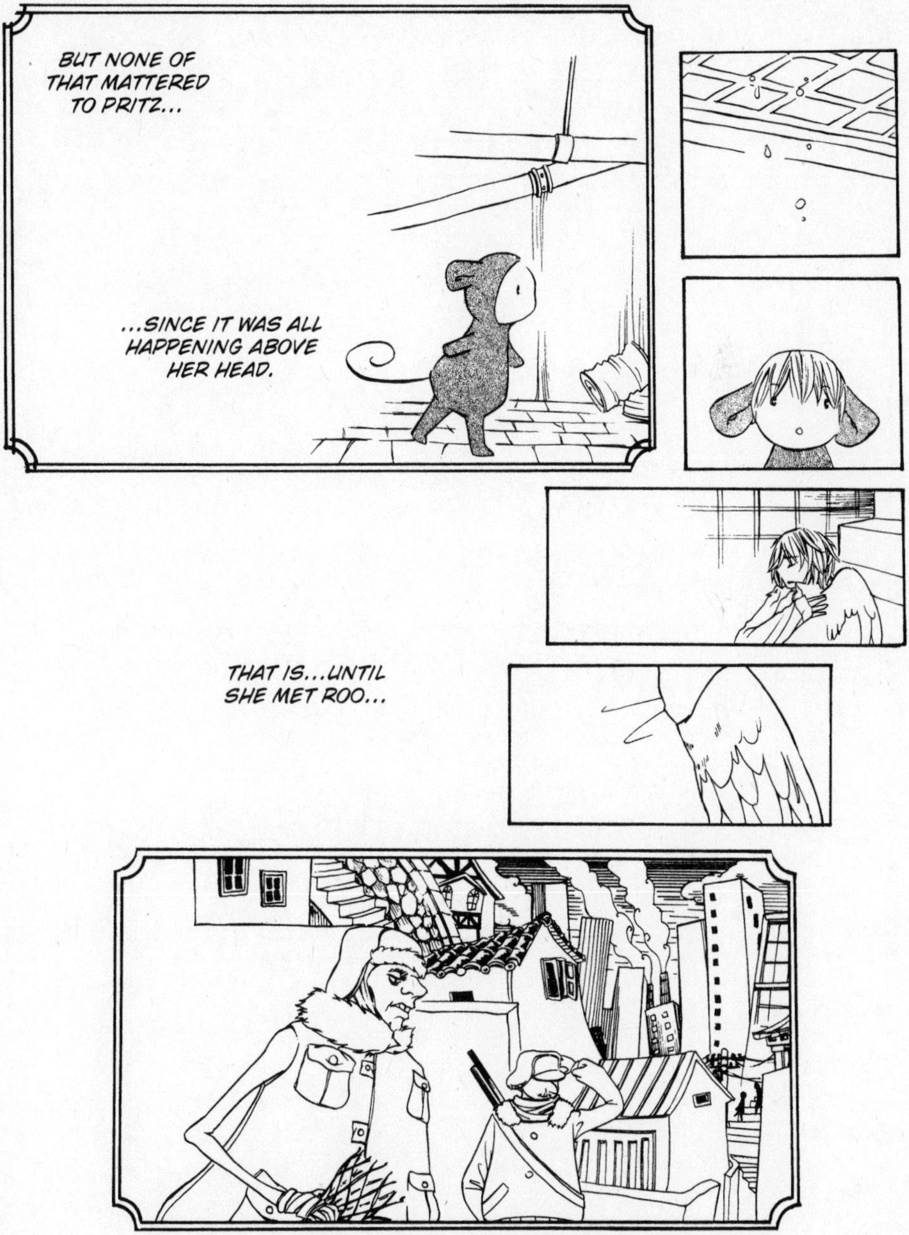
BUT NONE OF THAT MATTERED TO PRITZ...
...SINCE IT WAS ALL HAPPENING ABOVE HER HEAD.
THAT IS...UNTIL SHE MET ROO...
I SAW ONE OF THOSE PIGEONS FALL NEAR HERE. WHERE IS IT?
THE MAYOR PAID ONE SILVER COIN FOR EACH DEAD PIGEON, SO THE HUNTERS WERE CHASING THE PIGEONS LIKE MAD...

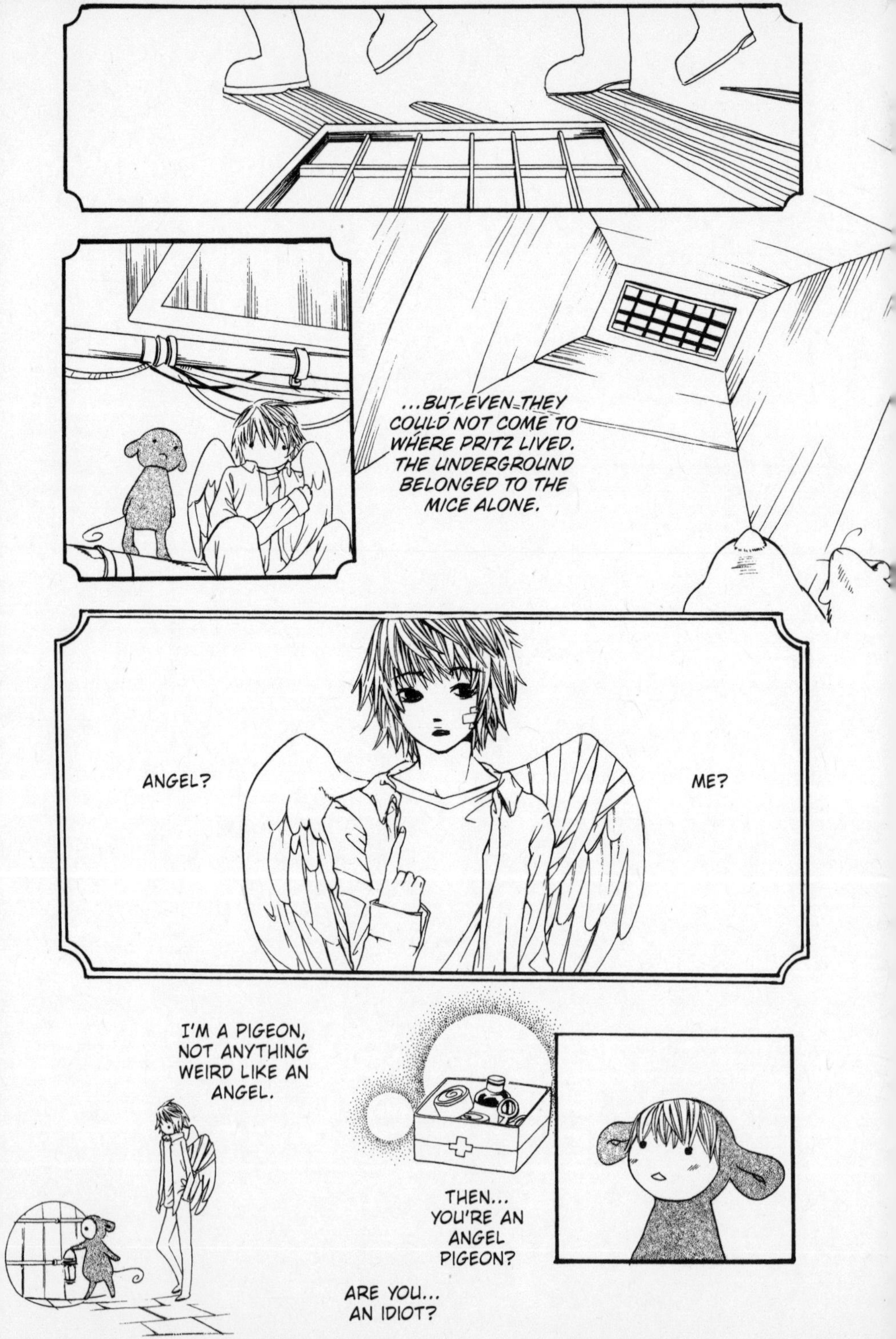
...BUT EVEN THEY COULD NOT COME TO WHERE PRITZ LIVED. THE UNDERGROUND BELONGED TO THE MICE ALONE.
ANGEL?
ME?
I'M A PIGEON, NOT ANYTHING WEIRD LIKE AN ANGEL.
THEN... YOU'RE AN ANGEL PIGEON?
ARE YOU... AN IDIOT?

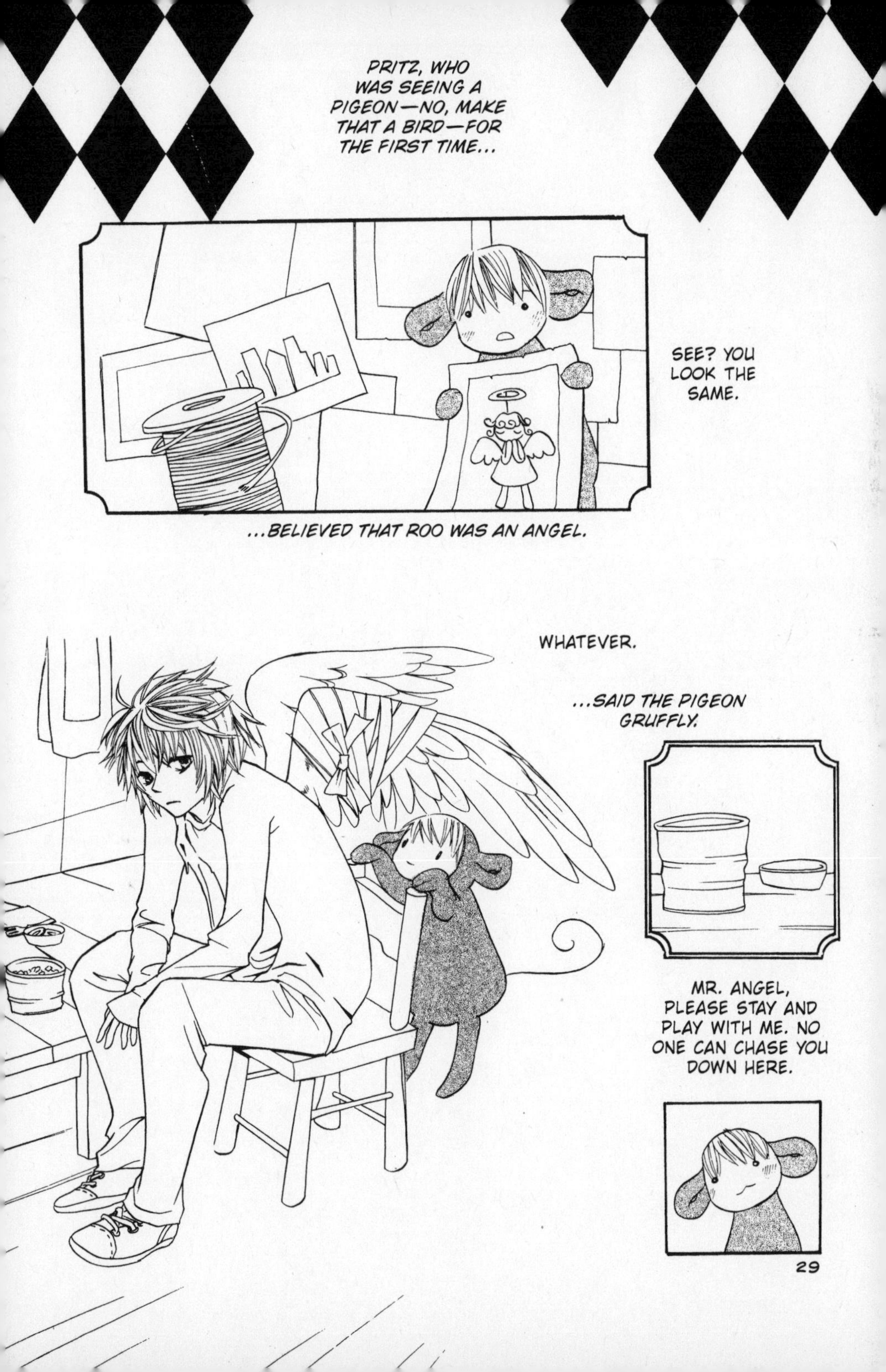
PRITZ, WHO WAS SEEING A PIGEON—NO, MAKE THAT A BIRD—FOR THE FIRST TIME...
SEE? YOU LOOK THE SAME.
...BELIEVED THAT ROO WAS AN ANGEL.
WHATEVER.
...SAID THE PIGEON GRUFFLY.
MR. ANGEL, PLEASE STAY AND PLAY WITH ME. NO ONE CAN CHASE YOU DOWN HERE.

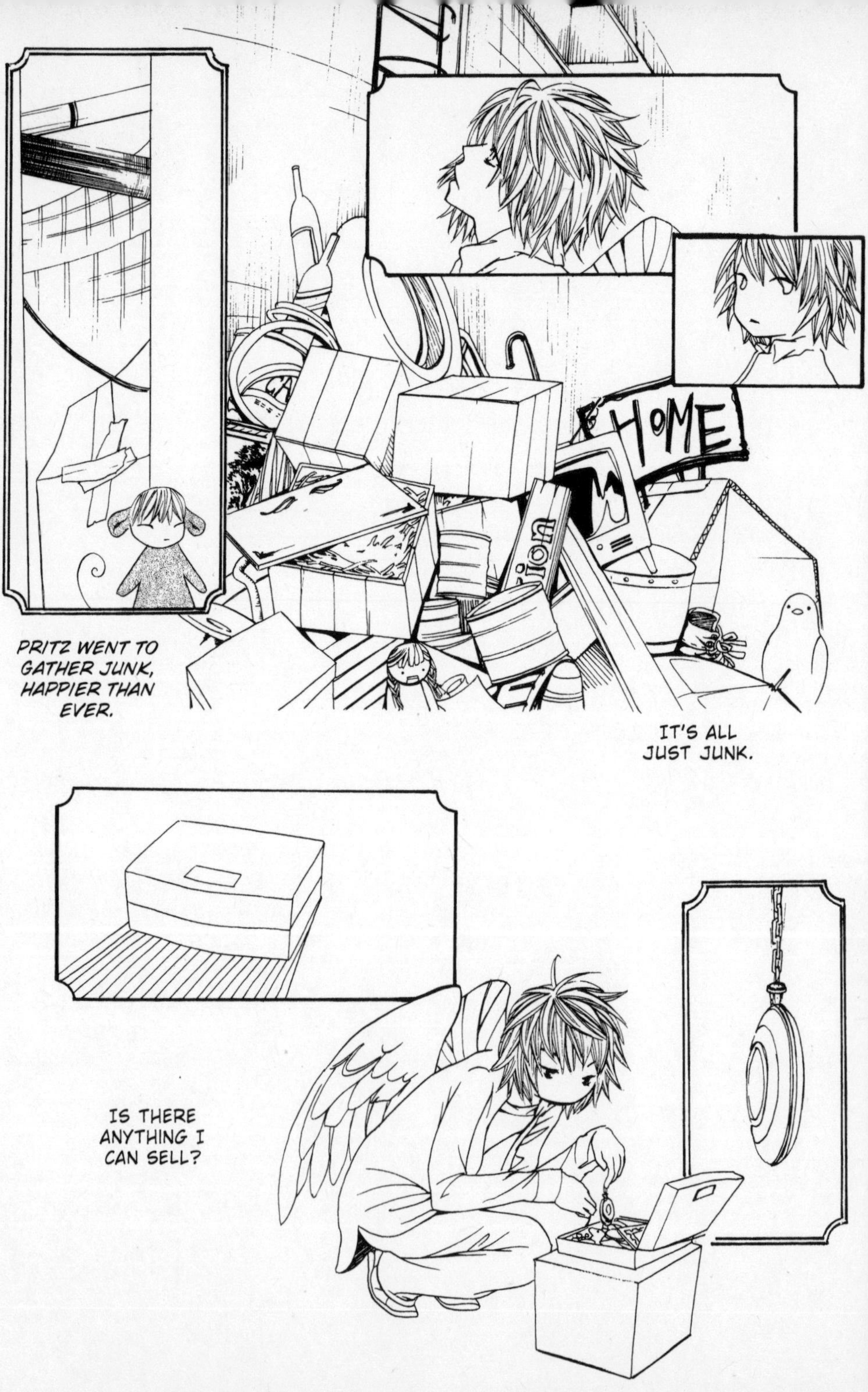
HOME
PRITZ WENT TO GATHER JUNK, HAPPIER THAN EVER.
IT'S ALL JUST JUNK.
IS THERE ANYTHING I CAN SELL?

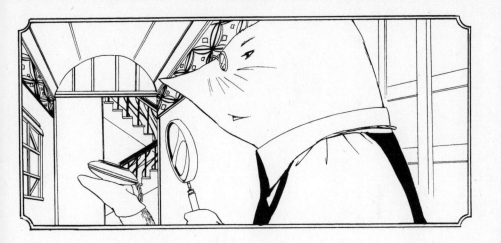

THIS IS BROKEN.
IT'S MADE OF
SILVER, BUT THE HANDS
DON'T MOVE.

YOU WON'T
GET ANY MONEY
FOR THIS.

BUT...

...YOU CAN GET A TICKET
OUT OF THIS CITY.

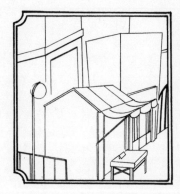

......

...WOULD ONE
OF THOSE LOOK
GOOD ON THAT
STUPID MOUSE?

WHAT AM I
THINKING...?

HERE. IT'S
A PRESENT.

IT WAS SOMETHING SMALL...

...BUT IT WAS THE
FIRST PRESENT
PRITZ HAD EVER
BEEN GIVEN...

...SOMETHING
THAT SHE DIDN'T
JUST PICK UP OFF
THE GROUND.

PRITZ
OPENED THE
BOX WHERE
SHE KEPT HER
TREASURES TO
PUT IT IN.

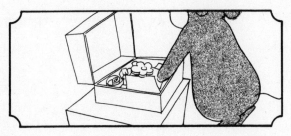

HUH?

BUT THE
SILVER CLOCK
THAT USUALLY
WELCOMED
PRITZ WITH ITS
SPARKLE WASN'T
THERE.

A THIEF MUST HAVE STOLEN IT.

...PRITZ SAID GLOOMILY.

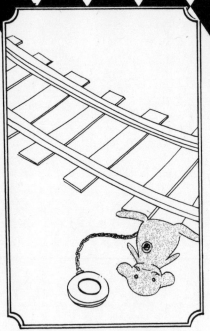

IT WAS THE
ONLY THING
SHE HAD
FROM HER
FATHER...

ROO.

IT HAD BELONGED TO
HER FATHER WHO WAS HIT
BY A TRAIN...PROBABLY
SOMETHING HE HAD PICKED
UP SOMEWHERE TOO...

IF IT WAS THAT
IMPORTANT, YOU
SHOULD'VE KEPT IT
IN A SAFER PLACE!
SAID ROO GRUFFLY.

I'M...   ...LEAVING.

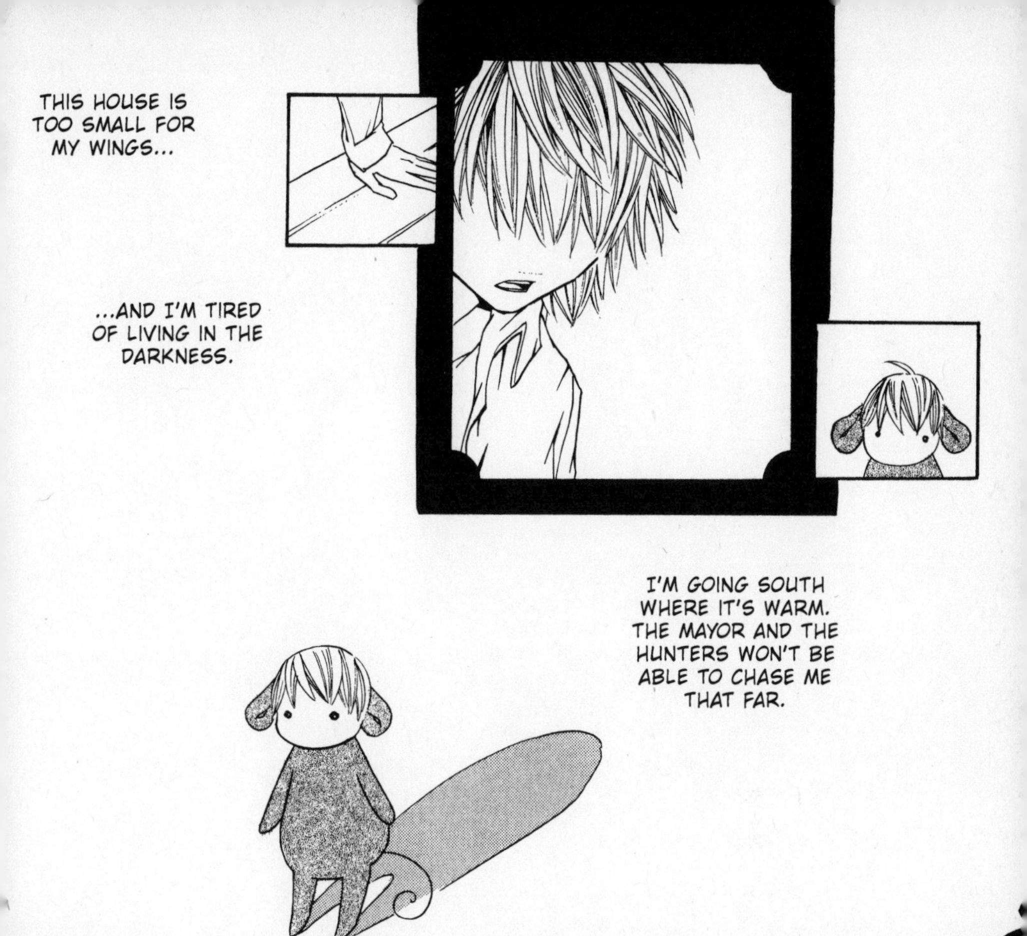
THIS HOUSE IS TOO SMALL FOR MY WINGS...
...AND I'M TIRED OF LIVING IN THE DARKNESS.
I'M GOING SOUTH WHERE IT'S WARM. THE MAYOR AND THE HUNTERS WON'T BE ABLE TO CHASE ME THAT FAR.
TAKE ME WITH YOU. I WANT TO SEE THE SKY. I WANT TO GO WITH MR. ANGEL.
YOU REALLY ARE AN IDIOT. A MOUSE BELONGS HERE, IN THE SEWERS.
YOU CAN'T EVEN FLY!

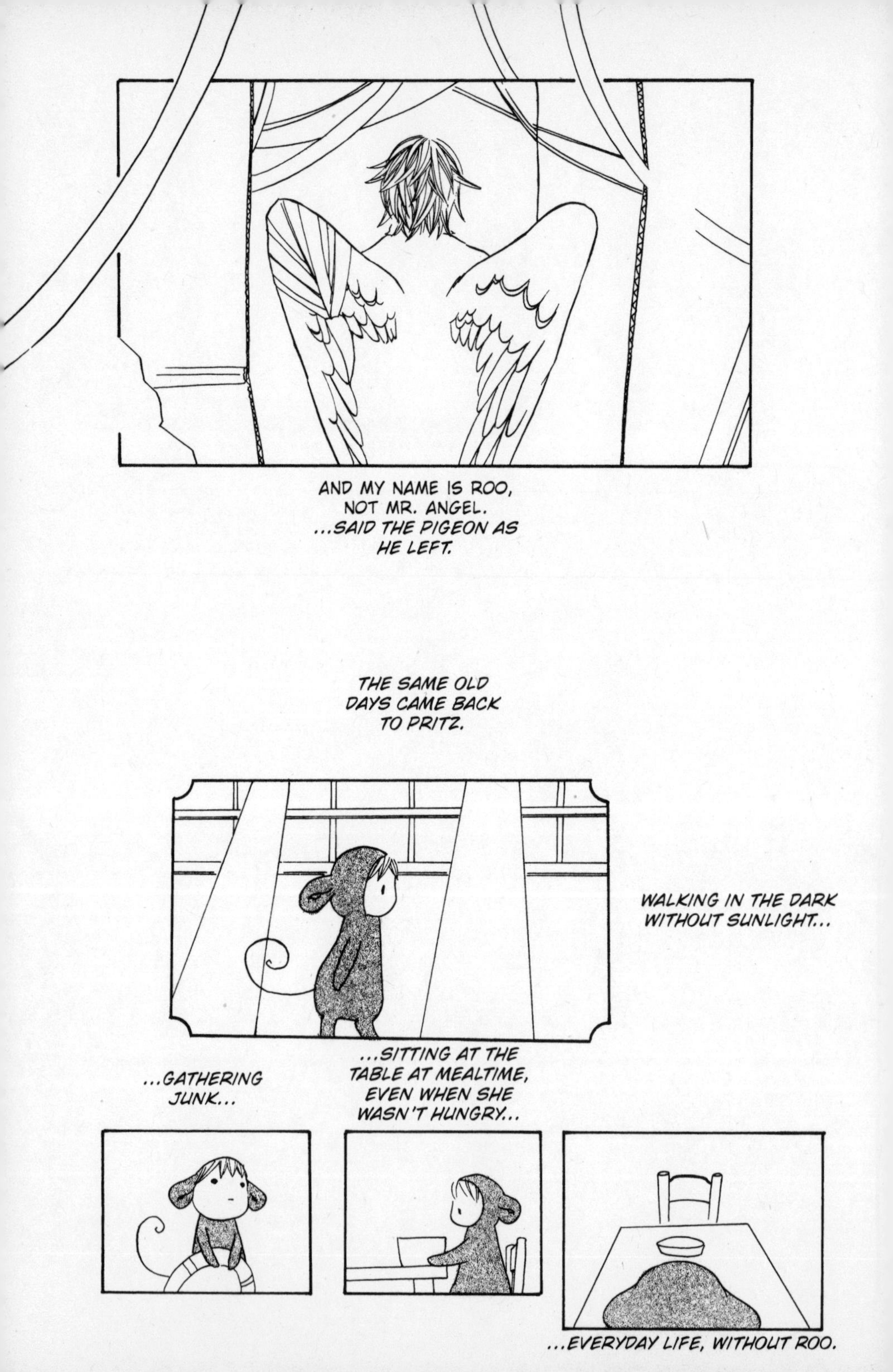
AND MY NAME IS ROO, NOT MR. ANGEL.
...SAID THE PIGEON AS HE LEFT.
THE SAME OLD DAYS CAME BACK TO PRITZ.
WALKING IN THE DARK WITHOUT SUNLIGHT...
...GATHERING JUNK...
...SITTING AT THE TABLE AT MEALTIME, EVEN WHEN SHE WASN'T HUNGRY...
...EVERYDAY LIFE, WITHOUT ROO.

PRITZ THOUGHT
OF THE ANGEL
SOMETIMES.

NO, SHE
THOUGHT ABOUT
ROO.

IS HE FLYING
FREELY IN THE
BIG BLUE SKY?

IN THE WARM SOUTH
FILLED WITH SUNSHINE,
IS HE SMILING HAPPILY
ON THE SHORE OF THE
BLUE SEA?

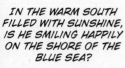

...NO, EVEN
JUST ONCE...

MR. PIGEON.

NICE TO SEE
YOU AGAIN.

SOMETIMES...

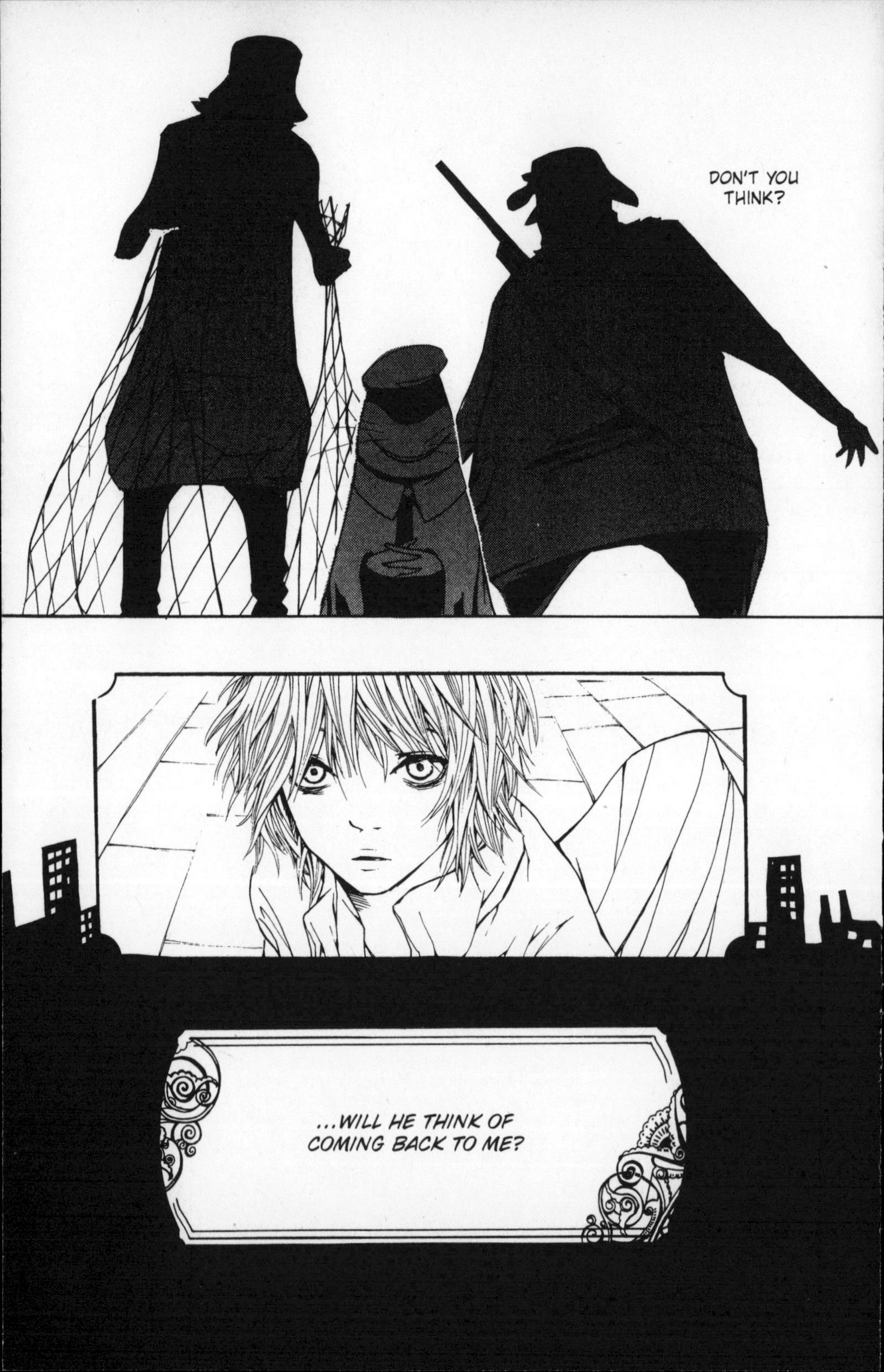
DON'T YOU THINK?
...WILL HE THINK OF COMING BACK TO ME?

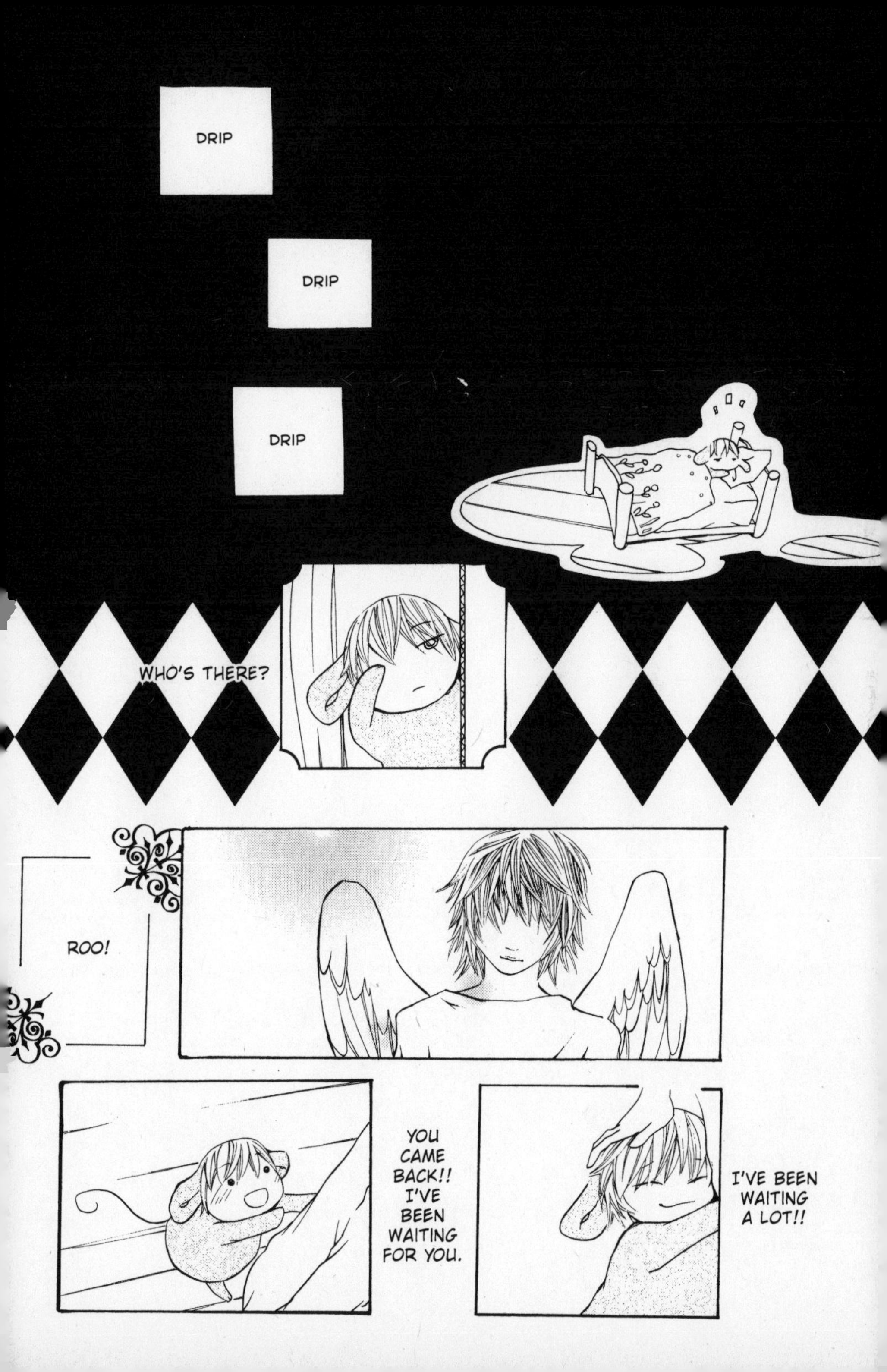
DRIP
DRIP
DRIP
WHO'S THERE?
ROO!
YOU CAME BACK!! I'VE BEEN WAITING FOR YOU.
I'VE BEEN WAITING A LOT!!

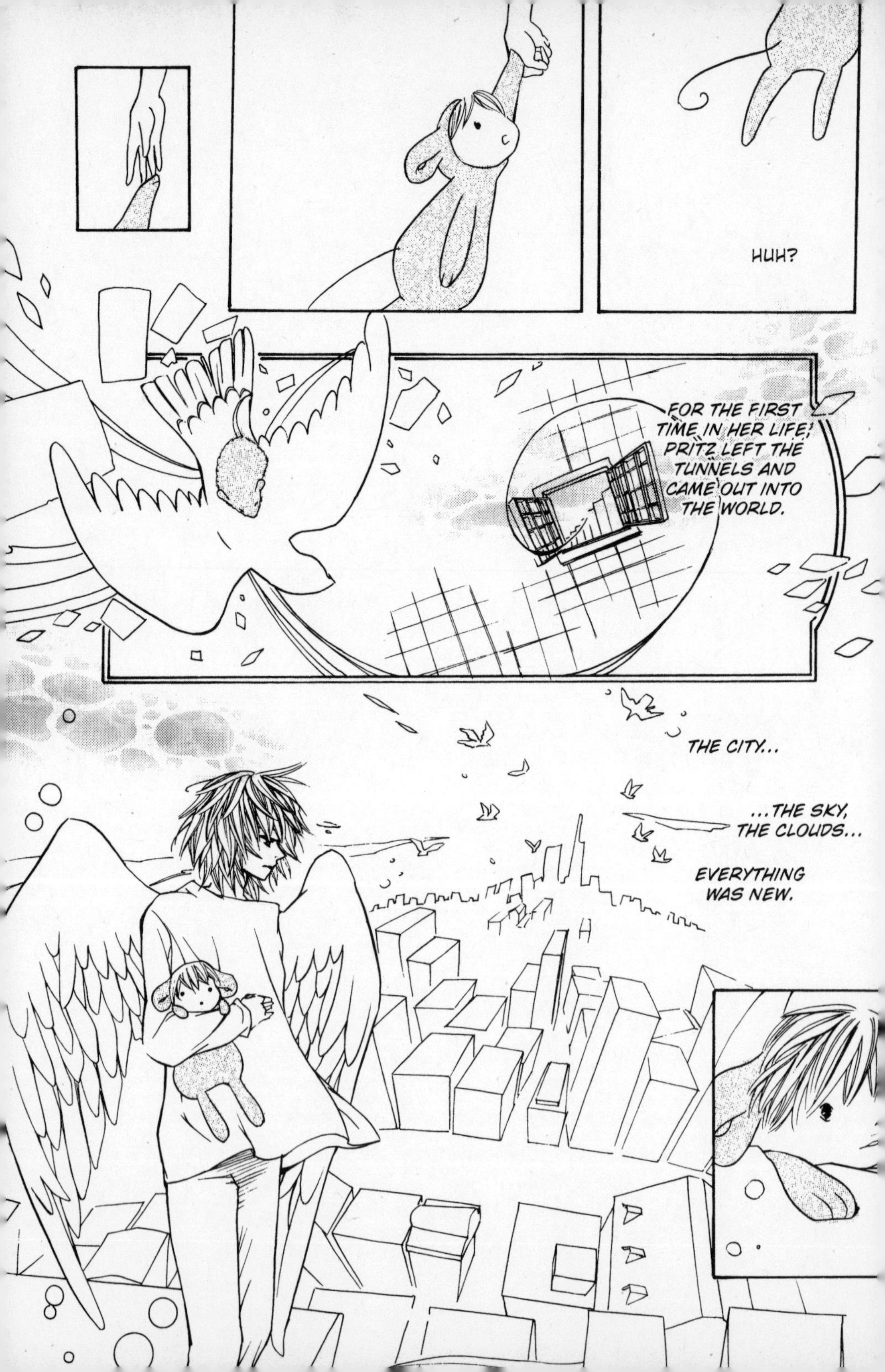
HUH?
FOR THE FIRST TIME IN HER LIFE, PRITZ LEFT THE TUNNELS AND CAME OUT INTO THE WORLD.
THE CITY...
...THE SKY, THE CLOUDS...
EVERYTHING WAS NEW.

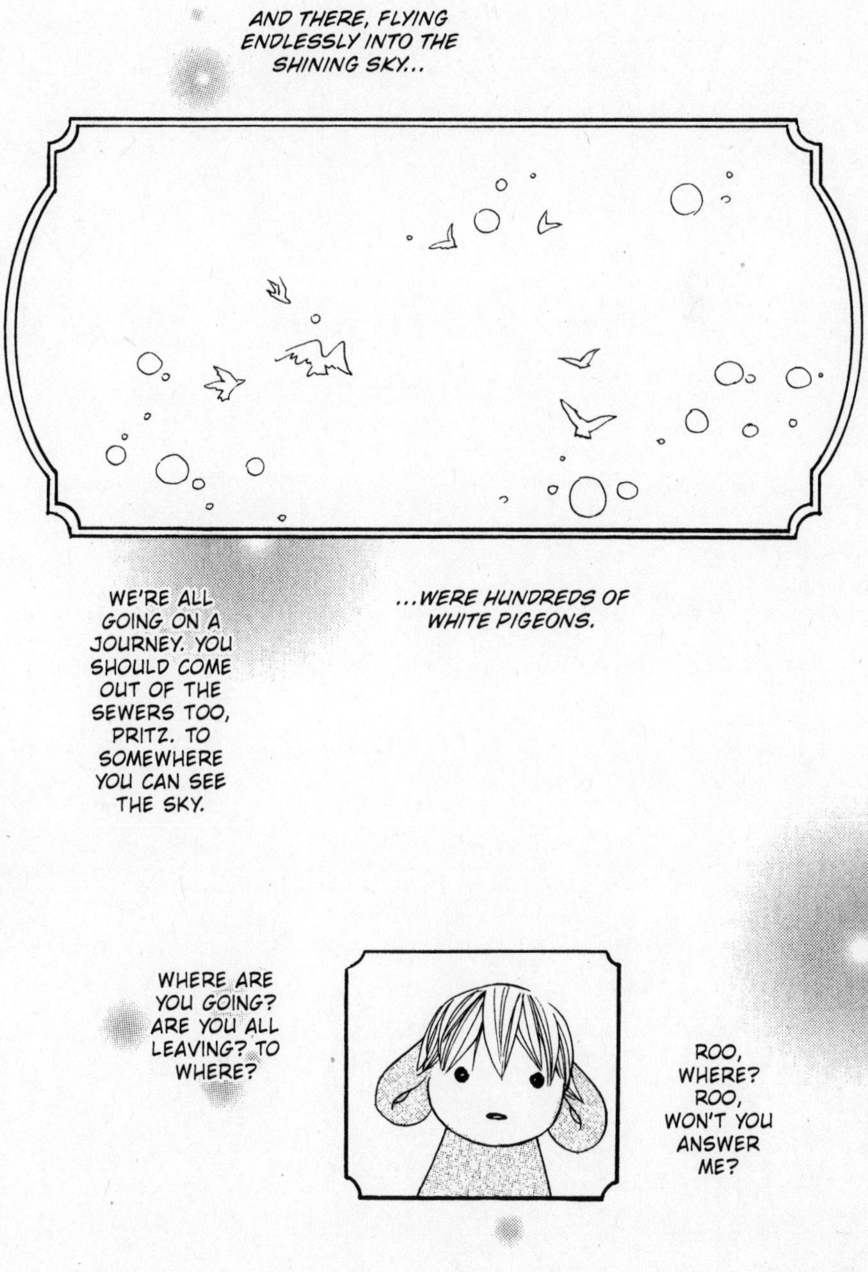
AND THERE, FLYING ENDLESSLY INTO THE SHINING SKY...
...WERE HUNDREDS OF WHITE PIGEONS.
WE'RE ALL GOING ON A JOURNEY. YOU SHOULD COME OUT OF THE SEWERS TOO, PRITZ. TO SOMEWHERE YOU CAN SEE THE SKY.
ROO, WHERE? ROO, WON'T YOU ANSWER ME?
WHERE ARE YOU GOING? ARE YOU ALL LEAVING? TO WHERE?

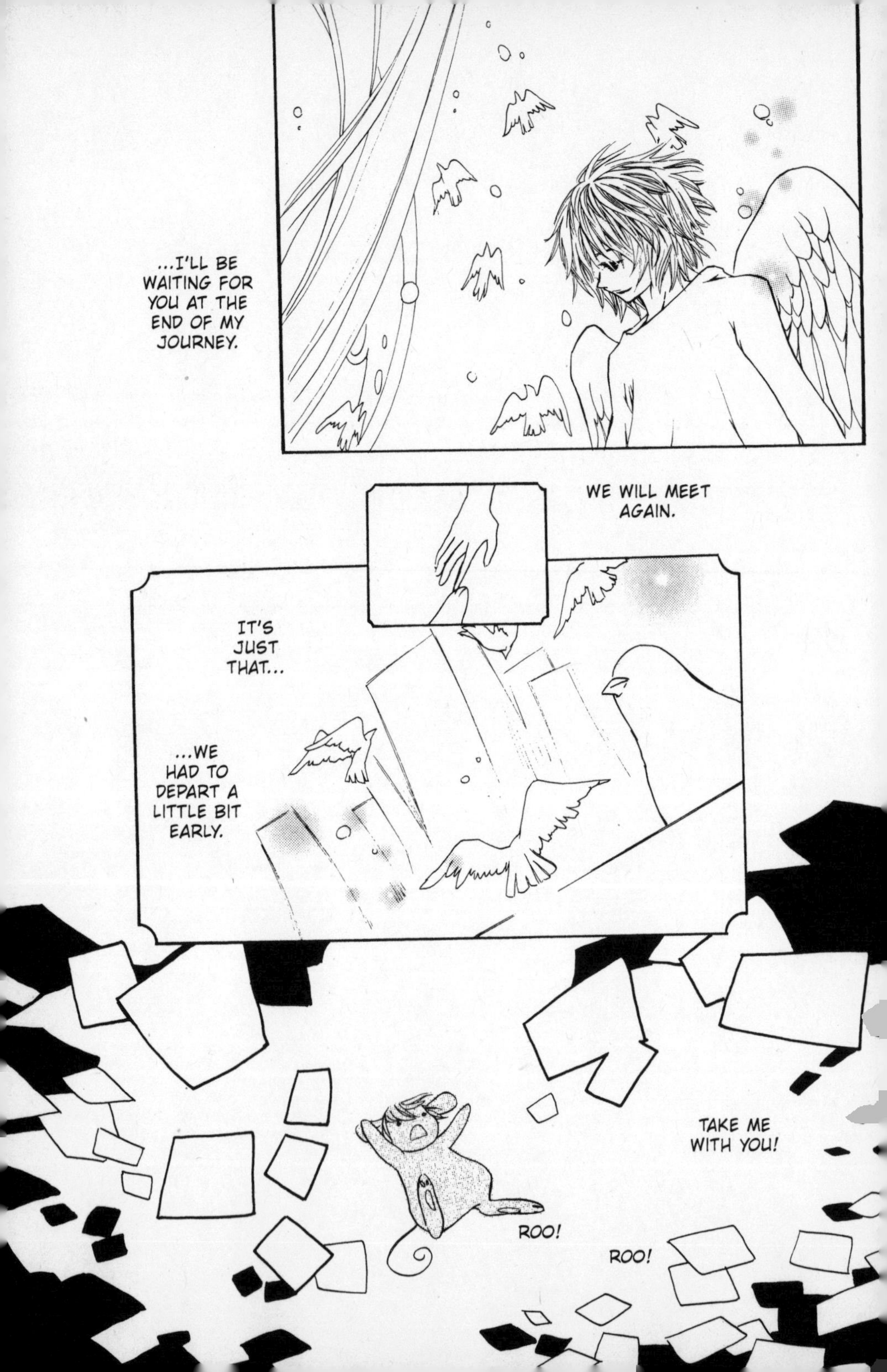
...I'LL BE WAITING FOR YOU AT THE END OF MY JOURNEY.
WE WILL MEET AGAIN.
IT'S JUST THAT...
...WE HAD TO DEPART A LITTLE BIT EARLY.
TAKE ME WITH YOU!
ROO!
ROO!

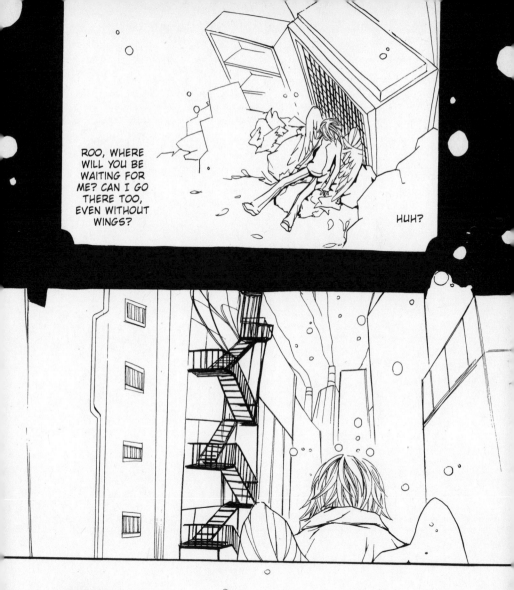

ROO, WHERE WILL YOU BE WAITING FOR ME? CAN I GO THERE TOO, EVEN WITHOUT WINGS?

HUH?

ANGEL, IF YOU REALLY DO EXIST, IF YOU REALLY DO LIVE UP THERE IN THE SKY, PLEASE TAKE GOOD CARE OF ROO.

UNTIL WE MEET AGAIN.

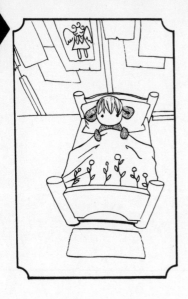

WHEN PRITZ
OPENED HER
EYES...

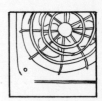

...SHE WAS
STILL IN HER
LITTLE ROOM IN
THE SEWERS.

DRIP

DRIP

PRITZ ONLY
HAD A SMALL
SUITCASE...

...BUT IT WAS ENOUGH.

A LITTLE MOUSE DOESN'T
NEED MUCH.

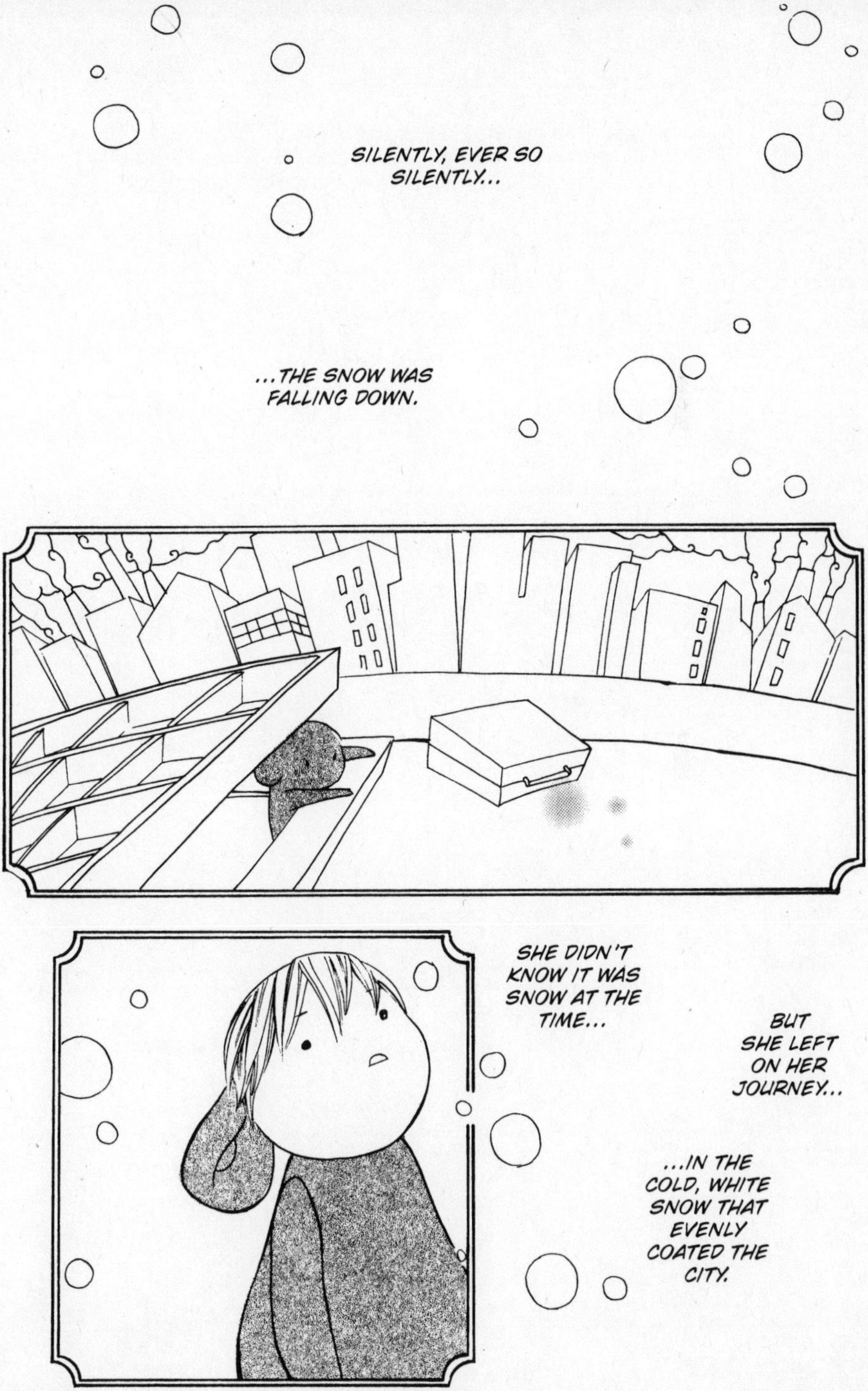
SILENTLY, EVER SO SILENTLY...
...THE SNOW WAS FALLING DOWN.
SHE DIDN'T KNOW IT WAS SNOW AT THE TIME...
BUT SHE LEFT ON HER JOURNEY...
...IN THE COLD, WHITE SNOW THAT EVENLY COATED THE CITY.

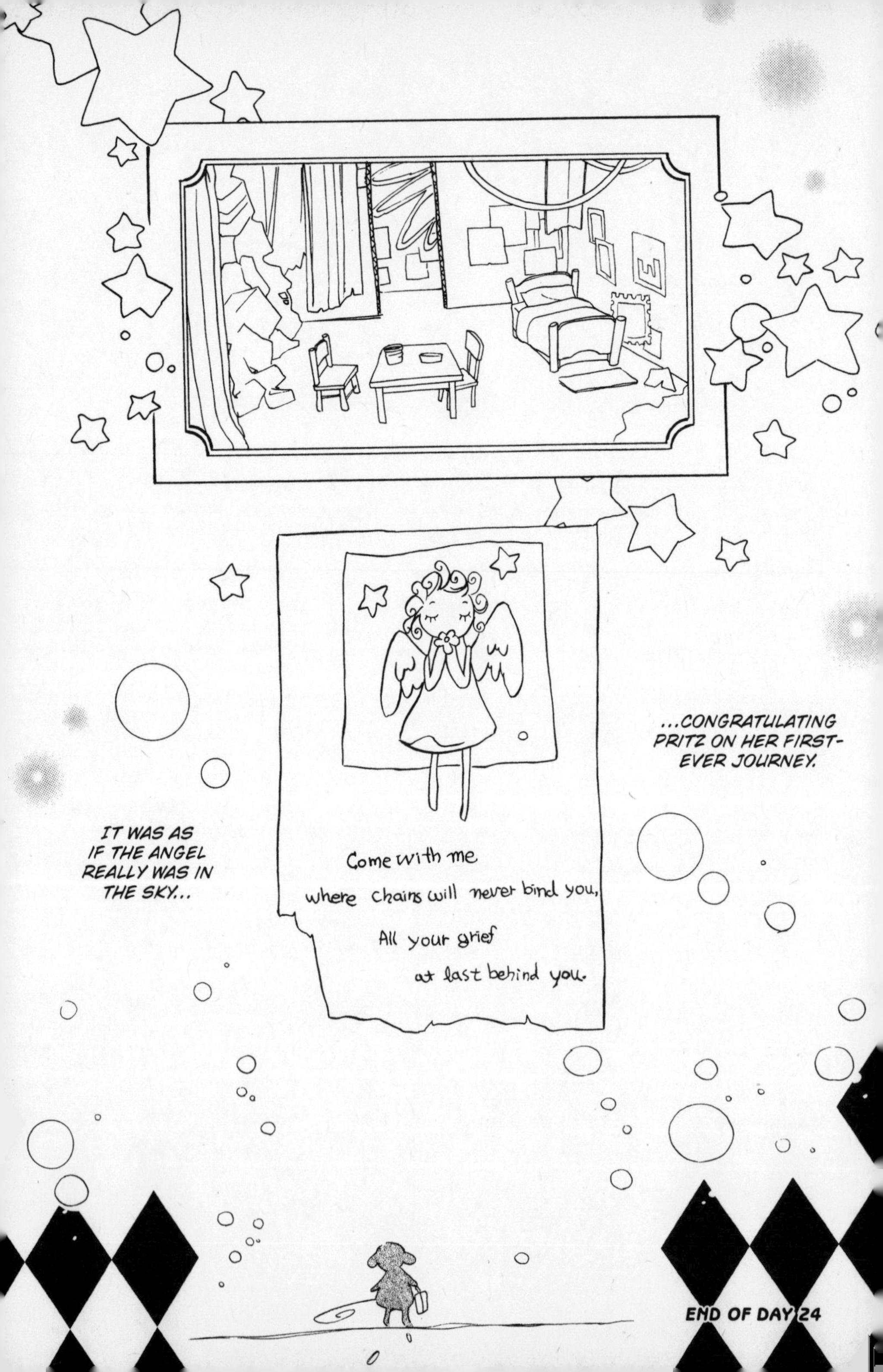

...CONGRATULATING PRITZ ON HER FIRST-EVER JOURNEY.
IT WAS AS IF THE ANGEL REALLY WAS IN THE SKY...
Come with me
where chains will never bind you,
All your grief
at last behind you.
END OF DAY 24

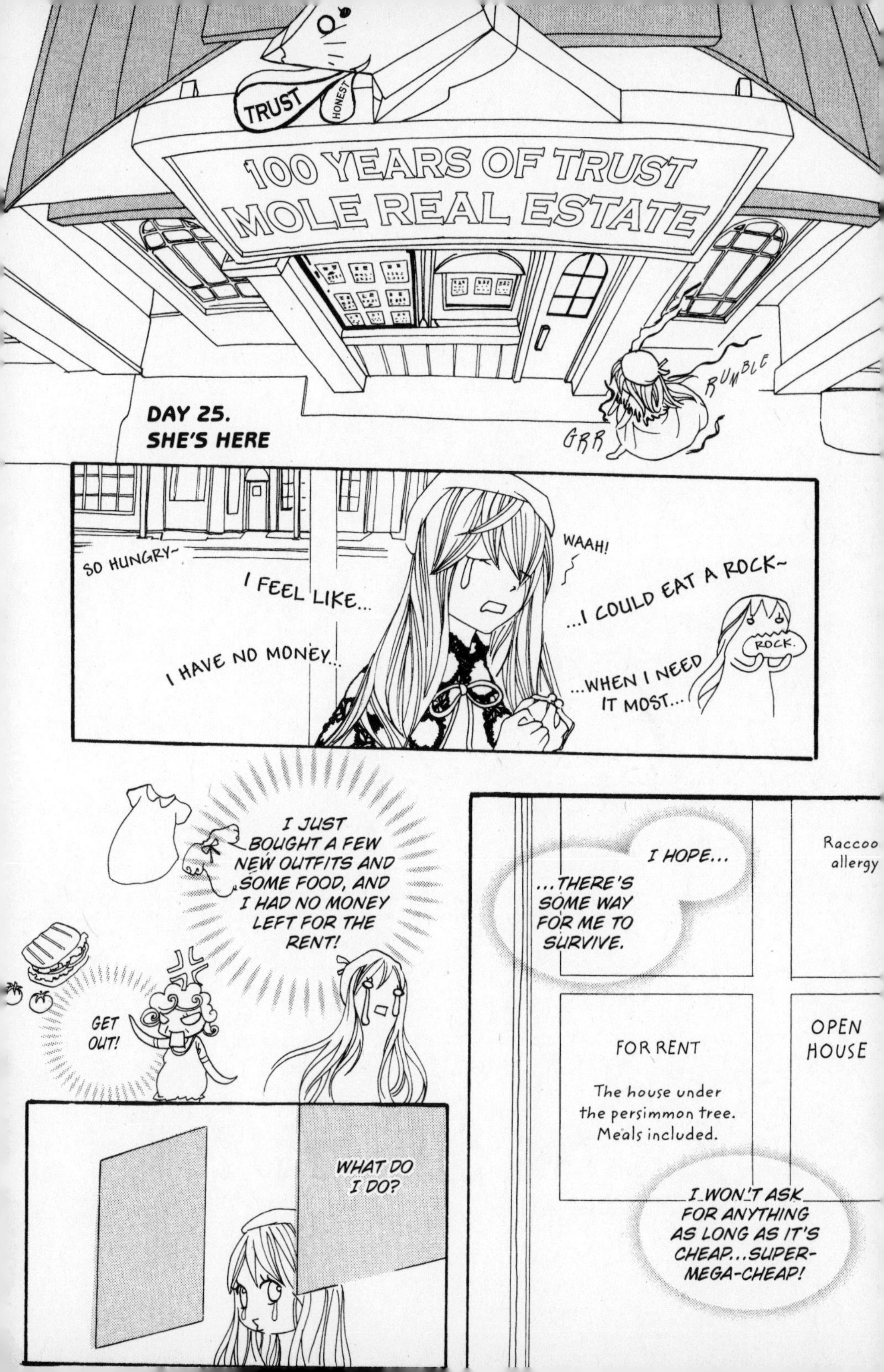
TRUST
HONEST
100 YEARS OF TRUST
MOLE REAL ESTATE
RUMBLE
GRR
DAY 25.
SHE'S HERE
SO HUNGRY~
I FEEL LIKE...
WAAH!
...I COULD EAT A ROCK~
ROCK.
I HAVE NO MONEY...
...WHEN I NEED IT MOST...
I JUST BOUGHT A FEW NEW OUTFITS AND SOME FOOD, AND I HAD NO MONEY LEFT FOR THE RENT!
GET OUT!
I HOPE...
...THERE'S SOME WAY FOR ME TO SURVIVE.
Raccoo
allergy
OPEN HOUSE
FOR RENT
The house under the persimmon tree. Meals included.
WHAT DO I DO?
I WON'T ASK FOR ANYTHING AS LONG AS IT'S CHEAP...SUPER-MEGA-CHEAP!

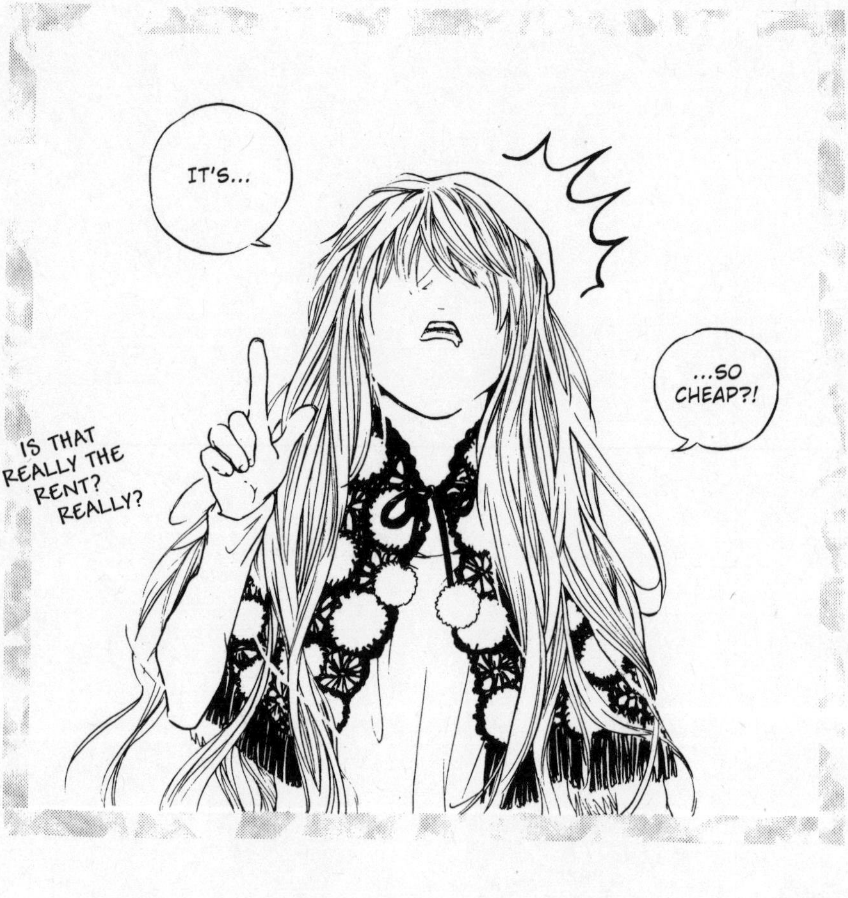
IT'S...
...SO CHEAP?!
IS THAT REALLY THE RENT? REALLY?

one fine day

DAY 25. SHE'S HERE

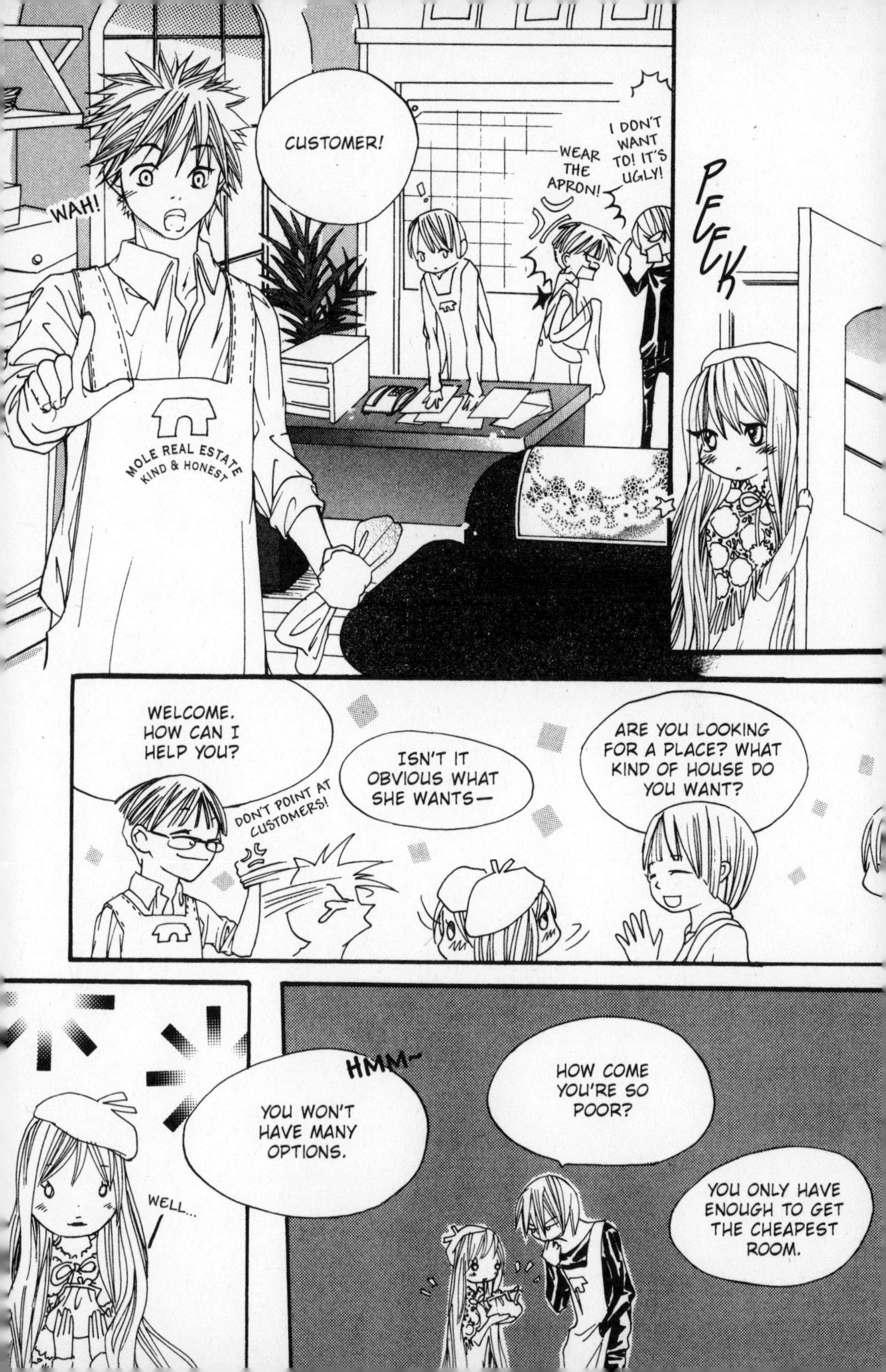
WAH!
CUSTOMER!
WEAR THE APRON!
I DON'T WANT TO! IT'S UGLY!
PFFK
MOLE REAL ESTATE KIND & HONEST
WELCOME. HOW CAN I HELP YOU?
DON'T POINT AT CUSTOMERS!
ISN'T IT OBVIOUS WHAT SHE WANTS—
ARE YOU LOOKING FOR A PLACE? WHAT KIND OF HOUSE DO YOU WANT?
HMM-
YOU WON'T HAVE MANY OPTIONS.
WELL...
HOW COME YOU'RE SO POOR?
YOU ONLY HAVE ENOUGH TO GET THE CHEAPEST ROOM.

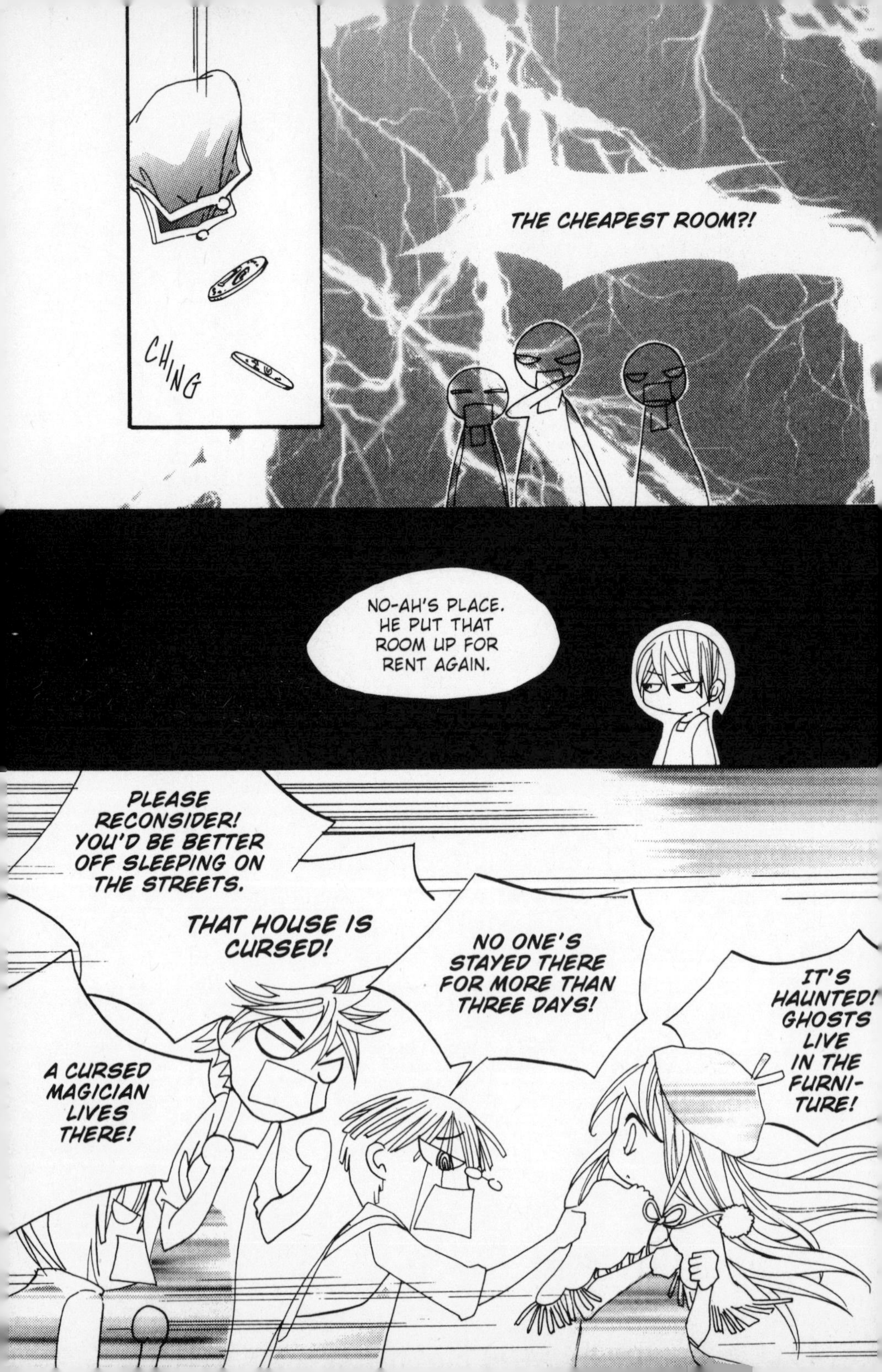
CHING
THE CHEAPEST ROOM?!
NO-AH'S PLACE. HE PUT THAT ROOM UP FOR RENT AGAIN.
PLEASE RECONSIDER! YOU'D BE BETTER OFF SLEEPING ON THE STREETS.
IT'S HAUNTED! GHOSTS LIVE IN THE FURNI-TURE!
NO ONE'S STAYED THERE FOR MORE THAN THREE DAYS!
THAT HOUSE IS CURSED!
A CURSED MAGICIAN LIVES THERE!

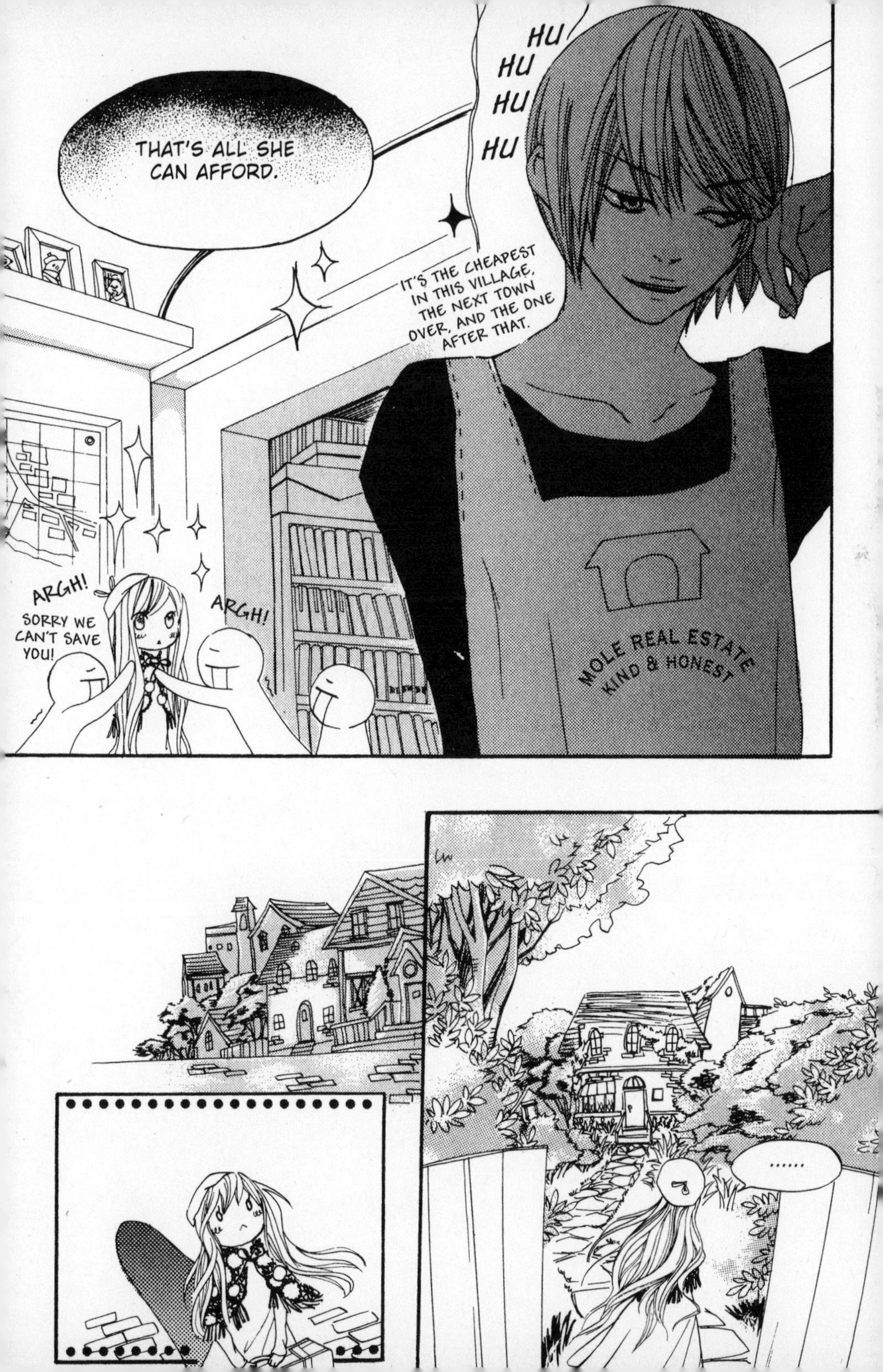
HU
HU
HU
HU
THAT'S ALL SHE CAN AFFORD.
IT'S THE CHEAPEST IN THIS VILLAGE, THE NEXT TOWN OVER, AND THE ONE AFTER THAT.
MOLE REAL ESTATE
KIND & HONEST
ARGH!
ARGH!
SORRY WE CAN'T SAVE YOU!
......

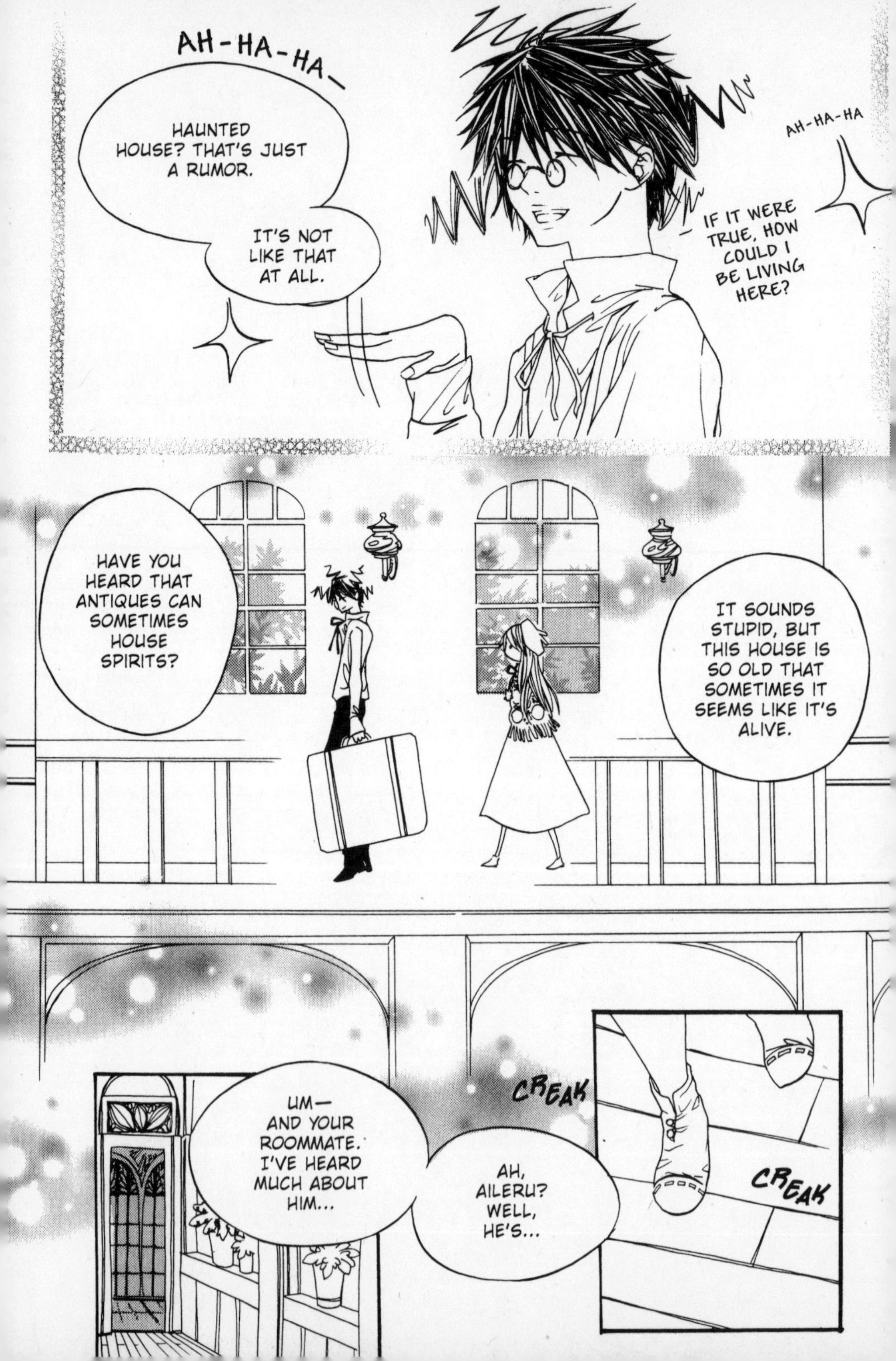
AH-HA-HA-
HAUNTED HOUSE? THAT'S JUST A RUMOR.
IT'S NOT LIKE THAT AT ALL.
AH-HA-HA
IF IT WERE TRUE, HOW COULD I BE LIVING HERE?
HAVE YOU HEARD THAT ANTIQUES CAN SOMETIMES HOUSE SPIRITS?
IT SOUNDS STUPID, BUT THIS HOUSE IS SO OLD THAT SOMETIMES IT SEEMS LIKE IT'S ALIVE.
UM— AND YOUR ROOMMATE. I'VE HEARD MUCH ABOUT HIM...
AH, AILERU? WELL, HE'S...
CREAK
CREAK

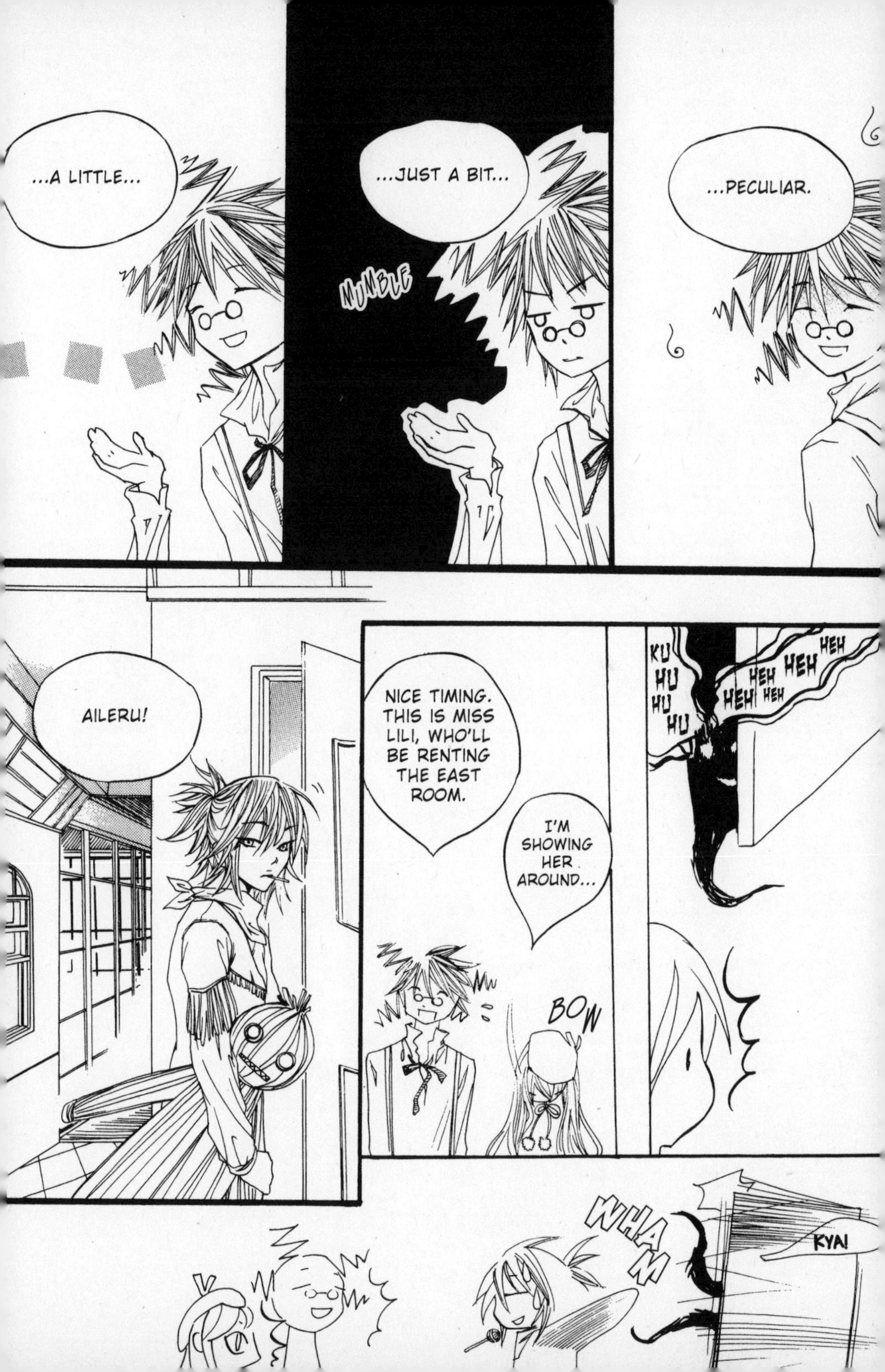
...A LITTLE...
...JUST A BIT...
MUMBLE
...PECULIAR.
AILERU!
NICE TIMING. THIS IS MISS LILI, WHO'LL BE RENTING THE EAST ROOM.
I'M SHOWING HER AROUND...
BOW
KU HU HU HU
HEH HEH HEH HEH HEH HEH
WHAM
KYA!

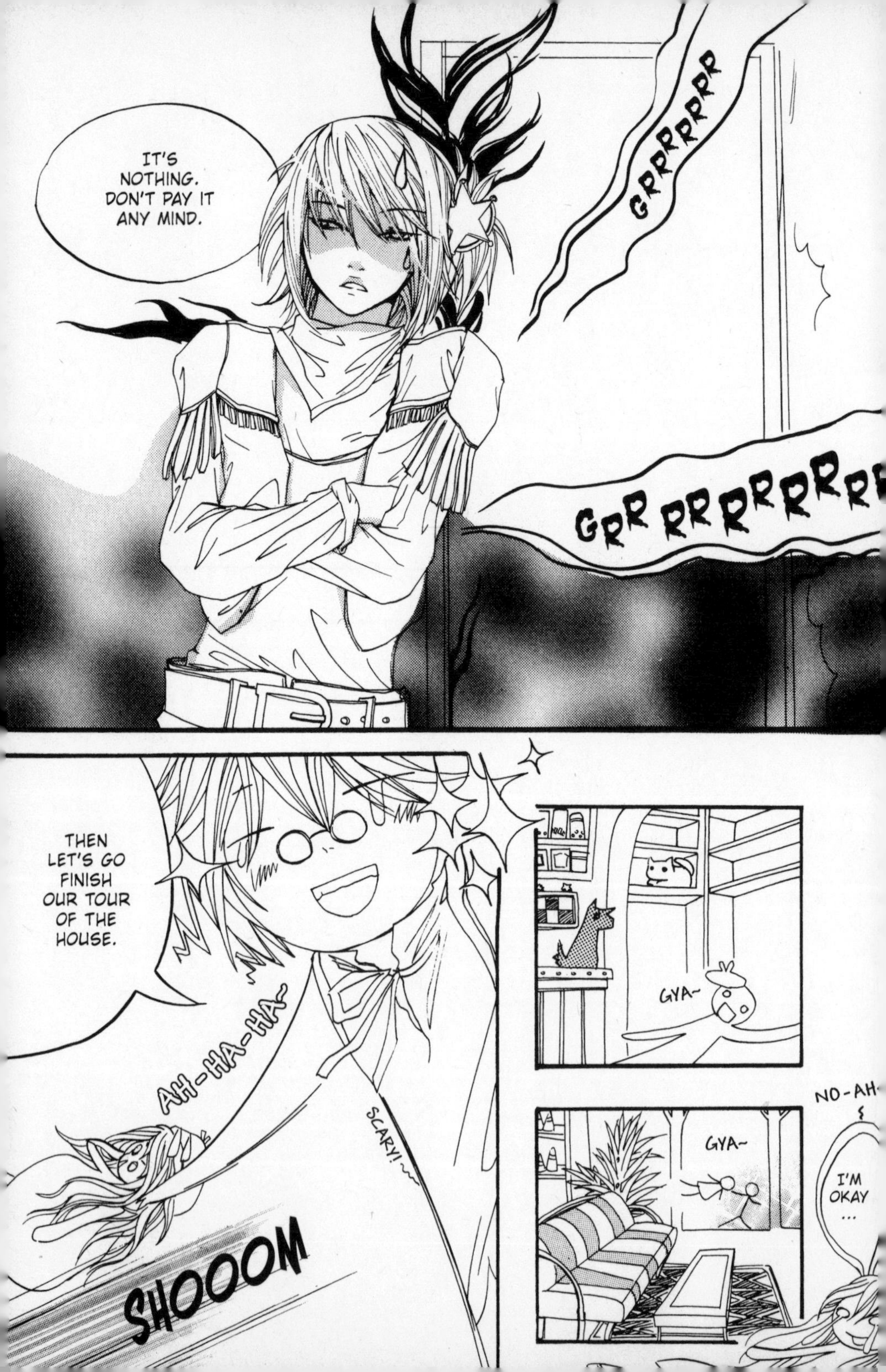
IT'S NOTHING. DON'T PAY IT ANY MIND.
GRRRRRRR
GRR RRRRRRR
THEN LET'S GO FINISH OUR TOUR OF THE HOUSE.
AH-HA-HA~
SCARY!~
SHOOOM
GYA~
GYA~
NO-AH~
I'M OKAY ...

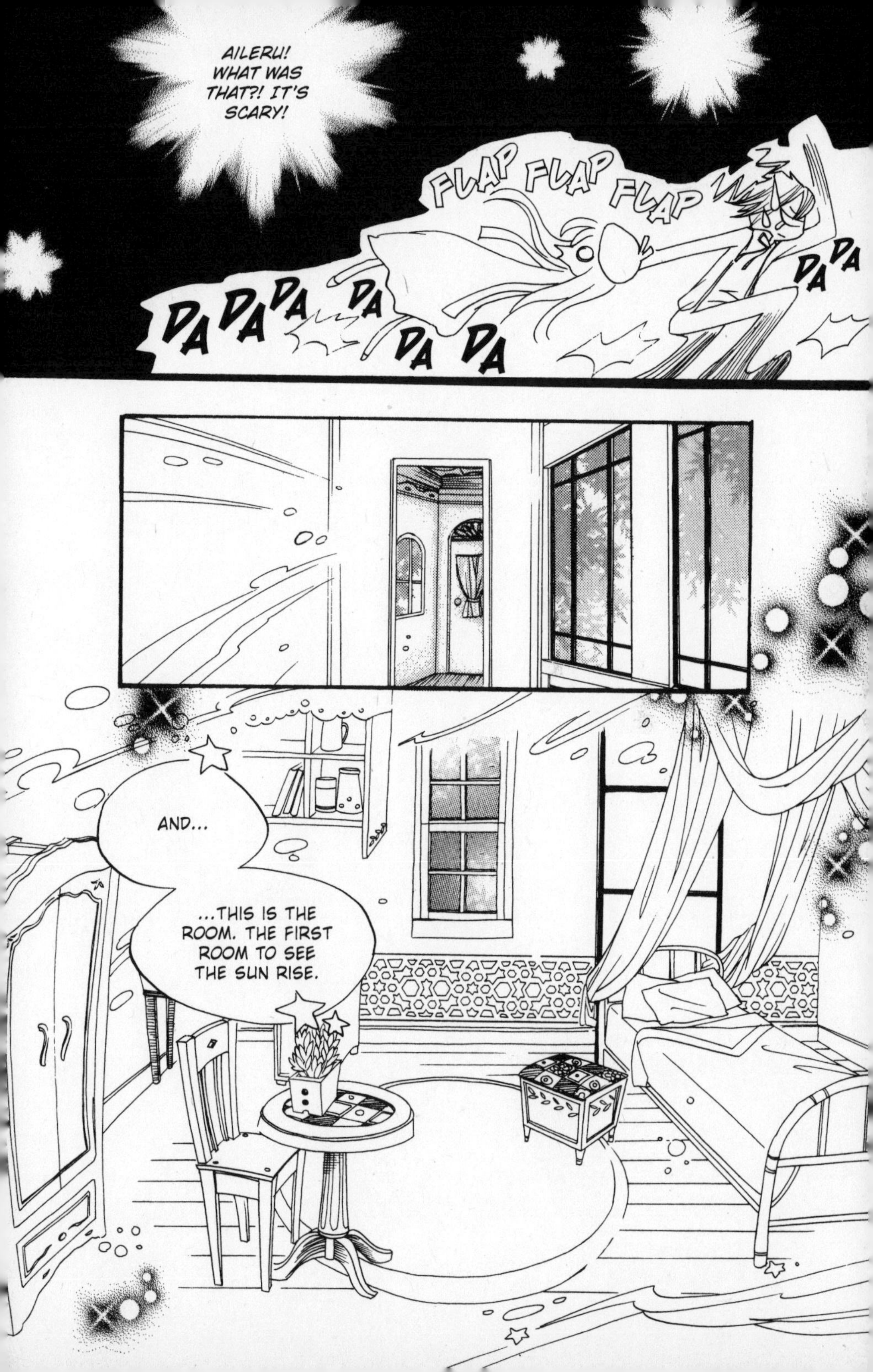
AILERU! WHAT WAS THAT?! IT'S SCARY!
FLAP FLAP FLAP
DA DA DA DA DA DA
DA DA
AND...
...THIS IS THE ROOM. THE FIRST ROOM TO SEE THE SUN RISE.

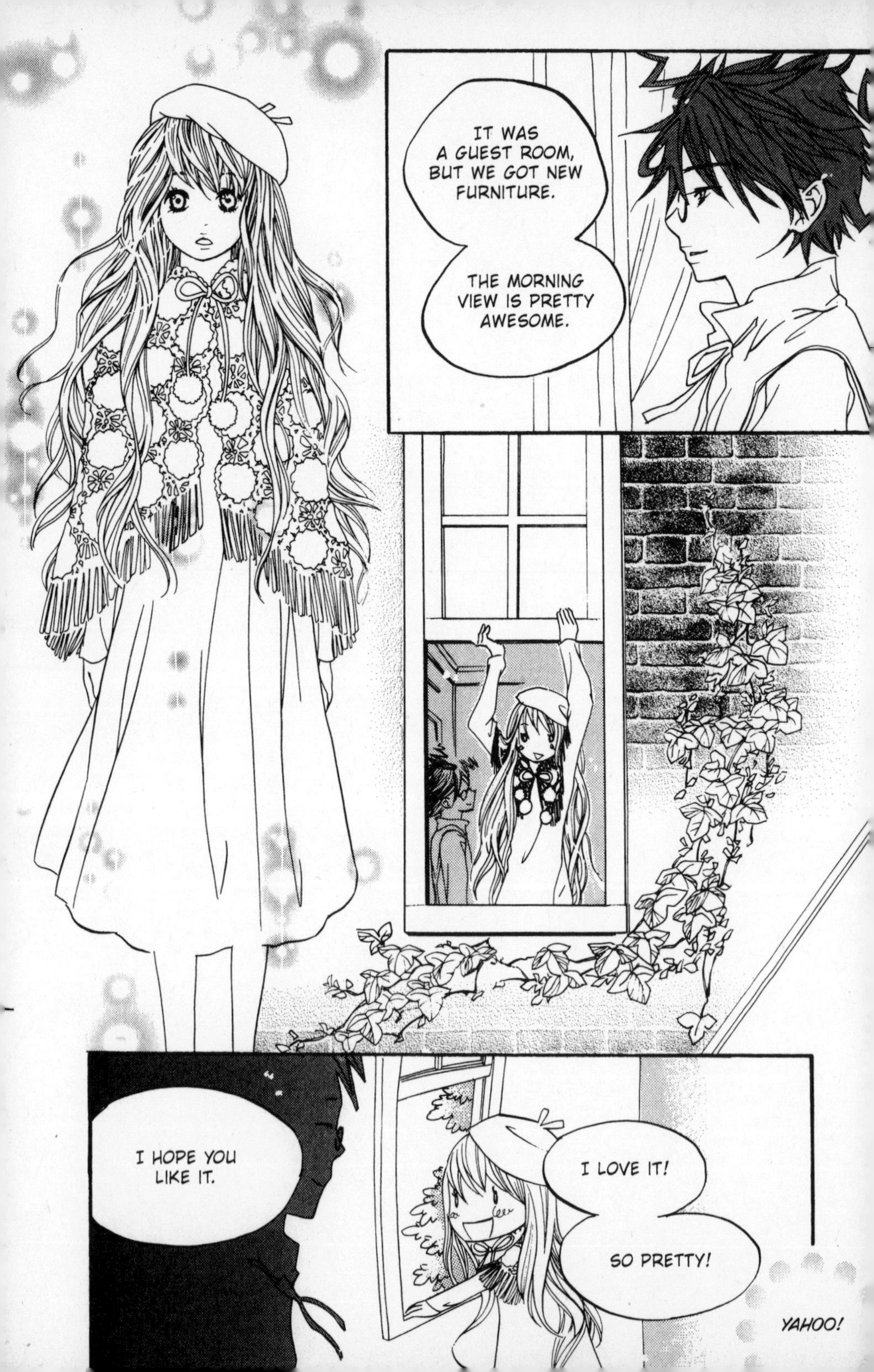
IT WAS A GUEST ROOM, BUT WE GOT NEW FURNITURE.
THE MORNING VIEW IS PRETTY AWESOME.
I HOPE YOU LIKE IT.
I LOVE IT!
SO PRETTY!
YAHOO!

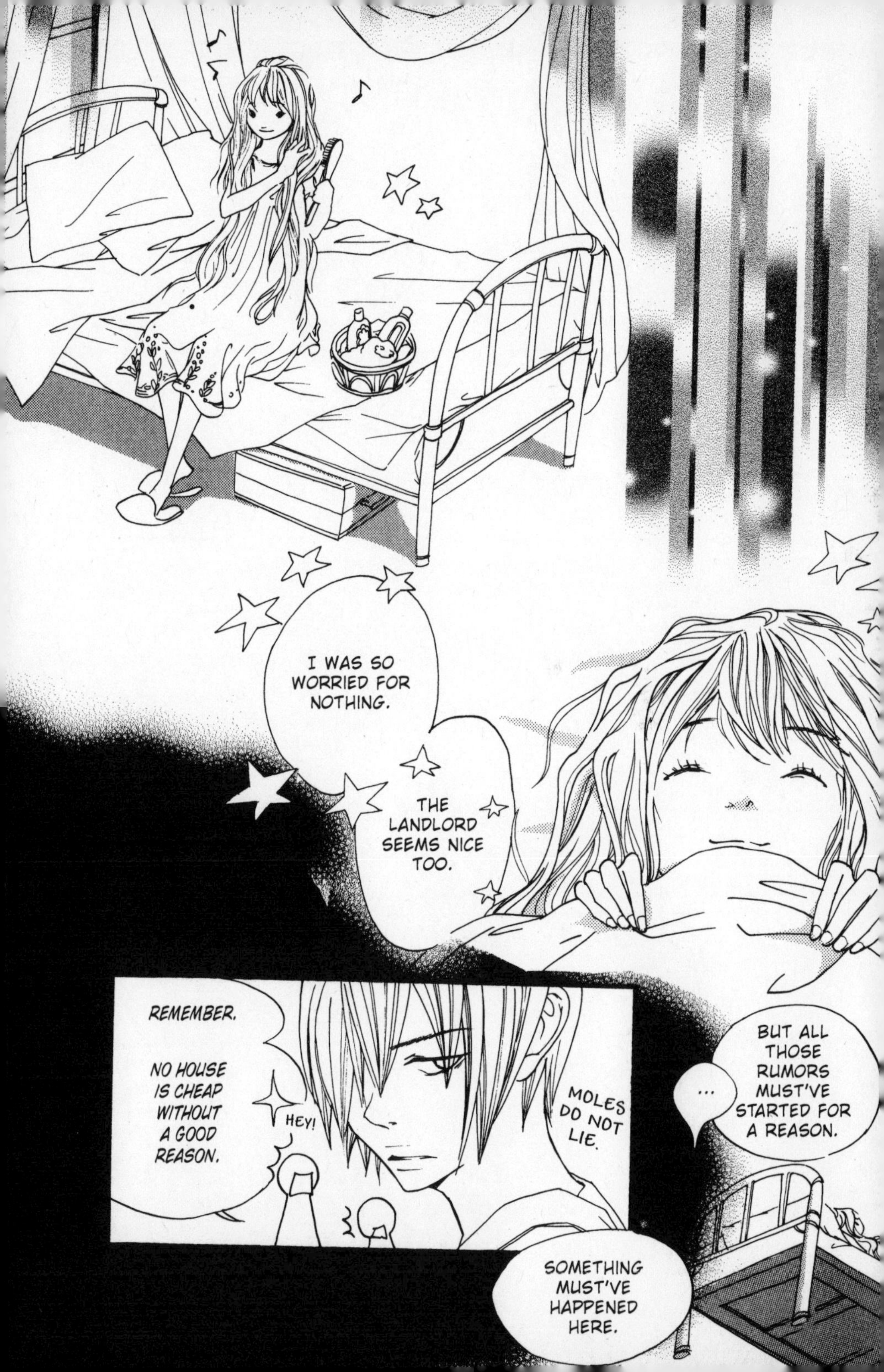
I WAS SO WORRIED FOR NOTHING.
THE LANDLORD SEEMS NICE TOO.
BUT ALL THOSE RUMORS MUST'VE STARTED FOR A REASON.
...
MOLES DO NOT LIE.
REMEMBER.
NO HOUSE IS CHEAP WITHOUT A GOOD REASON.
HEY!
SOMETHING MUST'VE HAPPENED HERE.

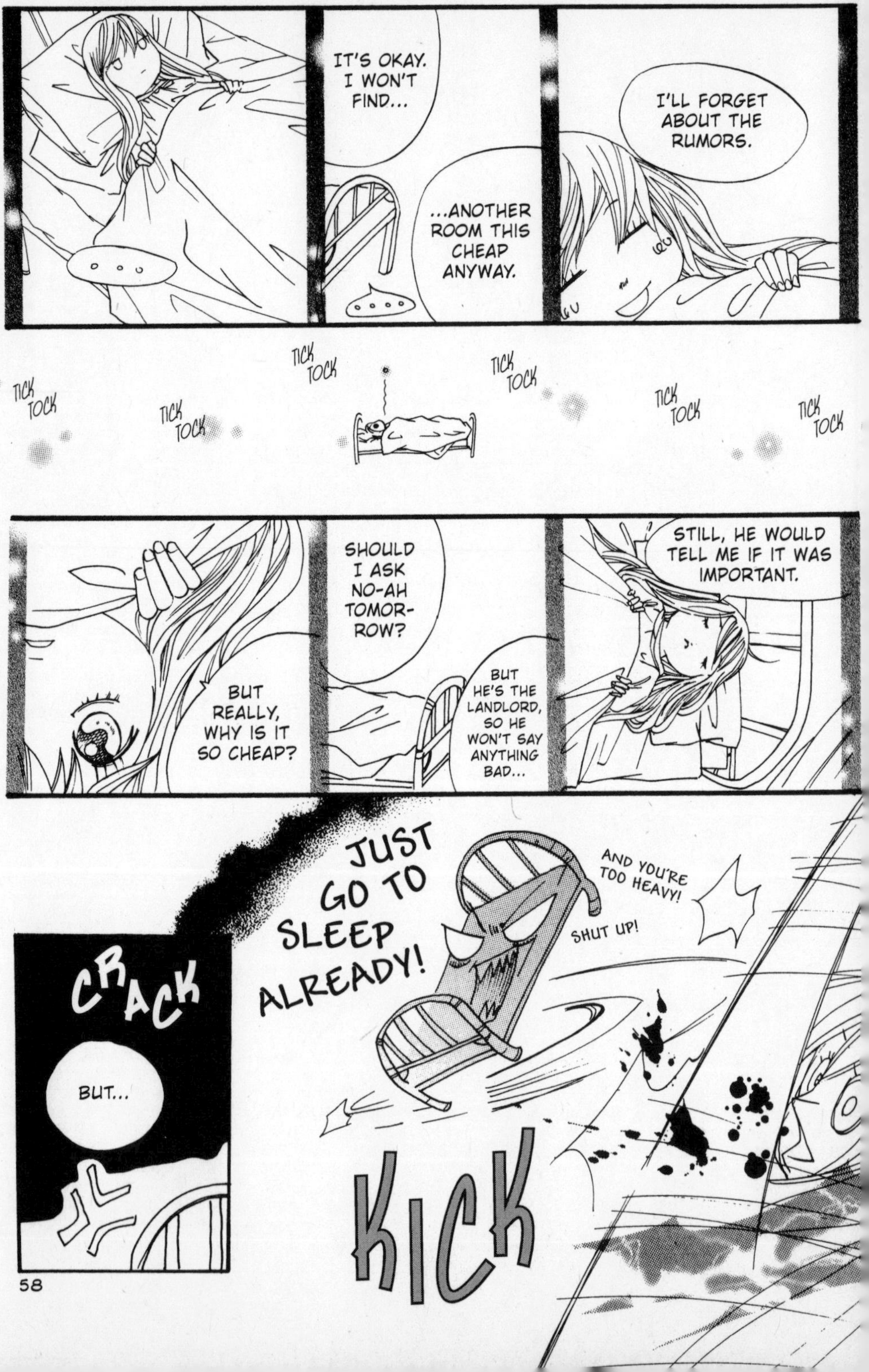
IT'S OKAY. I WON'T FIND...
...ANOTHER ROOM THIS CHEAP ANYWAY.
I'LL FORGET ABOUT THE RUMORS.
TICK TOCK
TICK TOCK
TICK TOCK
TICK TOCK
TICK TOCK
TICK TOCK
BUT REALLY, WHY IS IT SO CHEAP?
SHOULD I ASK NO-AH TOMOR-ROW?
BUT HE'S THE LANDLORD, SO HE WON'T SAY ANYTHING BAD...
STILL, HE WOULD TELL ME IF IT WAS IMPORTANT.
JUST GO TO SLEEP ALREADY!
AND YOU'RE TOO HEAVY!
SHUT UP!
KICK
CRACK
BUT...

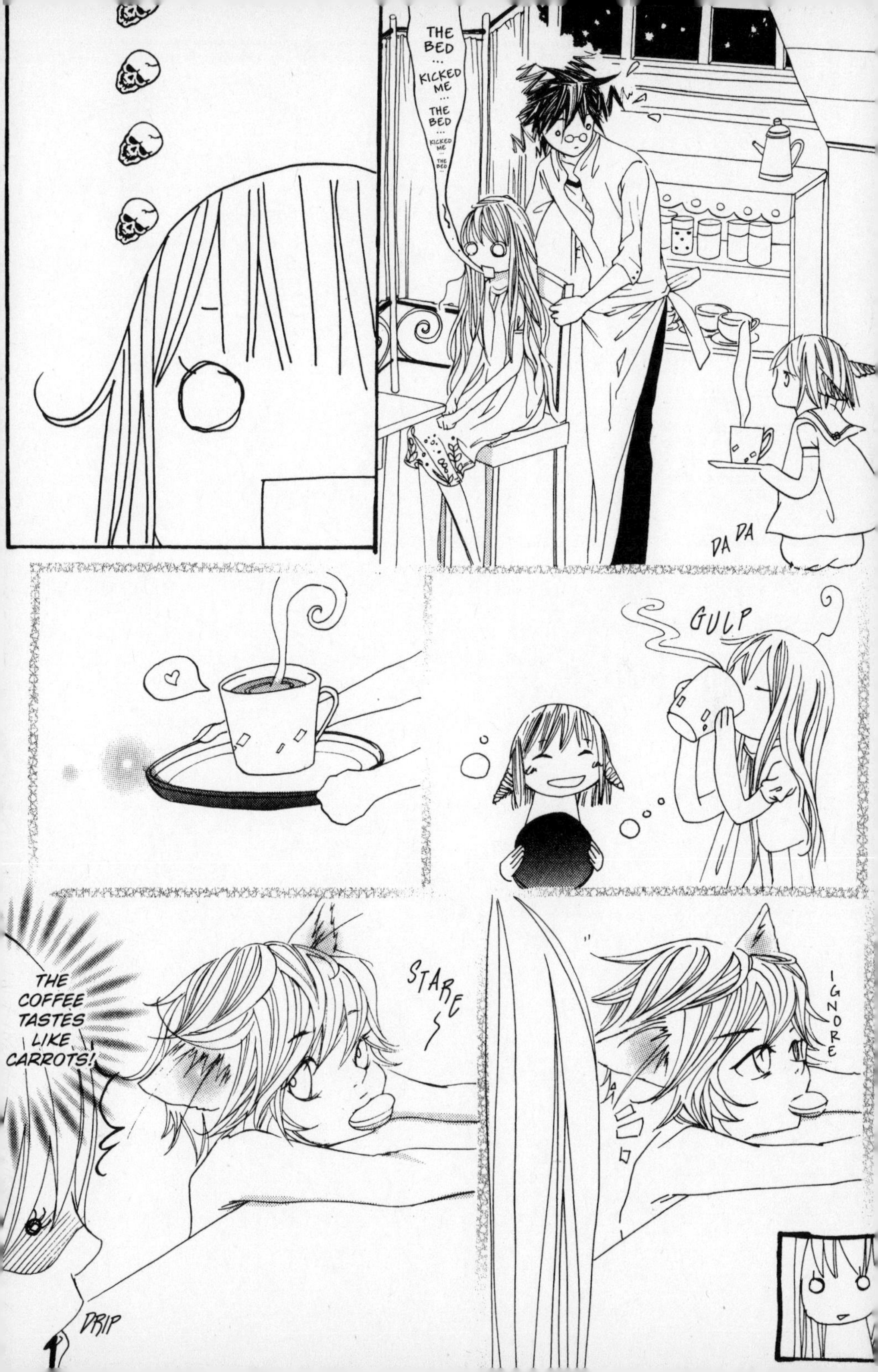
THE BED ... KICKED ME ... THE BED ... KICKED ME ... THE BED ...
DA DA
GULP
THE COFFEE TASTES LIKE CARROTS!
STARE
IGNORE
DRIP

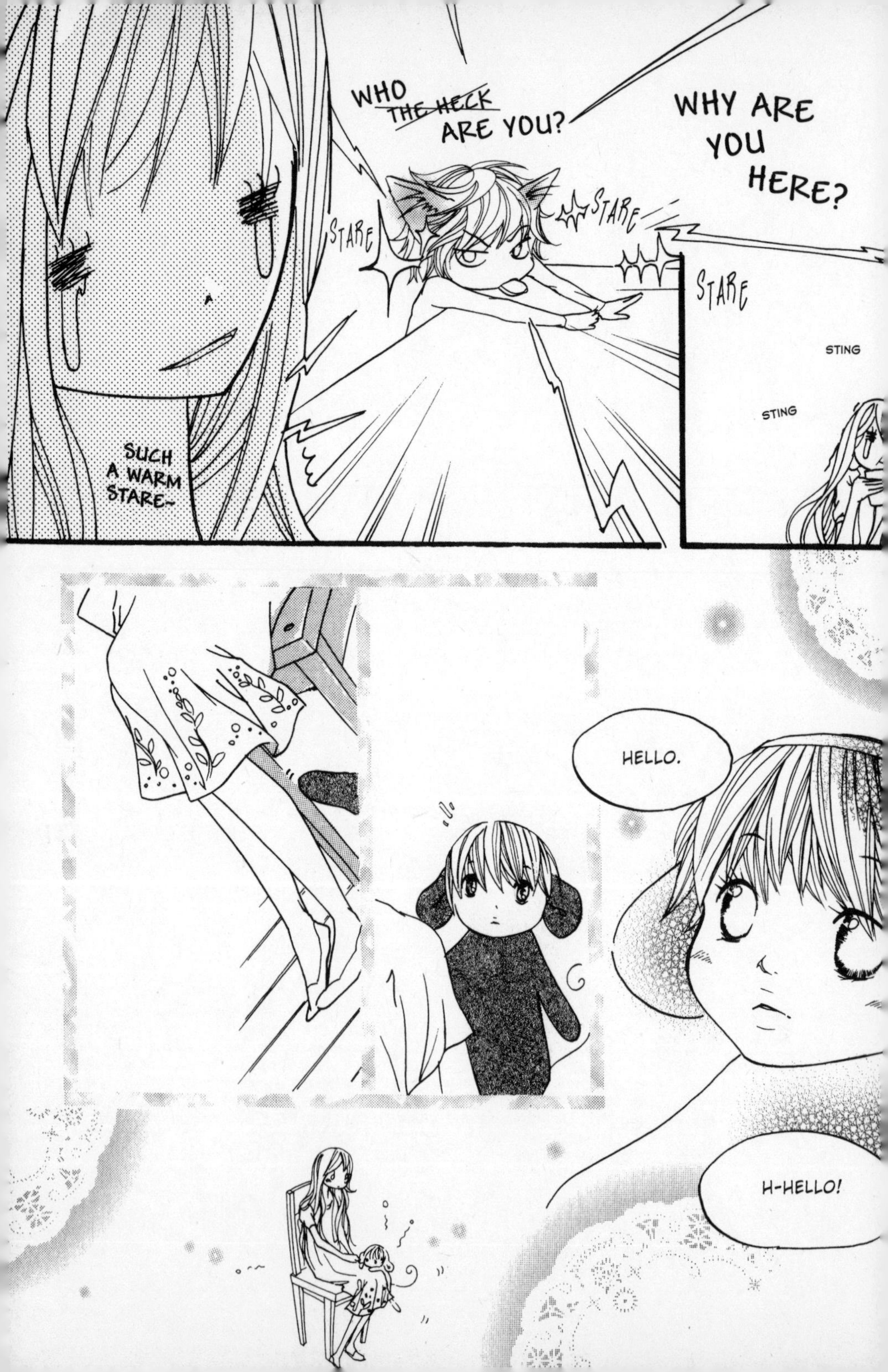
WHO THE HECK ARE YOU?
WHY ARE YOU HERE?
STARE
STARE
STARE
SUCH A WARM STARE~
STING
STING
HELLO.
H-HELLO!

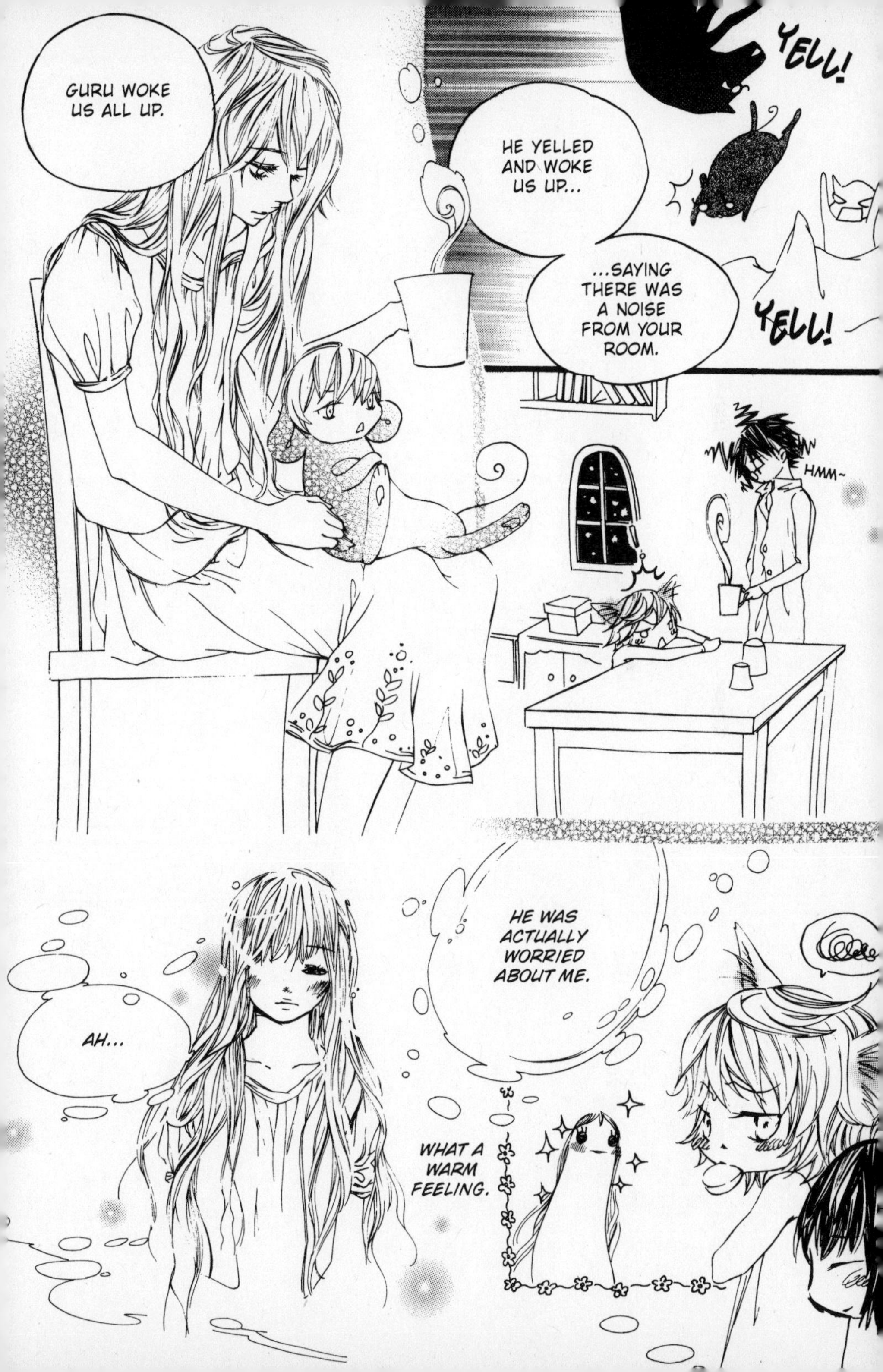
YELL!
YELL!
HE YELLED AND WOKE US UP...
...SAYING THERE WAS A NOISE FROM YOUR ROOM.
GURU WOKE US ALL UP.
HMM~
HE WAS ACTUALLY WORRIED ABOUT ME.
AH...
WHAT A WARM FEELING.

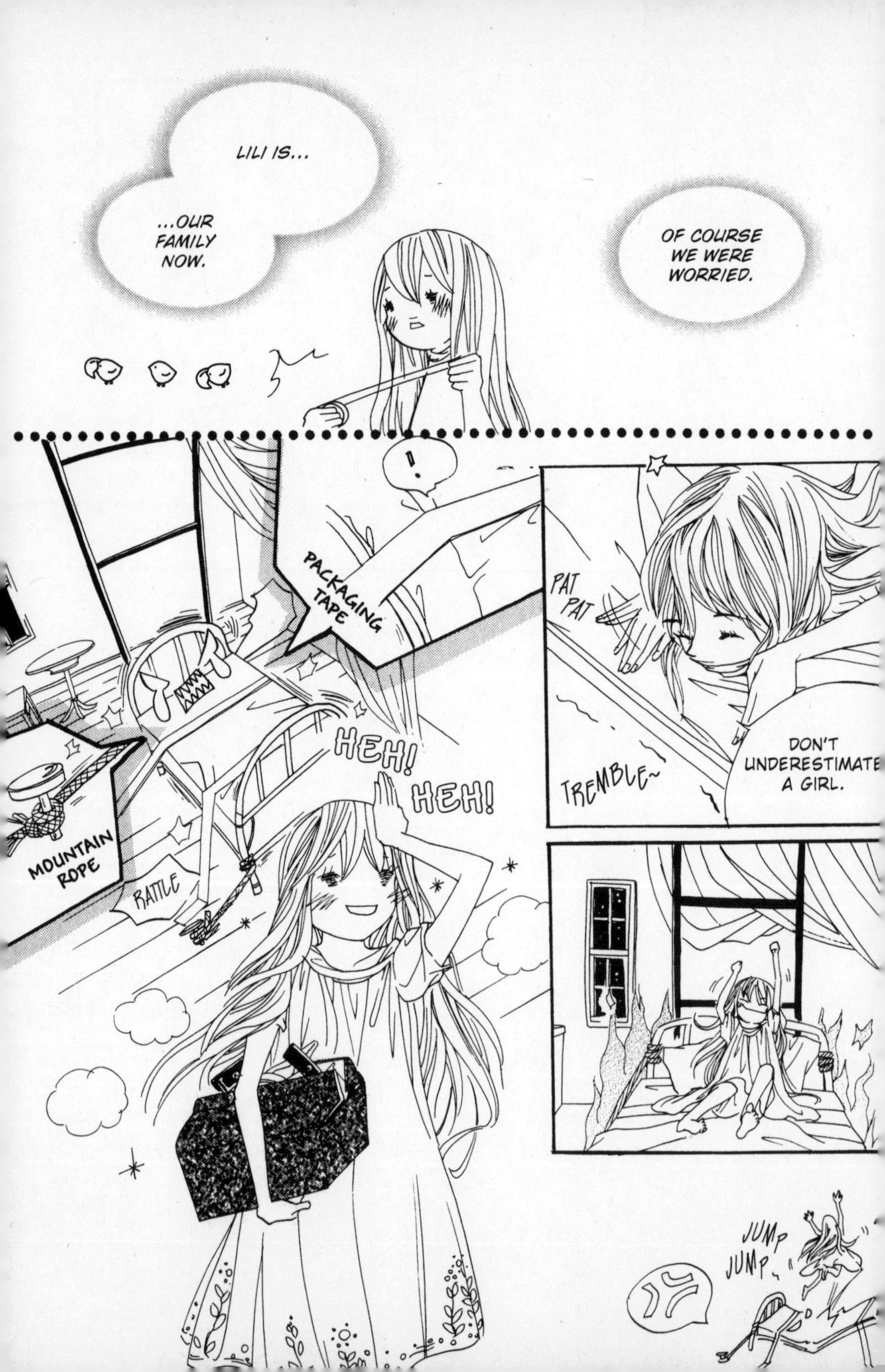
LILI IS...
...OUR FAMILY NOW.
OF COURSE WE WERE WORRIED.
!
PACKAGING TAPE
PAT PAT
TREMBLE~
DON'T UNDERESTIMATE A GIRL.
HEH! HEH!
MOUNTAIN ROPE
RATTLE
JUMP JUMP

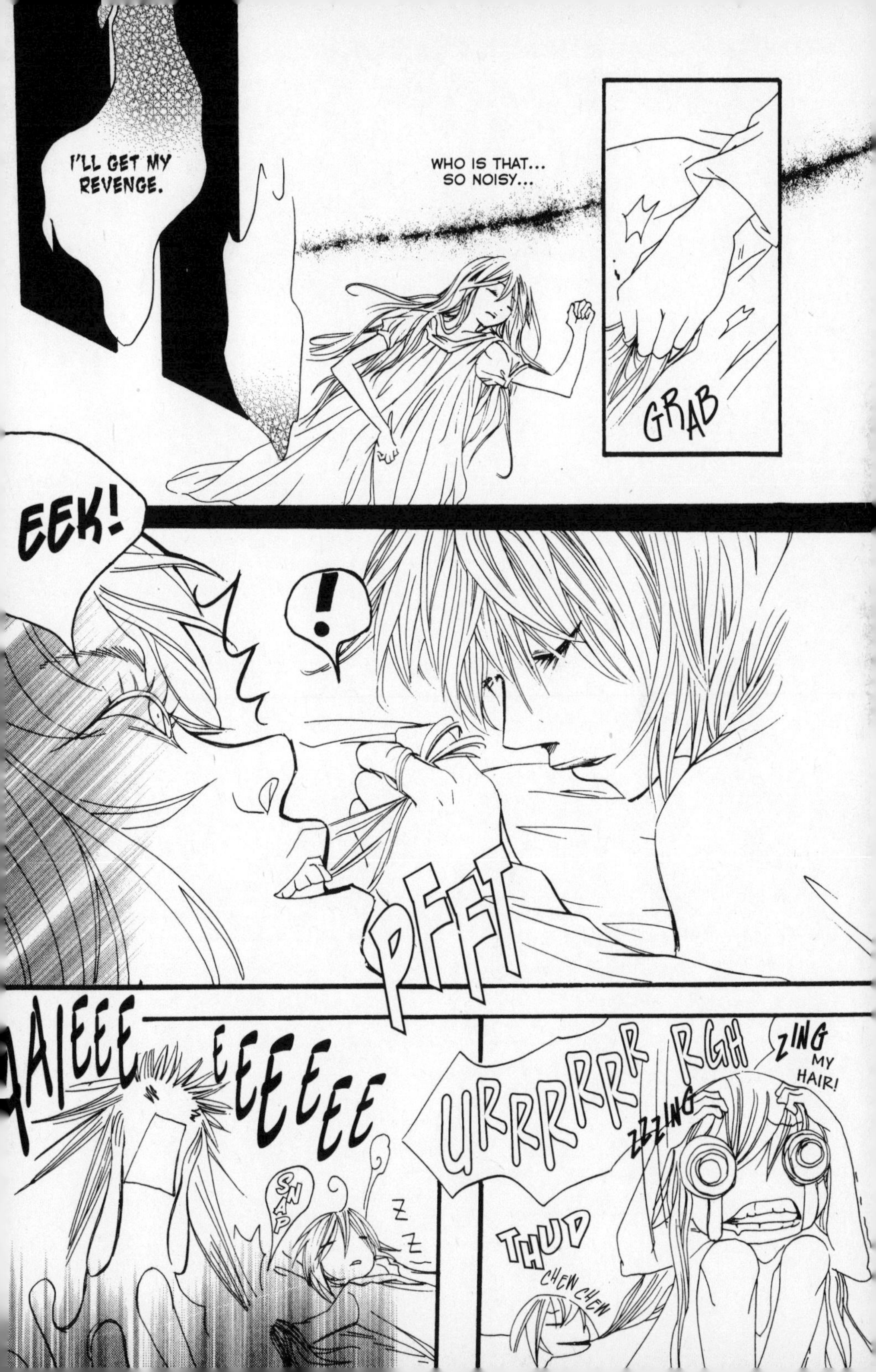

I'LL GET MY REVENGE.
WHO IS THAT... SO NOISY...
GRAB
EEK!
!
PFFT
AIEEE EEEEEE
SNAP
Z Z
URRRRRR RGH
ZING MY HAIR!
ZZZING
THUD
CHEW CHEW

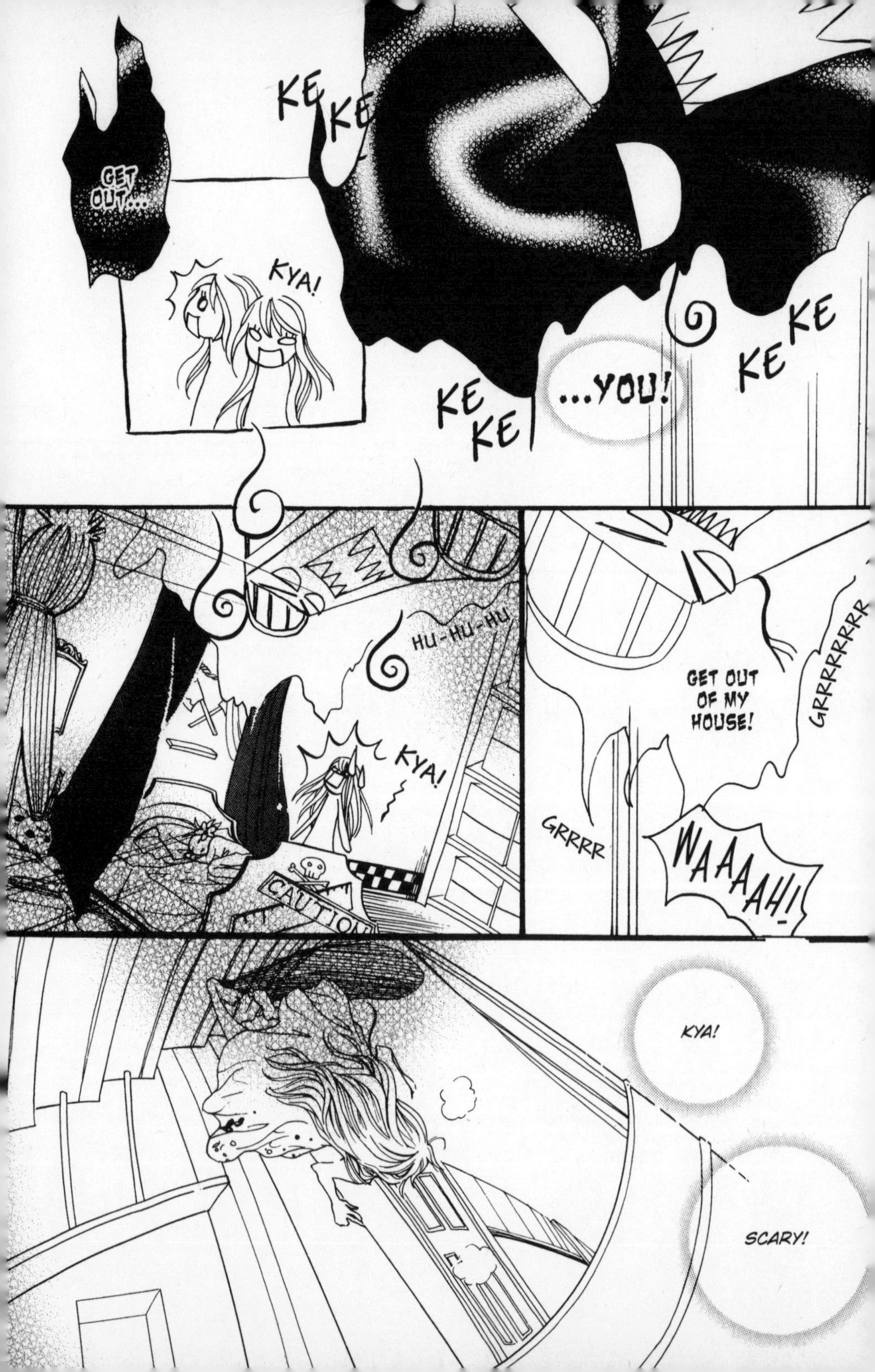

GET OUT...
KE KE
KYA!
KE KE
...YOU!
KE KE
GET OUT OF MY HOUSE!
GRRRRRRRRR
GRRRR
WAAAAAH!
HU-HU-HU
KYA!
CAUTION
KYA!
SCARY!

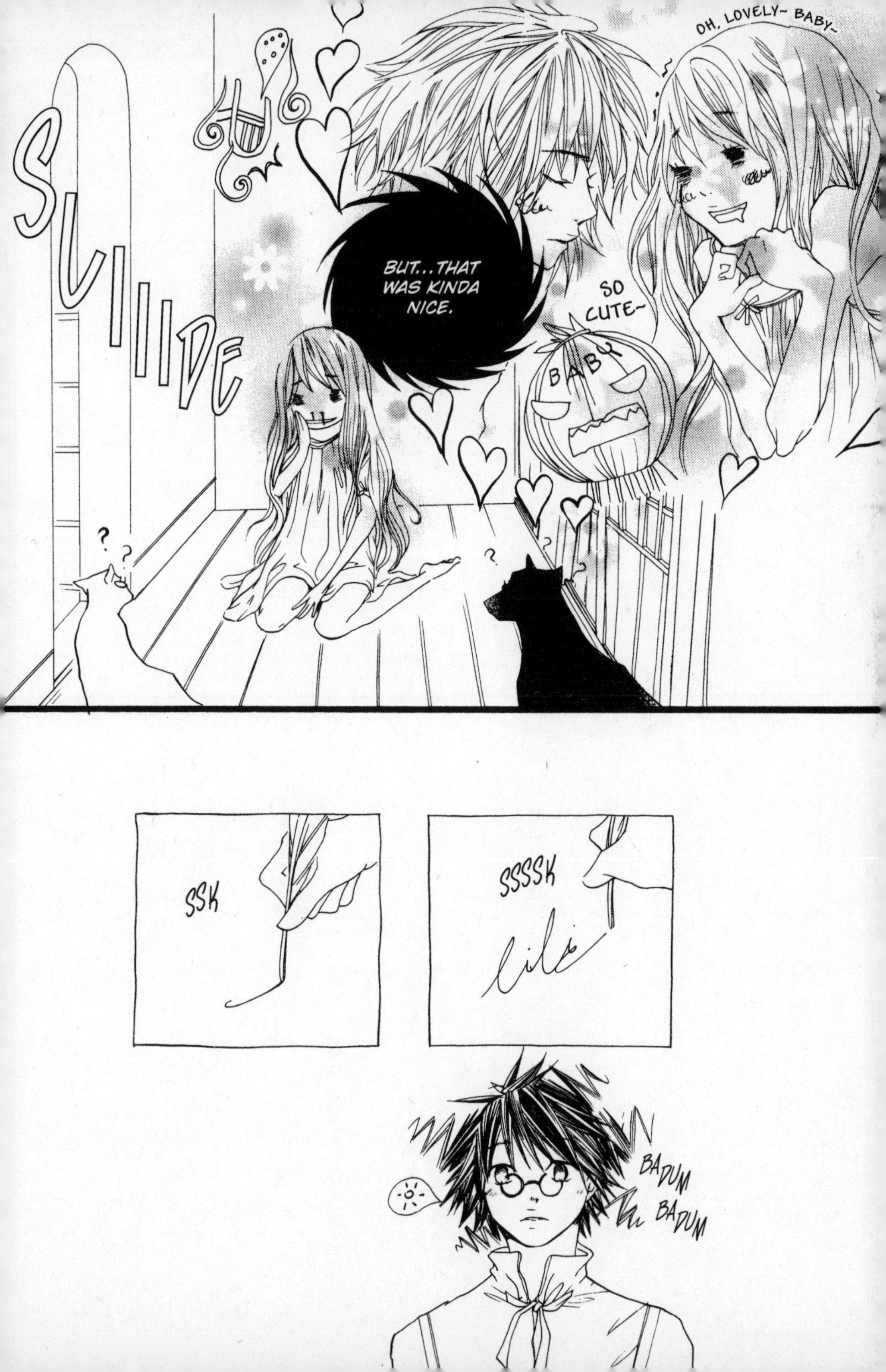
OH, LOVELY~ BABY~
SO CUTE~
BABY
BUT...THAT WAS KINDA NICE.
SLIIIDE
SSSSK
SSK
BADUM
BADUM

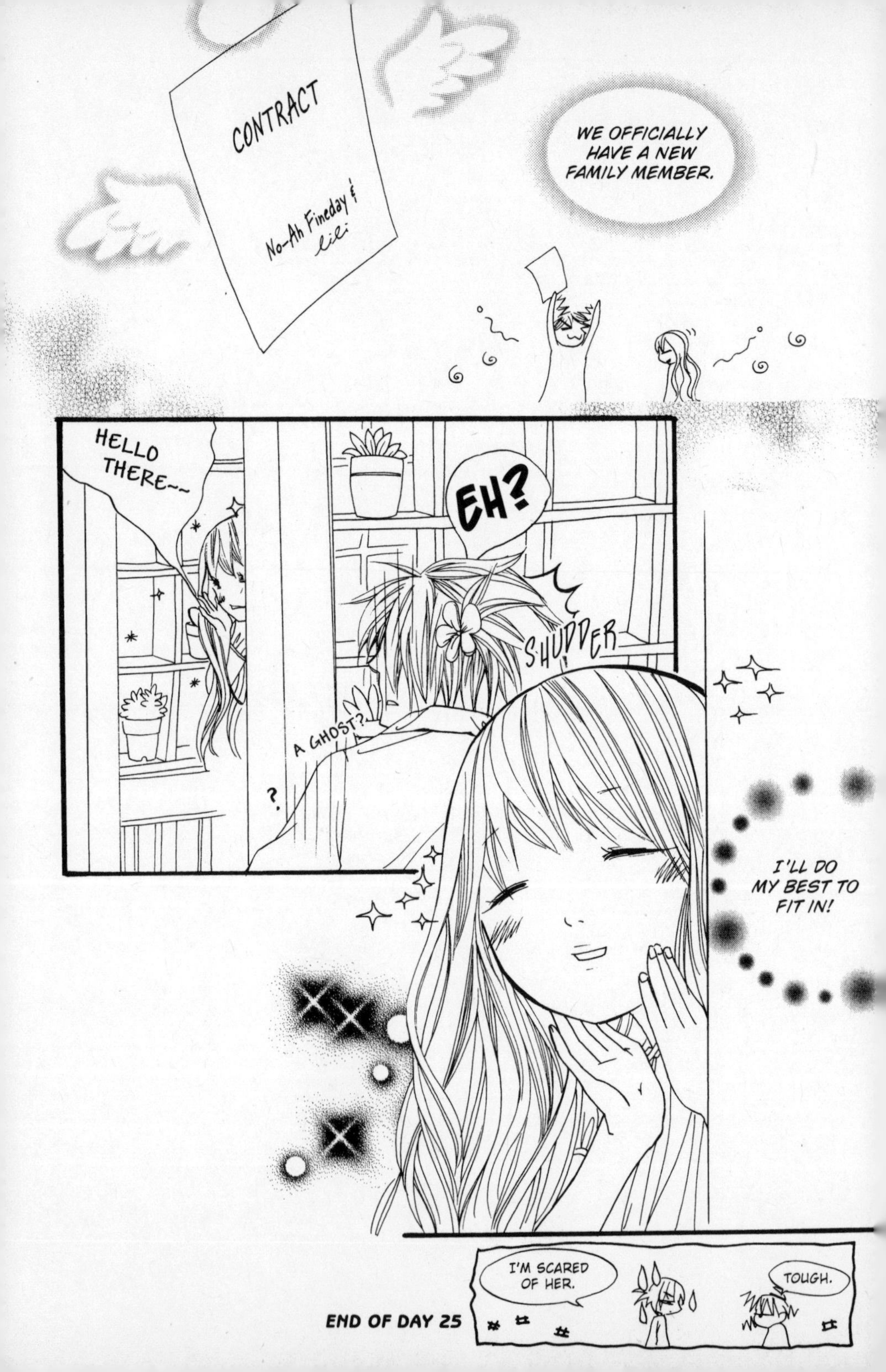
CONTRACT
No-Ah Fineday &
Lili
WE OFFICIALLY HAVE A NEW FAMILY MEMBER.
HELLO THERE~~
EH?
SHUDDER
A GHOST?
?
I'LL DO MY BEST TO FIT IN!
I'M SCARED OF HER.
TOUGH.
END OF DAY 25

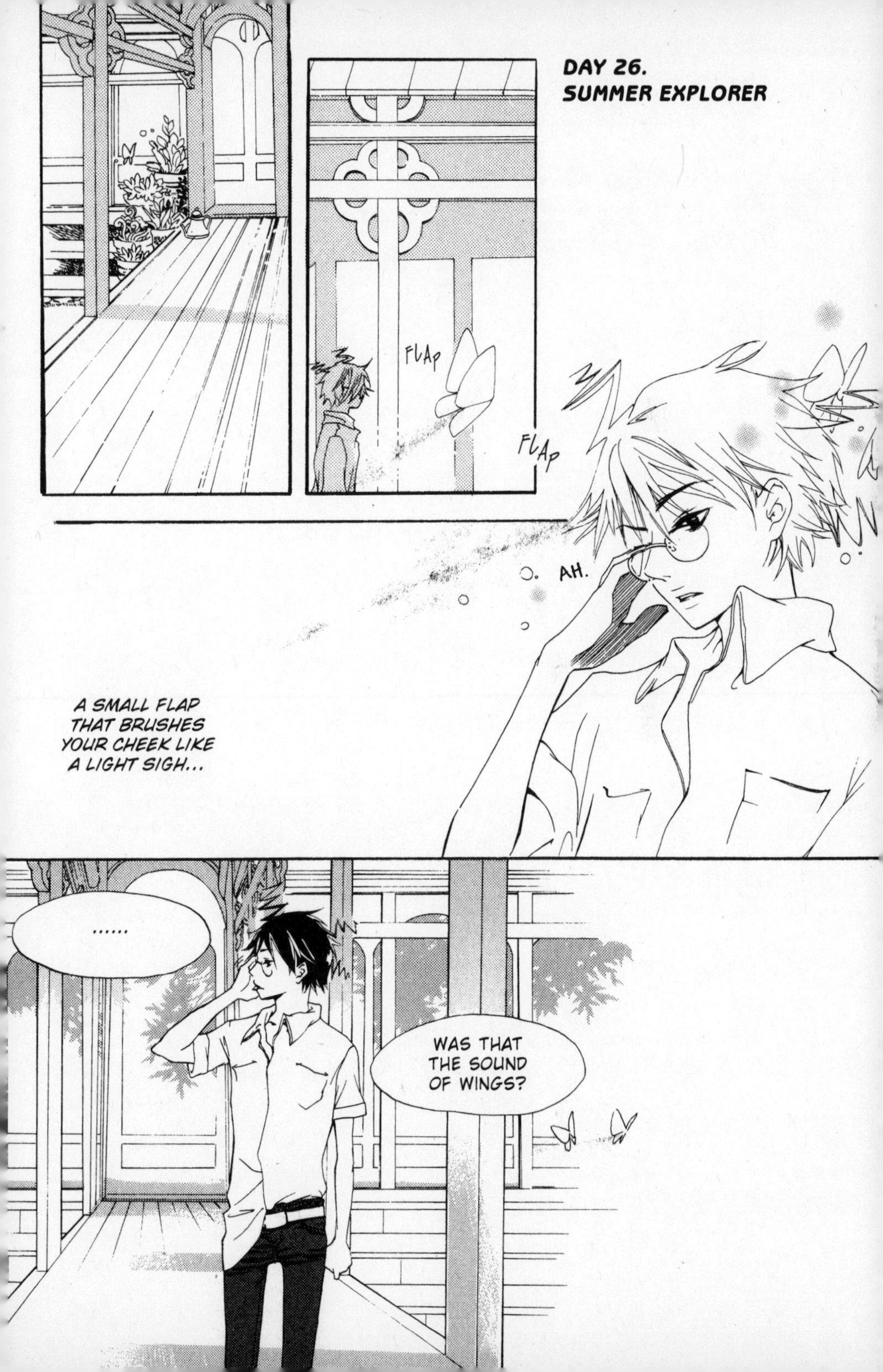
DAY 26.
SUMMER EXPLORER
FLAP
FLAP
AH.
A SMALL FLAP THAT BRUSHES YOUR CHEEK LIKE A LIGHT SIGH...
......
WAS THAT THE SOUND OF WINGS?

one fine day

DAY 26.
SUMMER EXPLORER

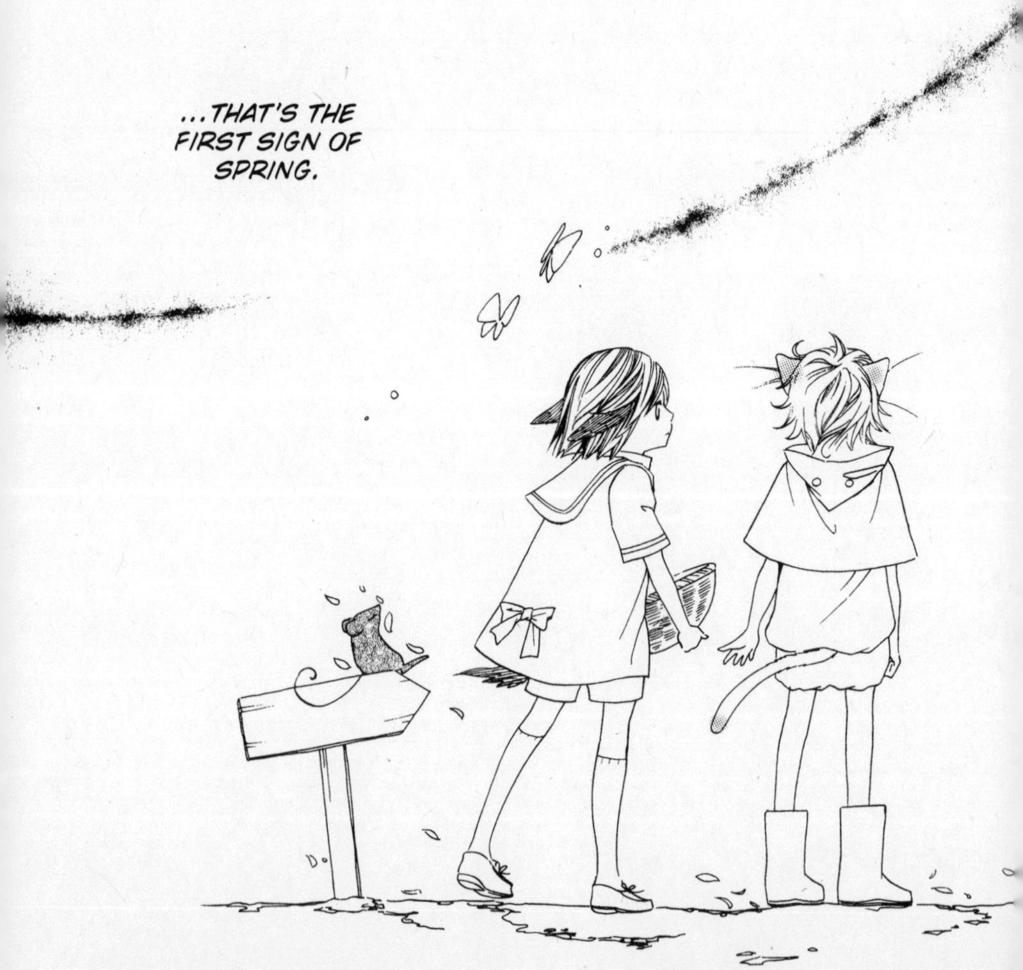
...THAT'S THE FIRST SIGN OF SPRING.

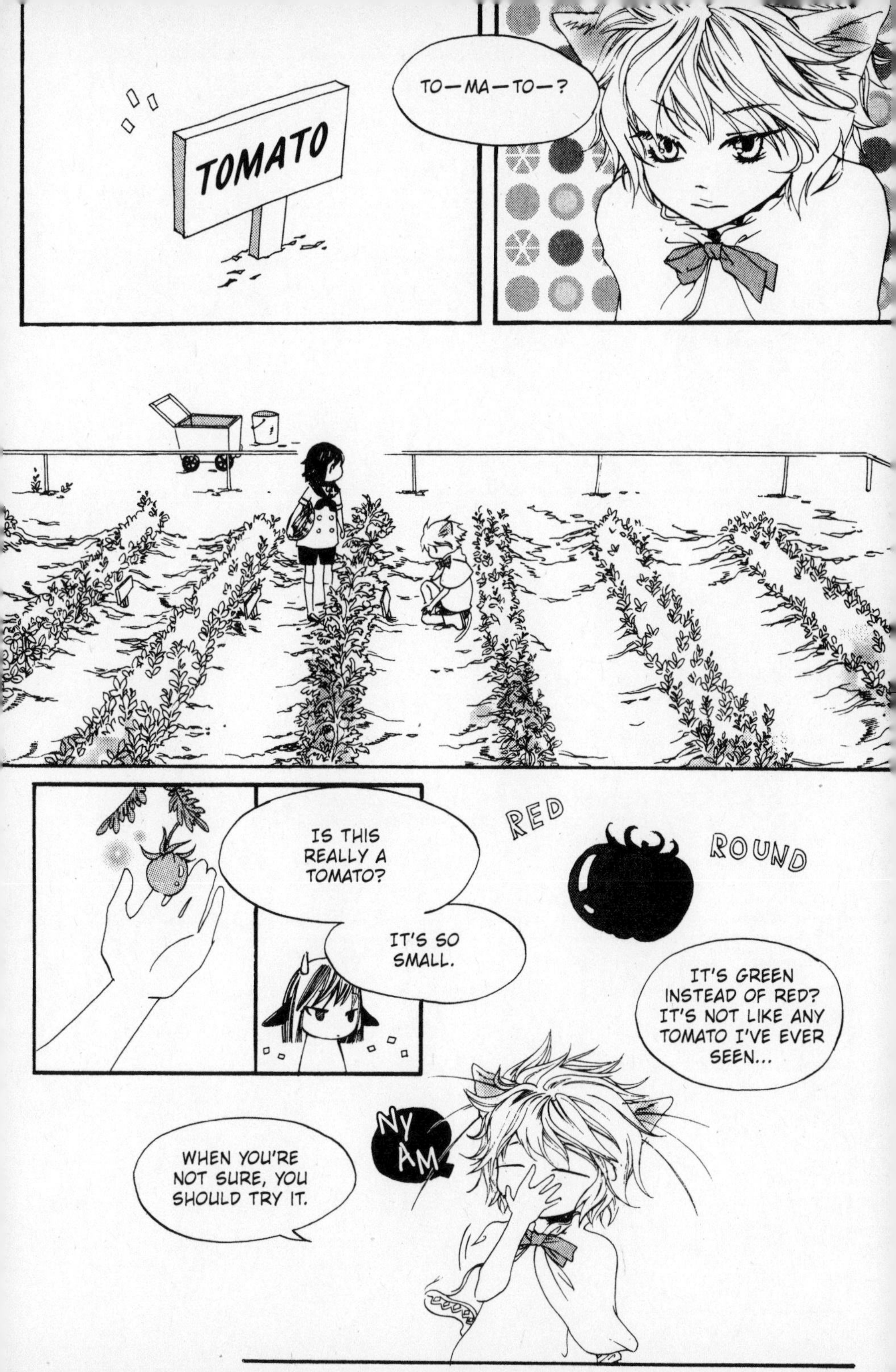
TOMATO
TO—MA—TO—?
IS THIS REALLY A TOMATO?
IT'S SO SMALL.
RED
ROUND
IT'S GREEN INSTEAD OF RED? IT'S NOT LIKE ANY TOMATO I'VE EVER SEEN...
NYAM
WHEN YOU'RE NOT SURE, YOU SHOULD TRY IT.

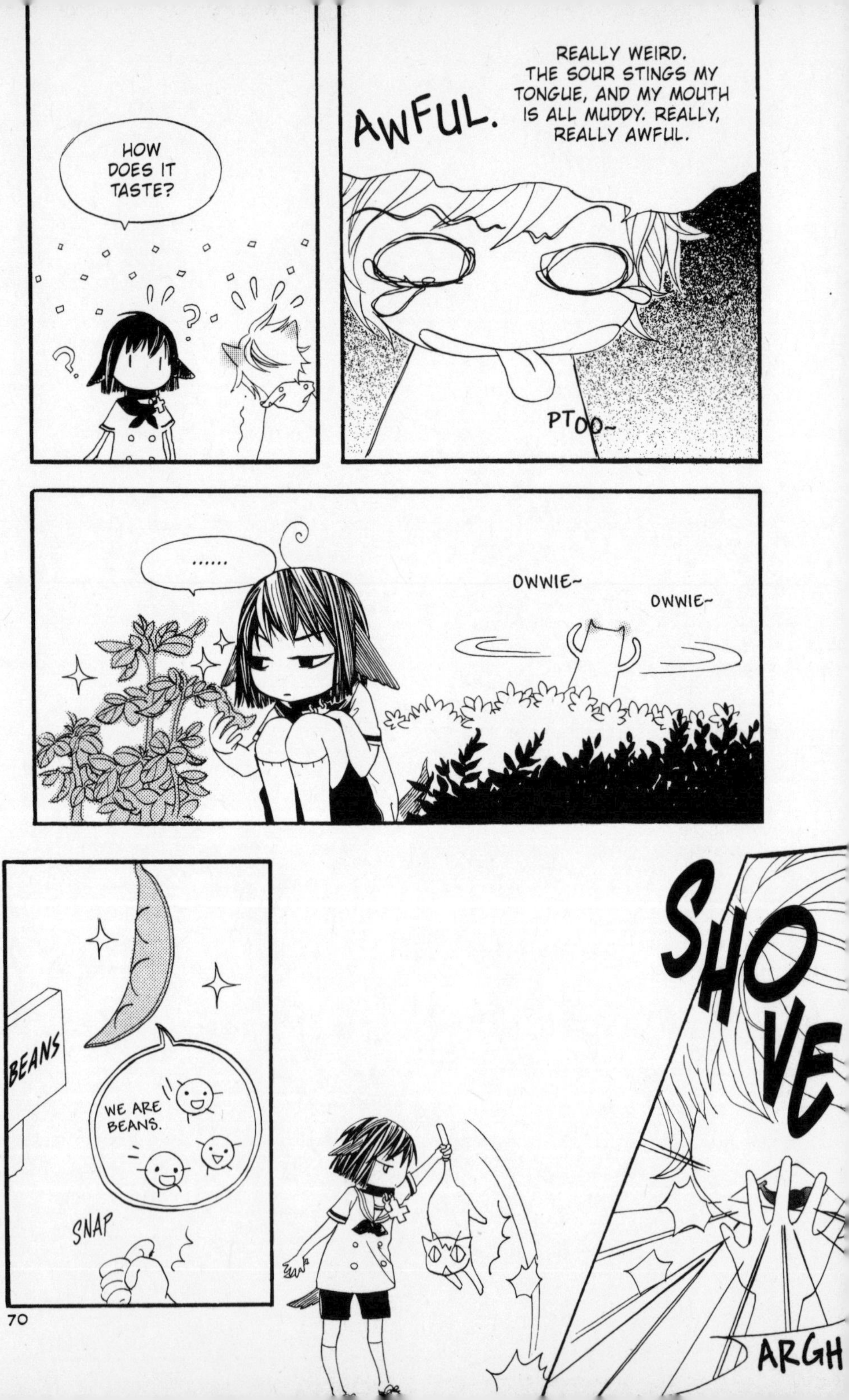
REALLY WEIRD. THE SOUR STINGS MY TONGUE, AND MY MOUTH IS ALL MUDDY. REALLY, REALLY AWFUL.
AWFUL.
PTOO~
HOW DOES IT TASTE?
......
OWWIE~
OWWIE~
SHOVE
ARGH
BEANS
WE ARE BEANS.
SNAP

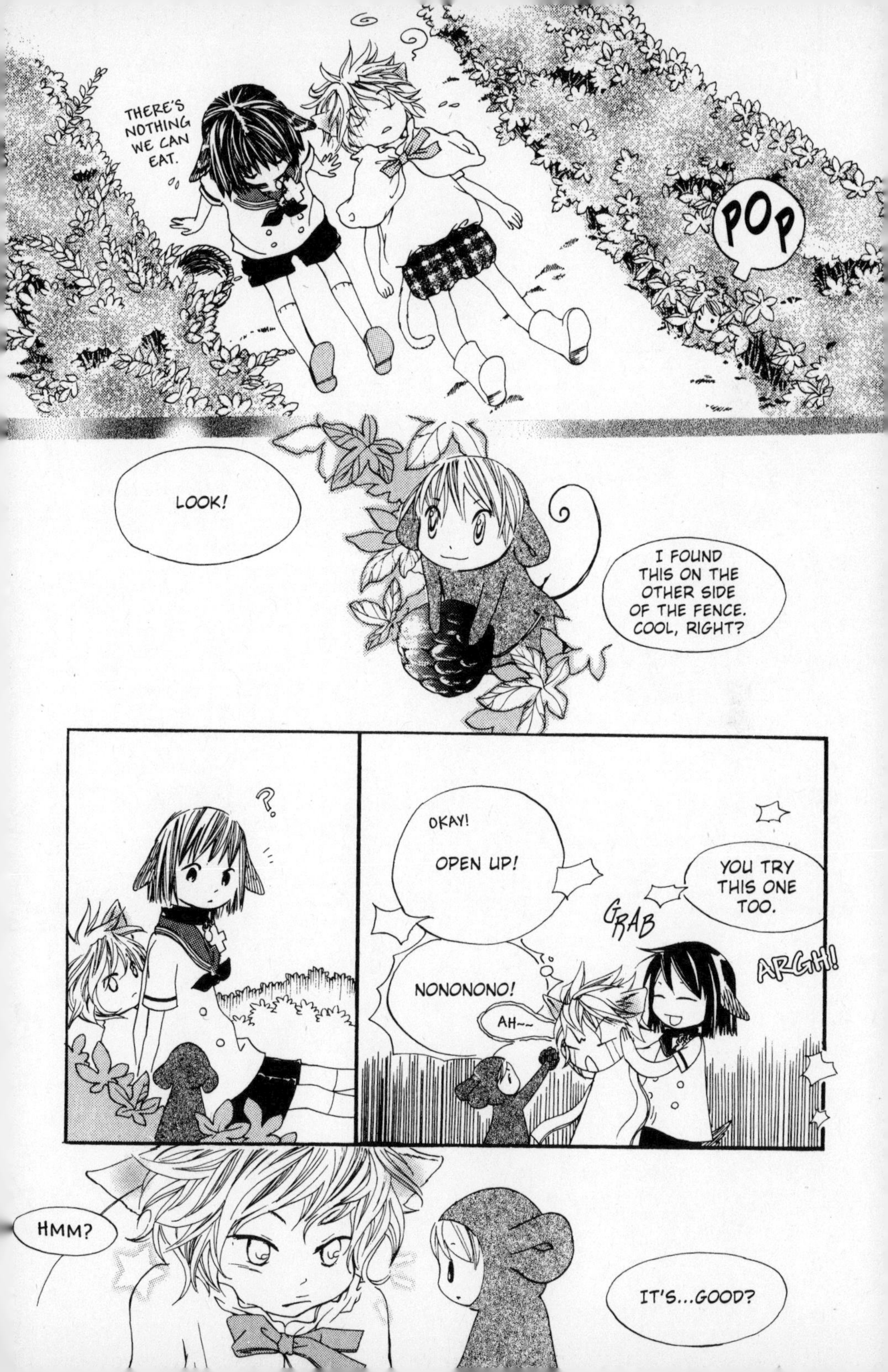
THERE'S NOTHING WE CAN EAT.
POP
I FOUND THIS ON THE OTHER SIDE OF THE FENCE. COOL, RIGHT?
LOOK!
YOU TRY THIS ONE TOO.
GRAB
ARGH!
OKAY!
OPEN UP!
NONONONO!
AH~~
IT'S...GOOD?
HMM?

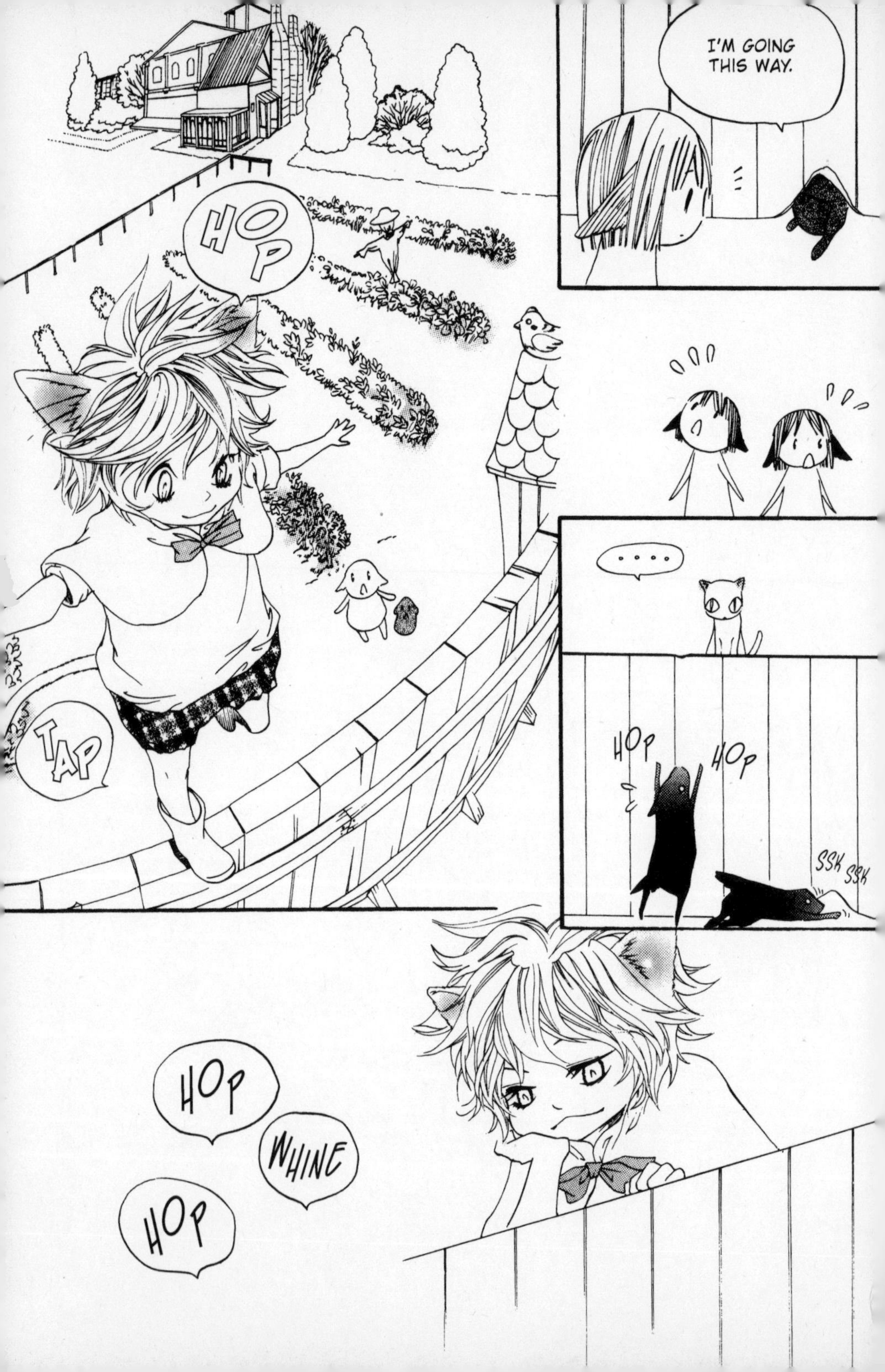
I'M GOING THIS WAY.
HOP
TAP
....
HOP
HOP
SSK SSK
HOP
WHINE
HOP

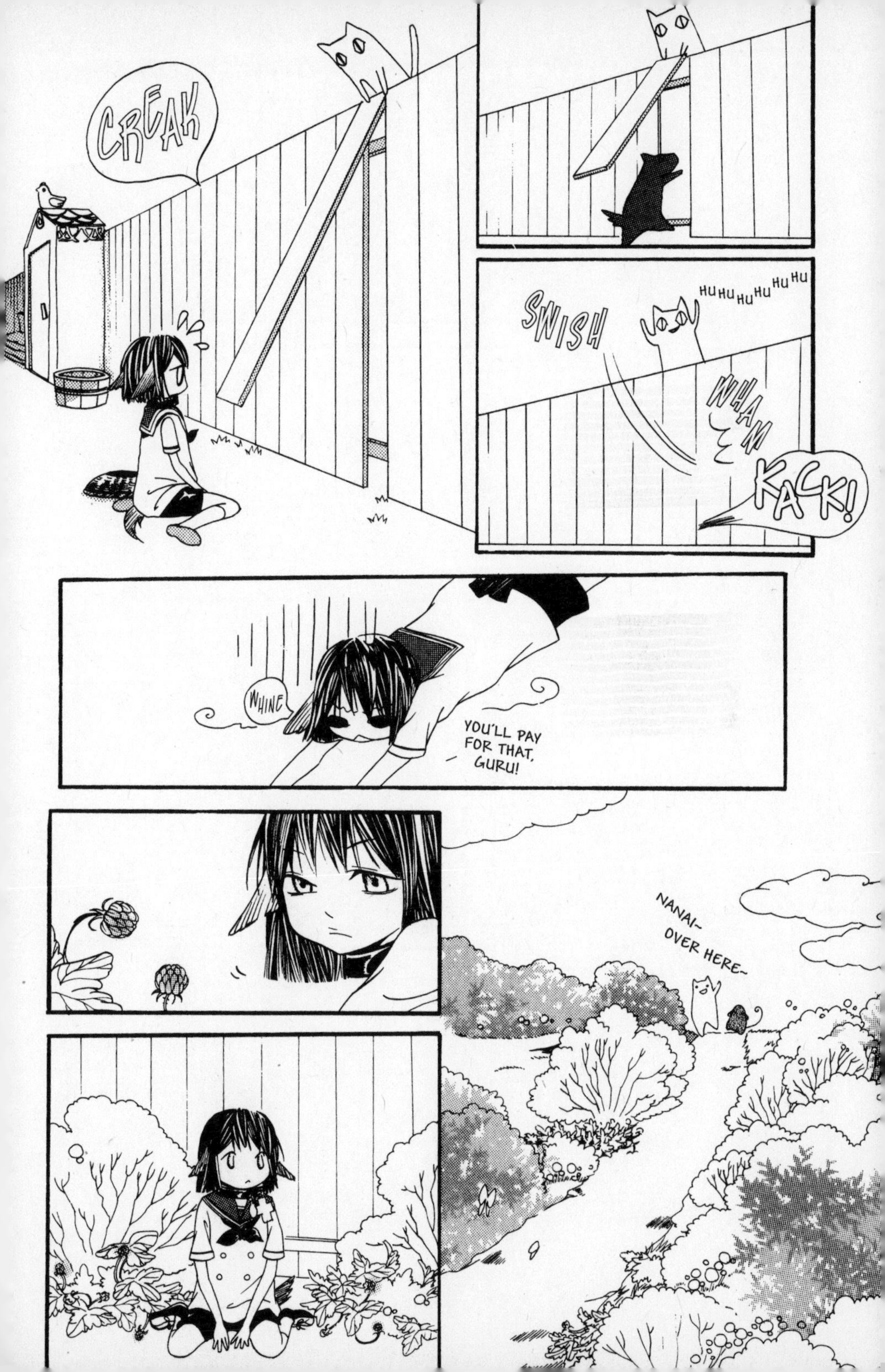
CREAK
SWISH
HUHUHUHUHUHU
WHAM
KACK!
WHINE
YOU'LL PAY FOR THAT, GURU!
NANAI~
OVER HERE~

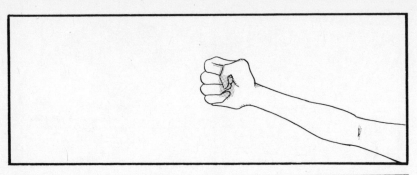

TA-DAA!

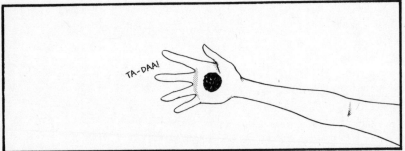

!

IT'S COOL, RIGHT? AWESOME, RIGHT? I FOUND THE KING BERRY!

THE KING of BERRIES

HU! HU! HU!

YOU WANT IT, DON'T YOU?

YOU WANT IT, DON'T YOU?

SAY PLEASE~ AND I MIGHT GIVE IT TO YOU.

HEE HEE HEE

CRACK

ACK

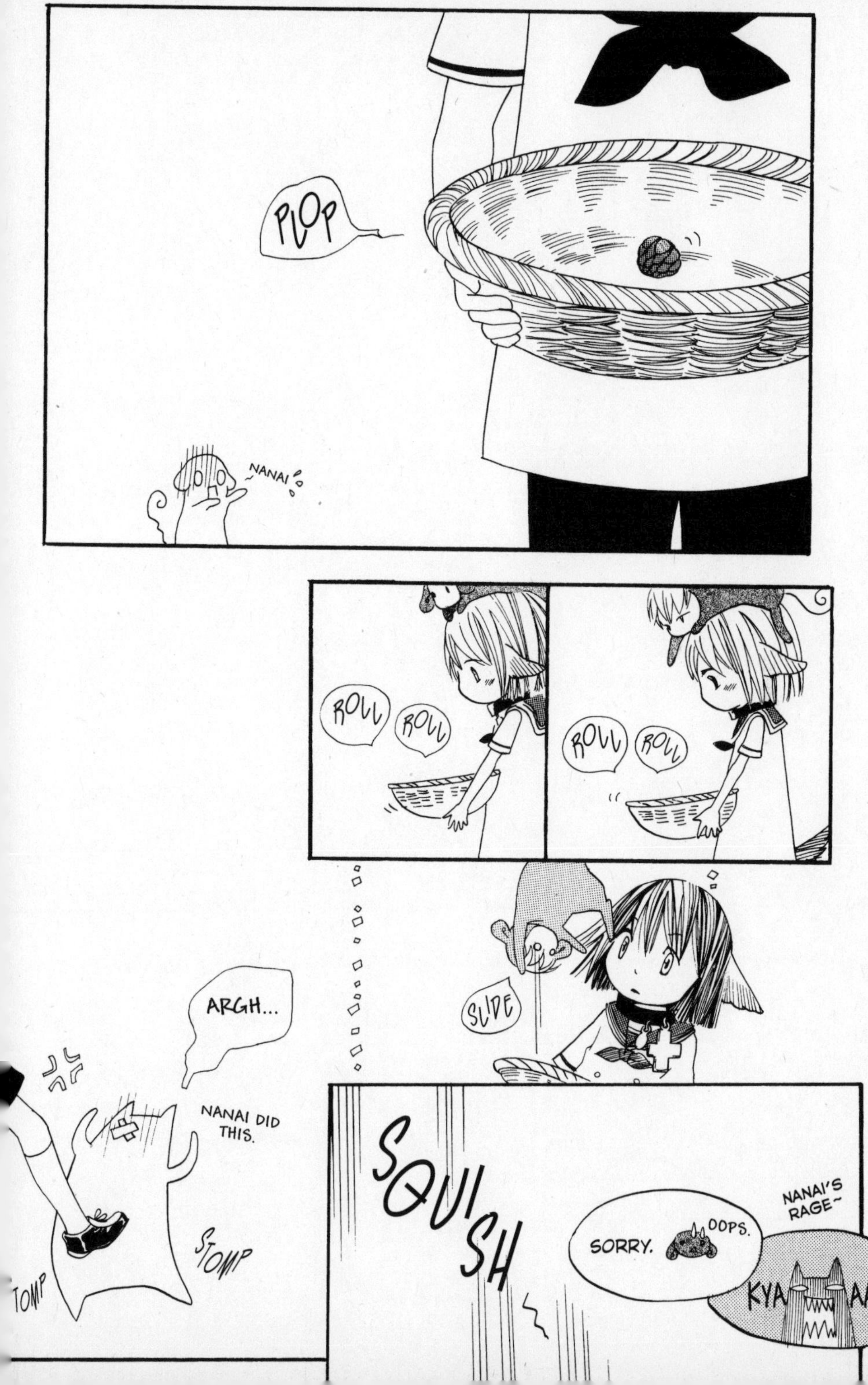
PLOP
NANAI
ROLL
ROLL
ROLL
ROLL
SLIDE
ARGH...
NANAI DID THIS.
STOMP
STOMP
SQUISH
NANAI'S RAGE~
KYA AAA!
OOPS.
SORRY.

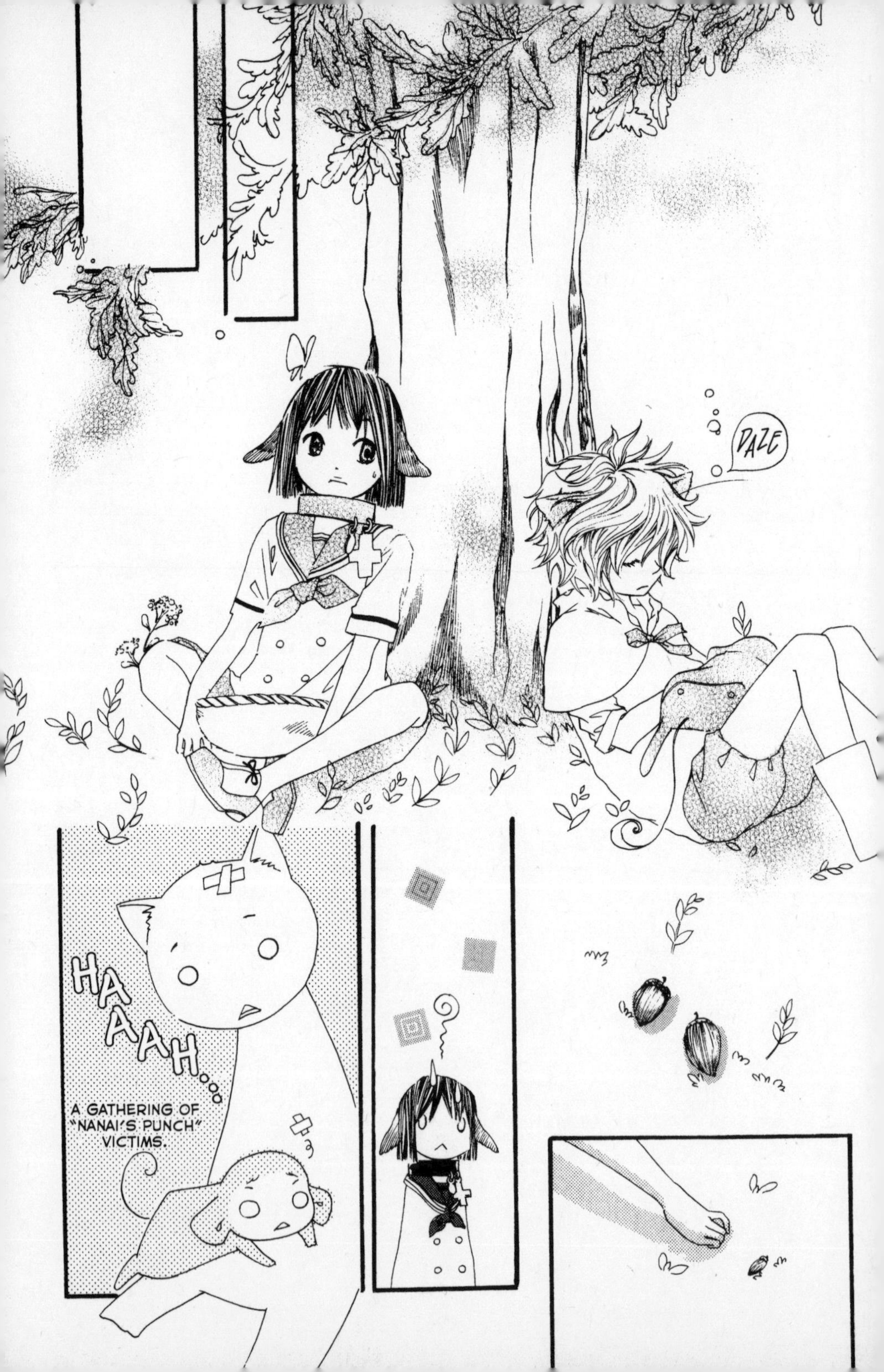
DAZE
HAAAAH...
A GATHERING OF "NANAI'S PUNCH" VICTIMS.

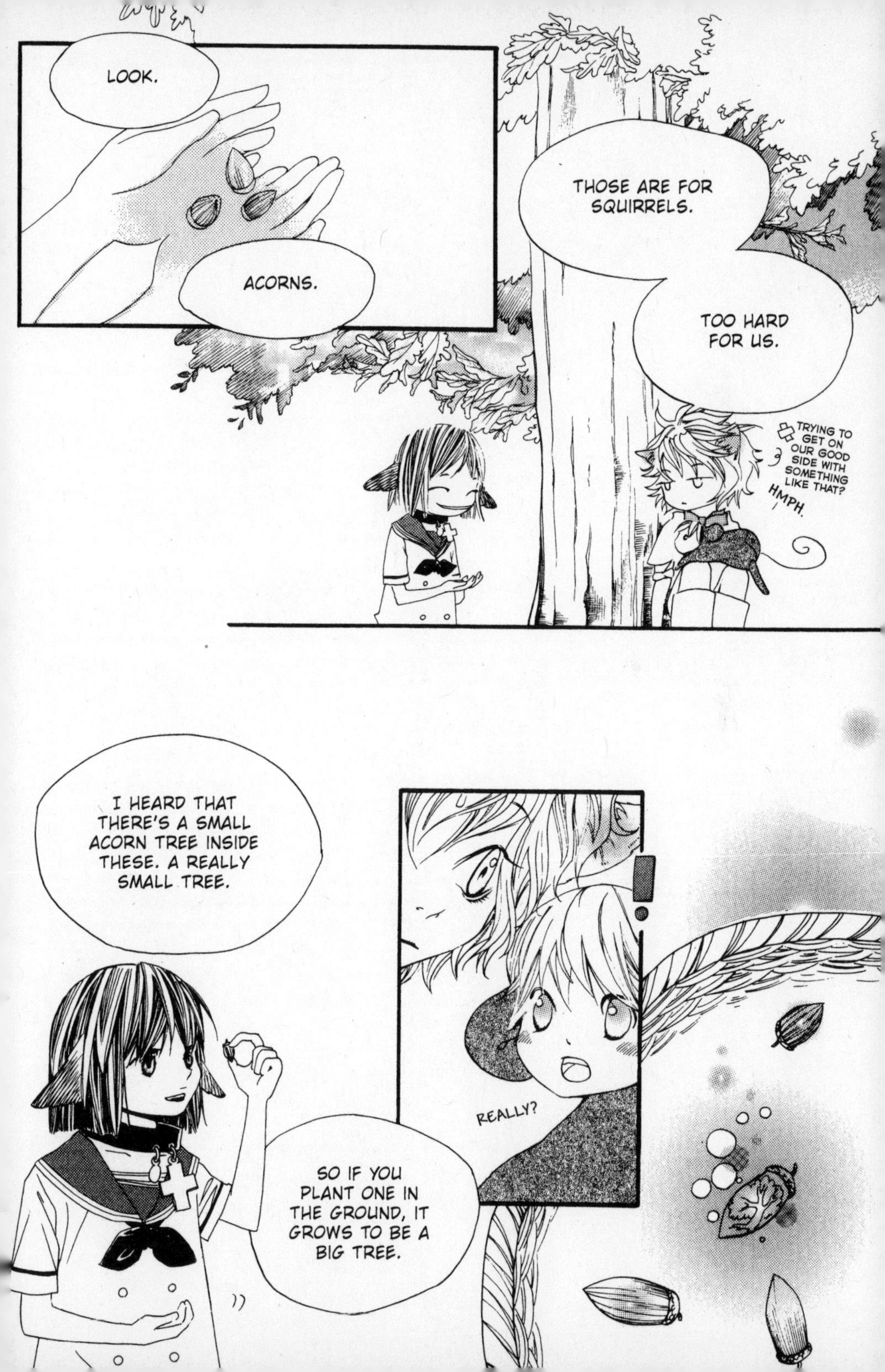
LOOK.
ACORNS.
THOSE ARE FOR SQUIRRELS.
TOO HARD FOR US.
TRYING TO GET ON OUR GOOD SIDE WITH SOMETHING LIKE THAT?
HMPH.
I HEARD THAT THERE'S A SMALL ACORN TREE INSIDE THESE. A REALLY SMALL TREE.
SO IF YOU PLANT ONE IN THE GROUND, IT GROWS TO BE A BIG TREE.
!
REALLY?

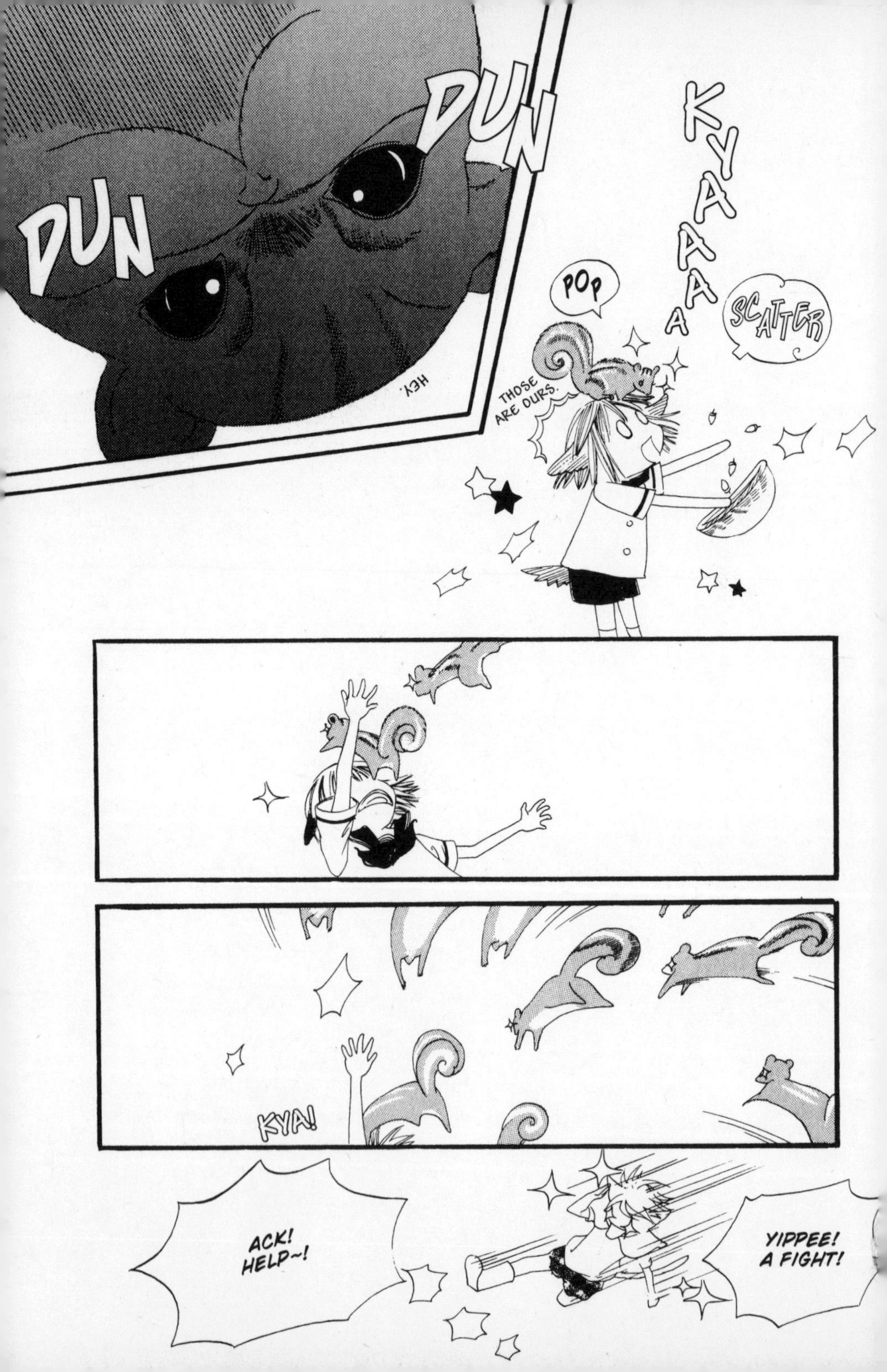
DUN
DUN
HEY.
KYAAAAA
POP
SCATTER
THOSE ARE OURS.
KYA!
YIPPEE! A FIGHT!
ACK! HELP~!

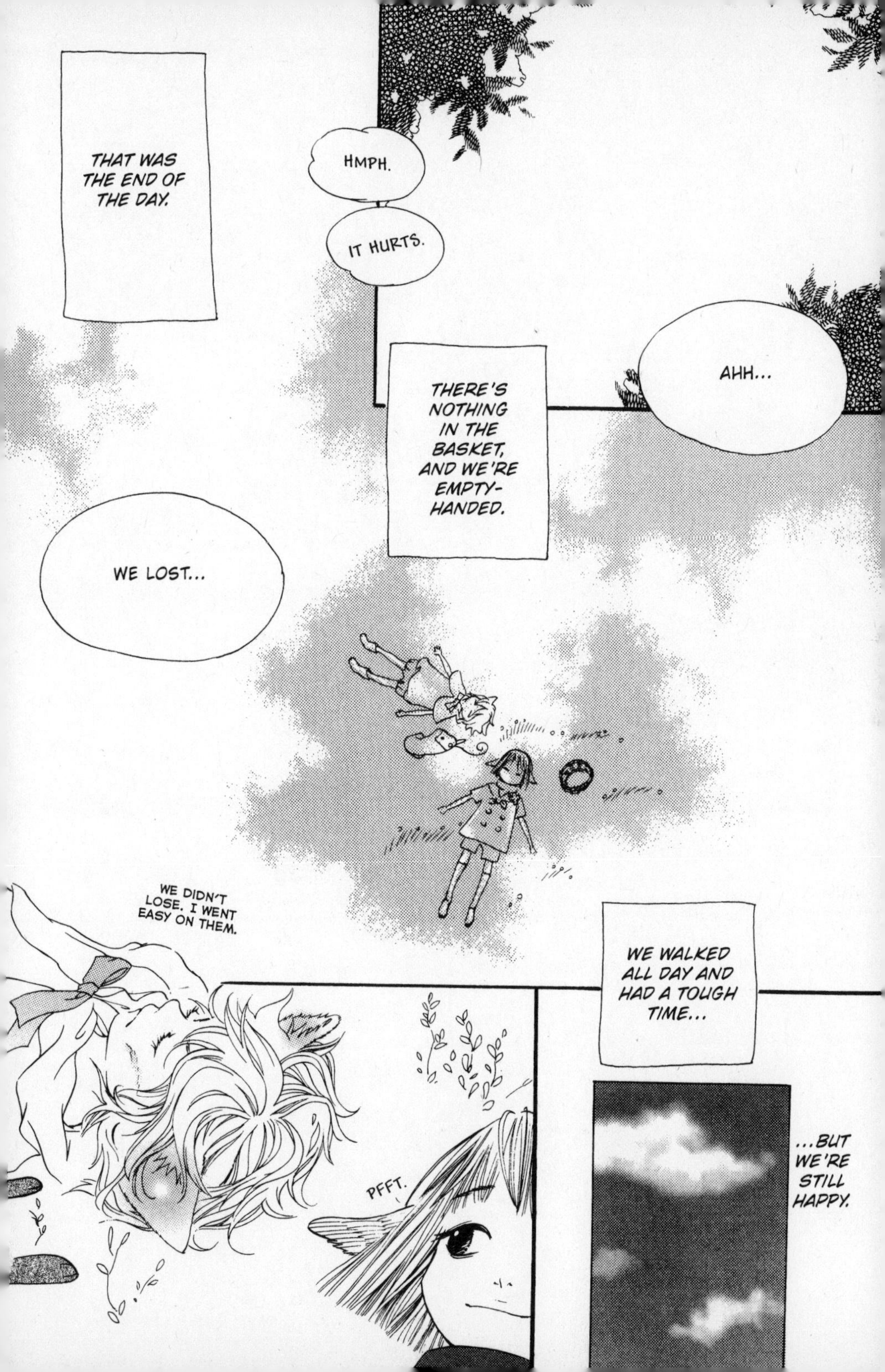
THAT WAS THE END OF THE DAY.
HMPH.
IT HURTS.
AHH...
THERE'S NOTHING IN THE BASKET, AND WE'RE EMPTY-HANDED.
WE LOST...
WE DIDN'T LOSE. I WENT EASY ON THEM.
WE WALKED ALL DAY AND HAD A TOUGH TIME...
...BUT WE'RE STILL HAPPY.
PFFT.

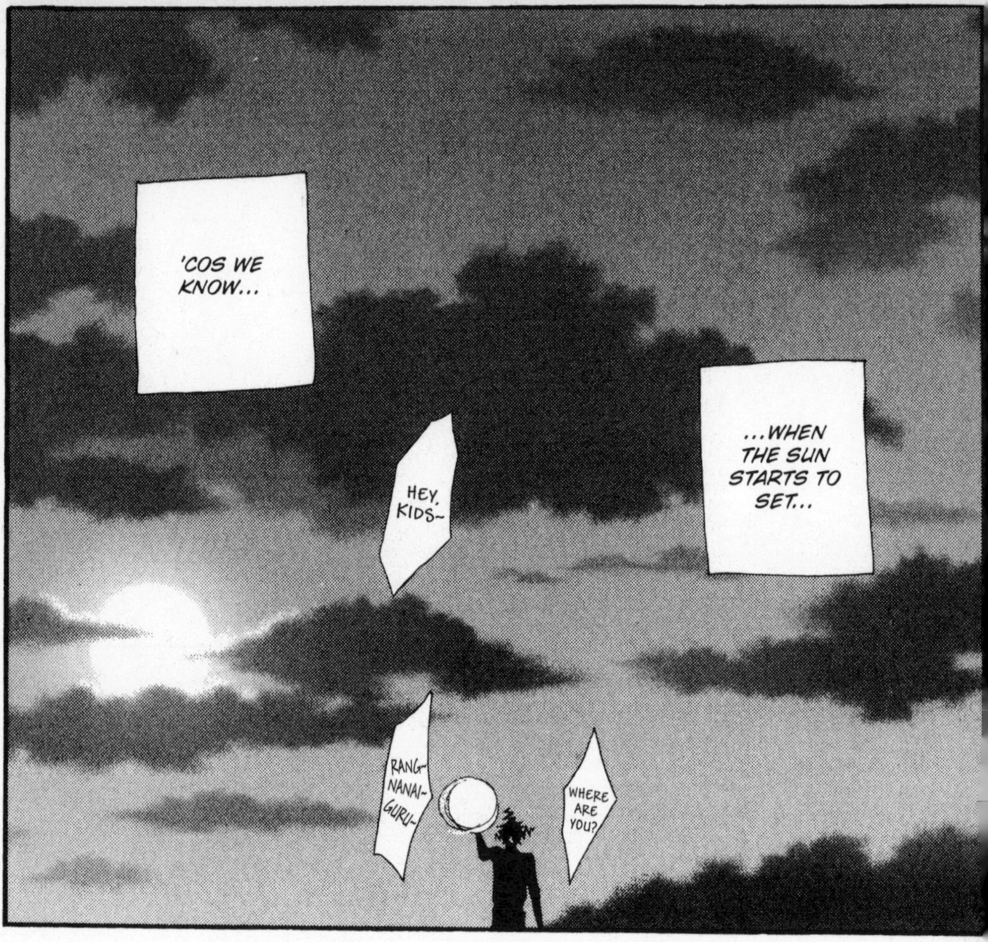
...WHEN THE SUN STARTS TO SET...
'COS WE KNOW...
HEY, KIDS~
WHERE ARE YOU?
RANG~ NANAI~ GURU~

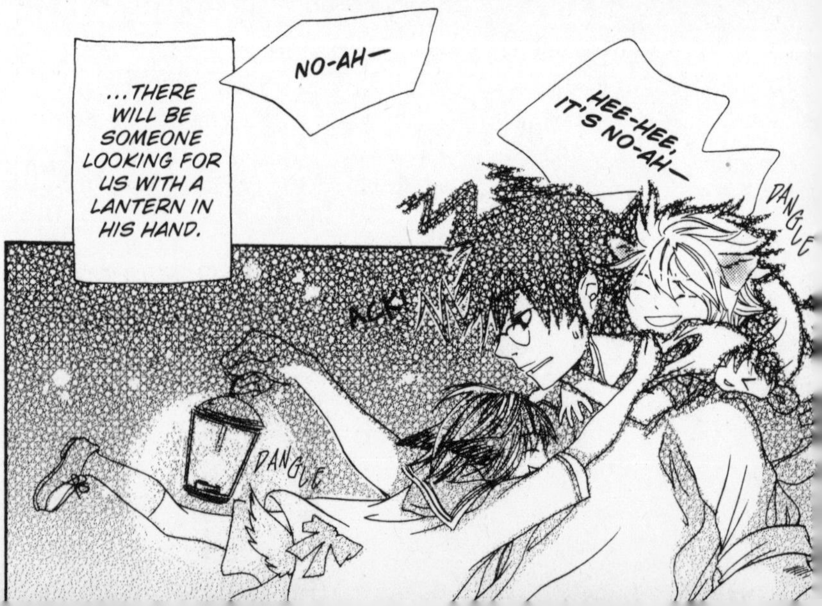
HEE-HEE, IT'S NO-AH—
NO-AH—
...THERE WILL BE SOMEONE LOOKING FOR US WITH A LANTERN IN HIS HAND.
DANGLE
ACK!
DANGLE

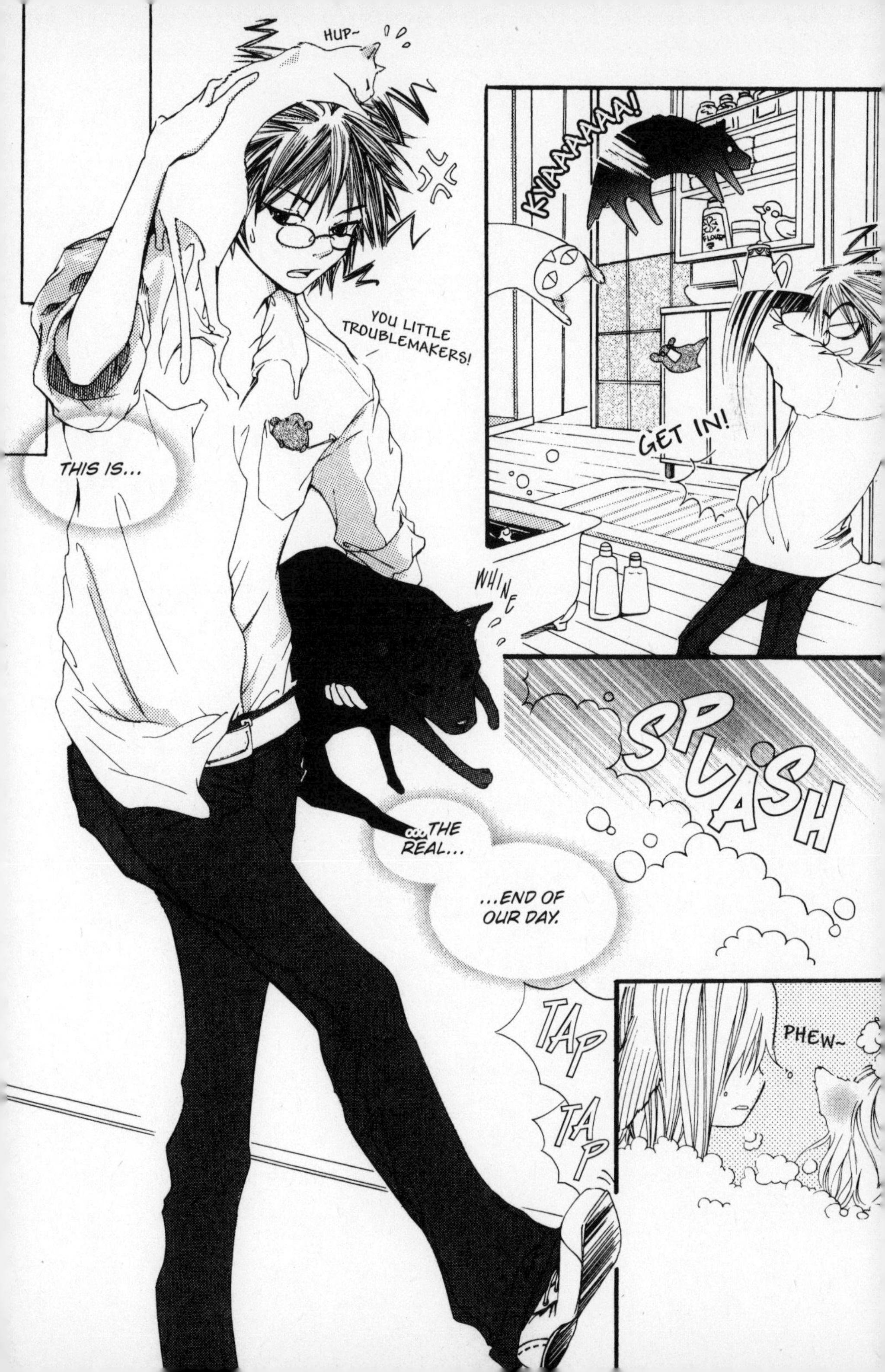

HUP~
KYAAAAAAA!
YOU LITTLE TROUBLEMAKERS!
GET IN!
THIS IS...
WHINE
SPLASH
...THE REAL...
...END OF OUR DAY.
TAP TAP
PHEW~

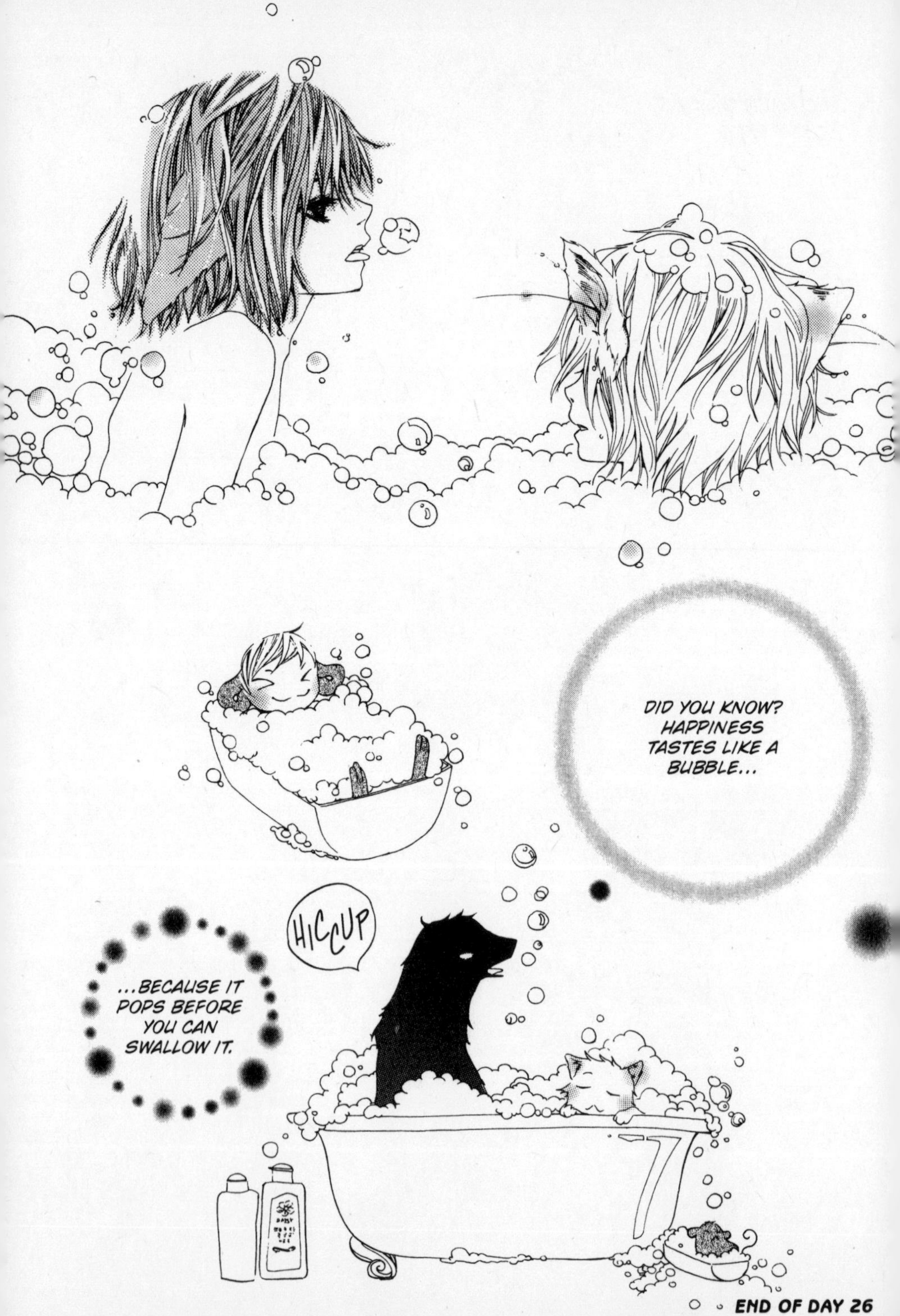
DID YOU KNOW? HAPPINESS TASTES LIKE A BUBBLE...
HICCUP
...BECAUSE IT POPS BEFORE YOU CAN SWALLOW IT.

END OF DAY 26

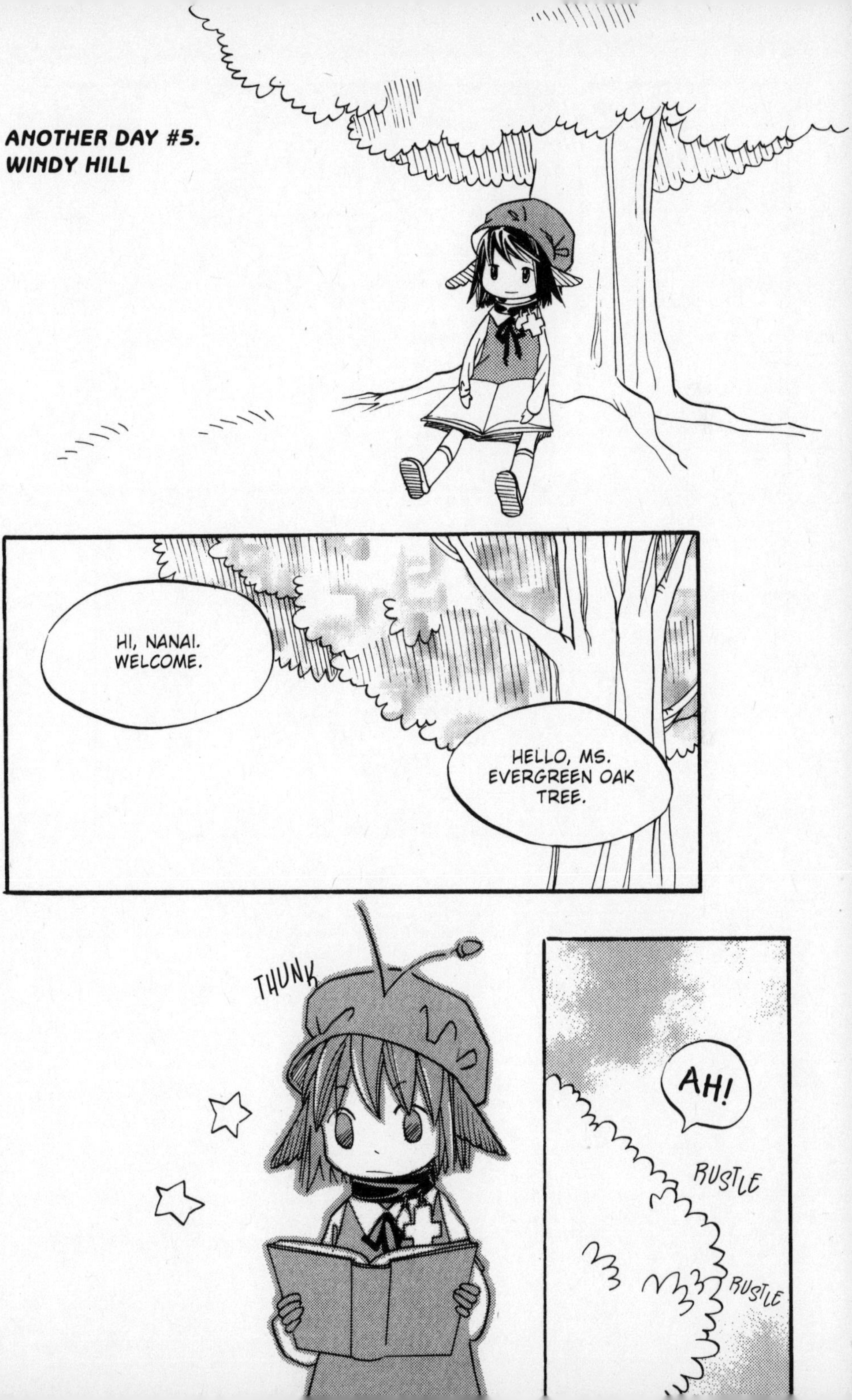
ANOTHER DAY #5.
WINDY HILL
HI, NANAI.
WELCOME.
HELLO, MS.
EVERGREEN OAK
TREE.
AH!
RUSTLE
RUSTLE
THUNK

ACORNS.

THERE ARE STILL MANY THAT THE SQUIRRELS DIDN'T TAKE.

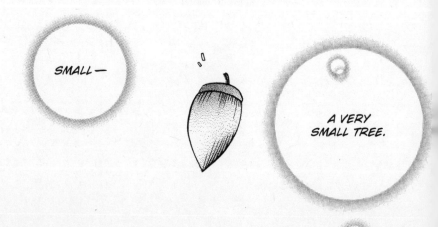

SMALL —

A VERY SMALL TREE.

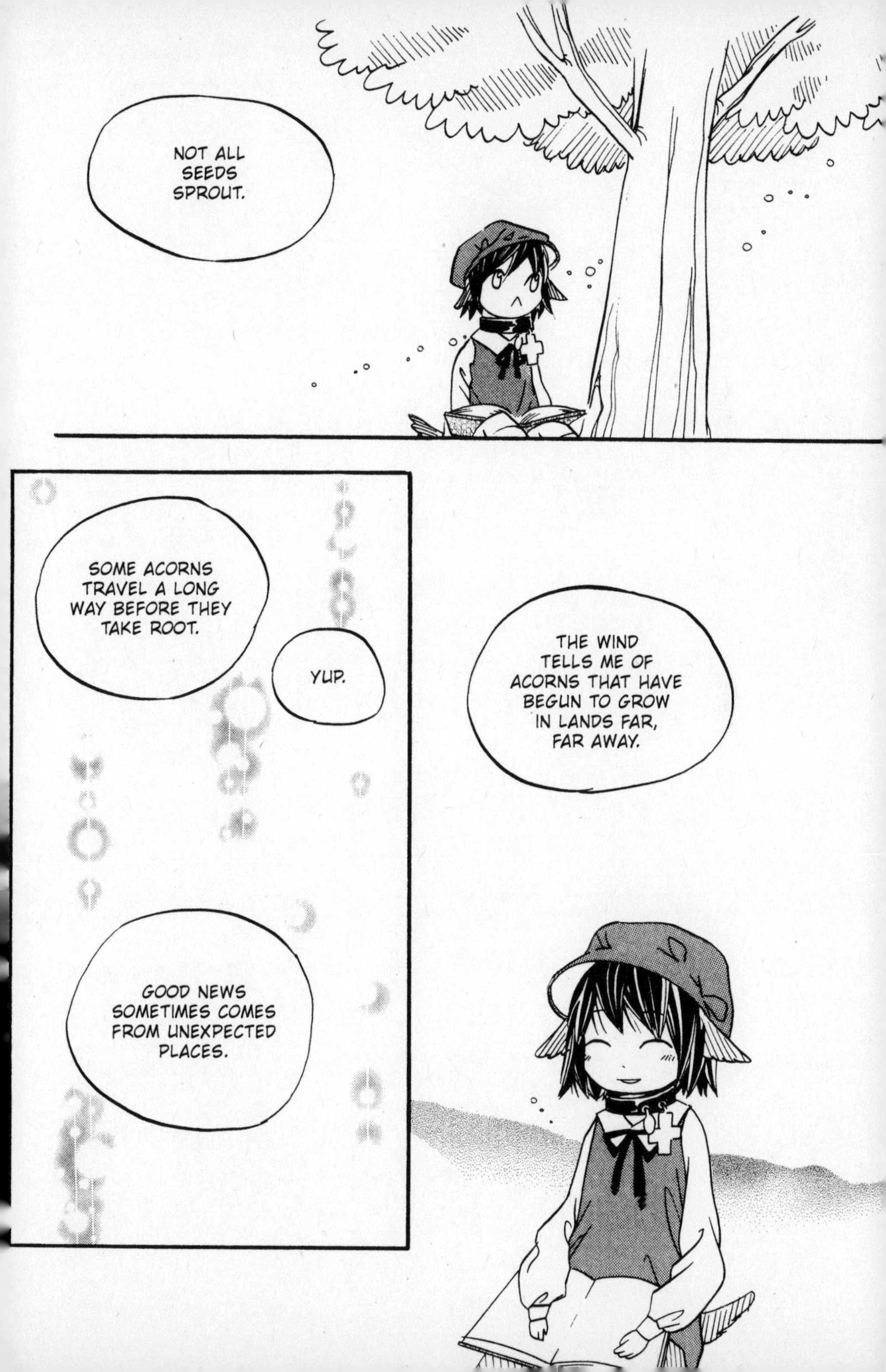
NOT ALL SEEDS SPROUT.
THE WIND TELLS ME OF ACORNS THAT HAVE BEGUN TO GROW IN LANDS FAR, FAR AWAY.
SOME ACORNS TRAVEL A LONG WAY BEFORE THEY TAKE ROOT.
YUP.
GOOD NEWS SOMETIMES COMES FROM UNEXPECTED PLACES.

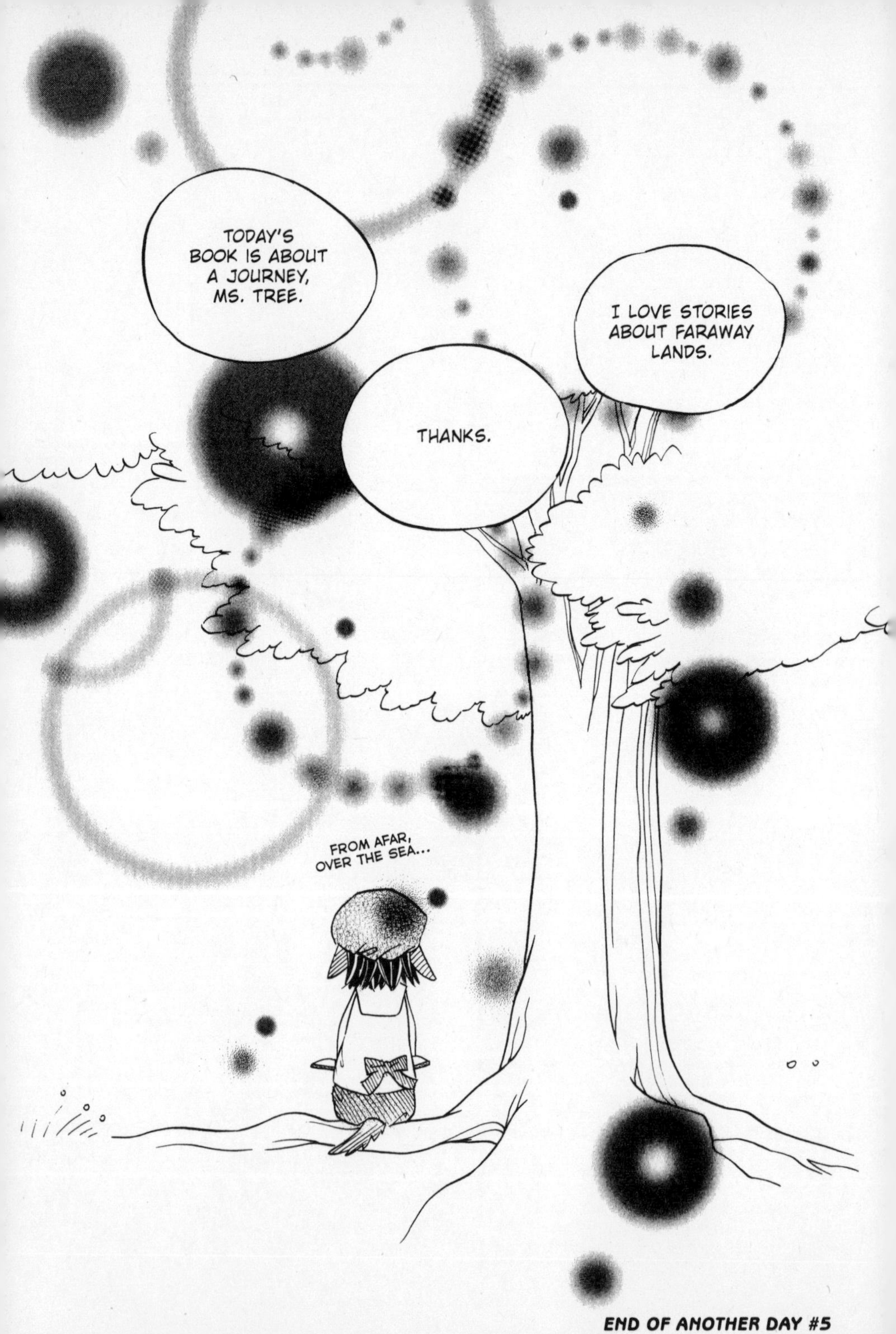
TODAY'S BOOK IS ABOUT A JOURNEY, MS. TREE.
I LOVE STORIES ABOUT FARAWAY LANDS.
THANKS.
FROM AFAR, OVER THE SEA...

END OF ANOTHER DAY #5

DAY 27.
ONE SUNNY DAY

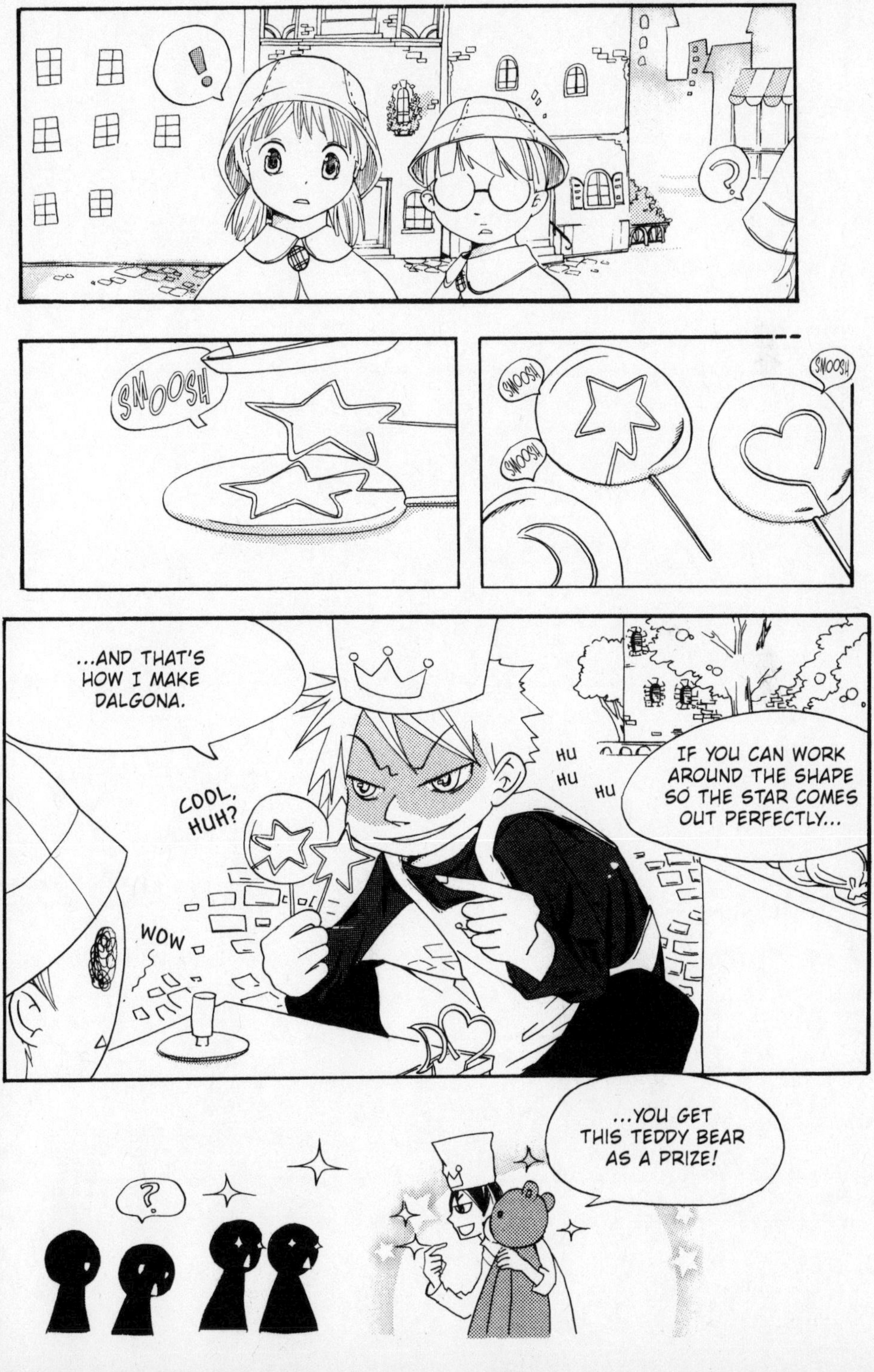
!
?
SMOOSH
SMOOSH
SMOOSH
SMOOSH
...AND THAT'S HOW I MAKE DALGONA.
COOL, HUH?
HU
HU
HU
IF YOU CAN WORK AROUND THE SHAPE SO THE STAR COMES OUT PERFECTLY...
WOW
...YOU GET THIS TEDDY BEAR AS A PRIZE!
?

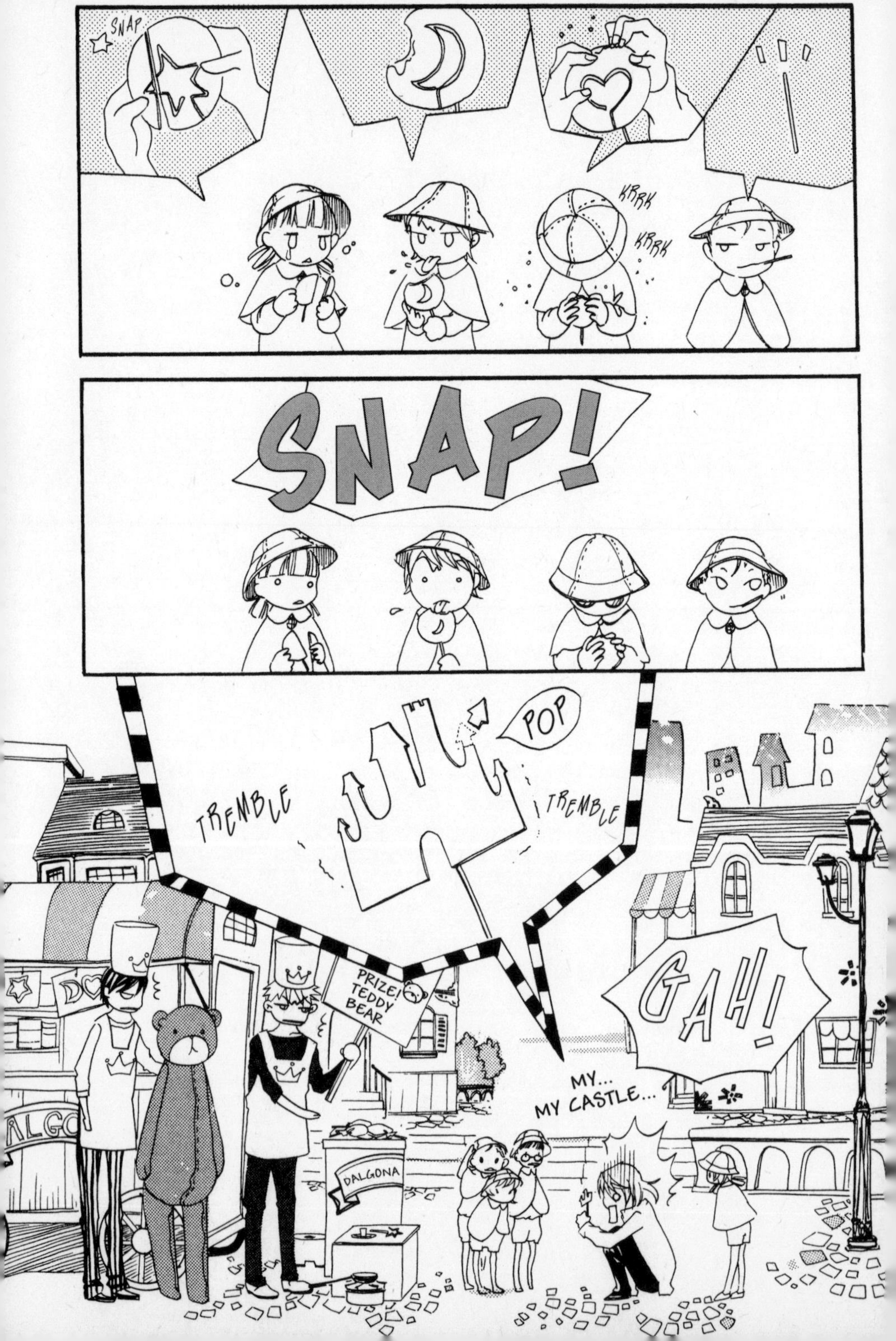
SNAP
KRRK
KRRK
SNAP!
TREMBLE
POP
TREMBLE
PRIZE! TEDDY BEAR
DALGONA
GAH!
MY... MY CASTLE...

one fine day

DAY 27.
ONE SUNNY DAY

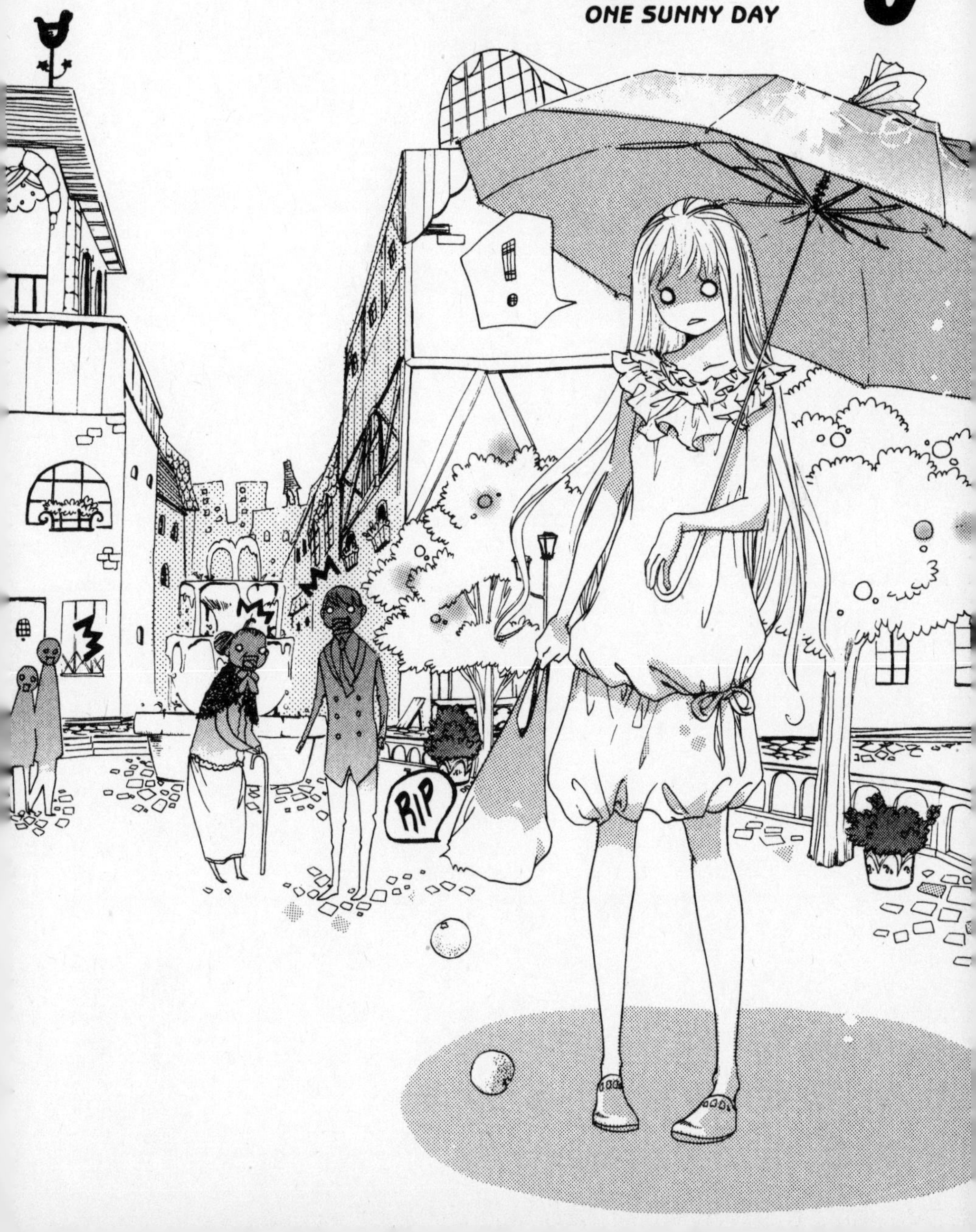
RIP

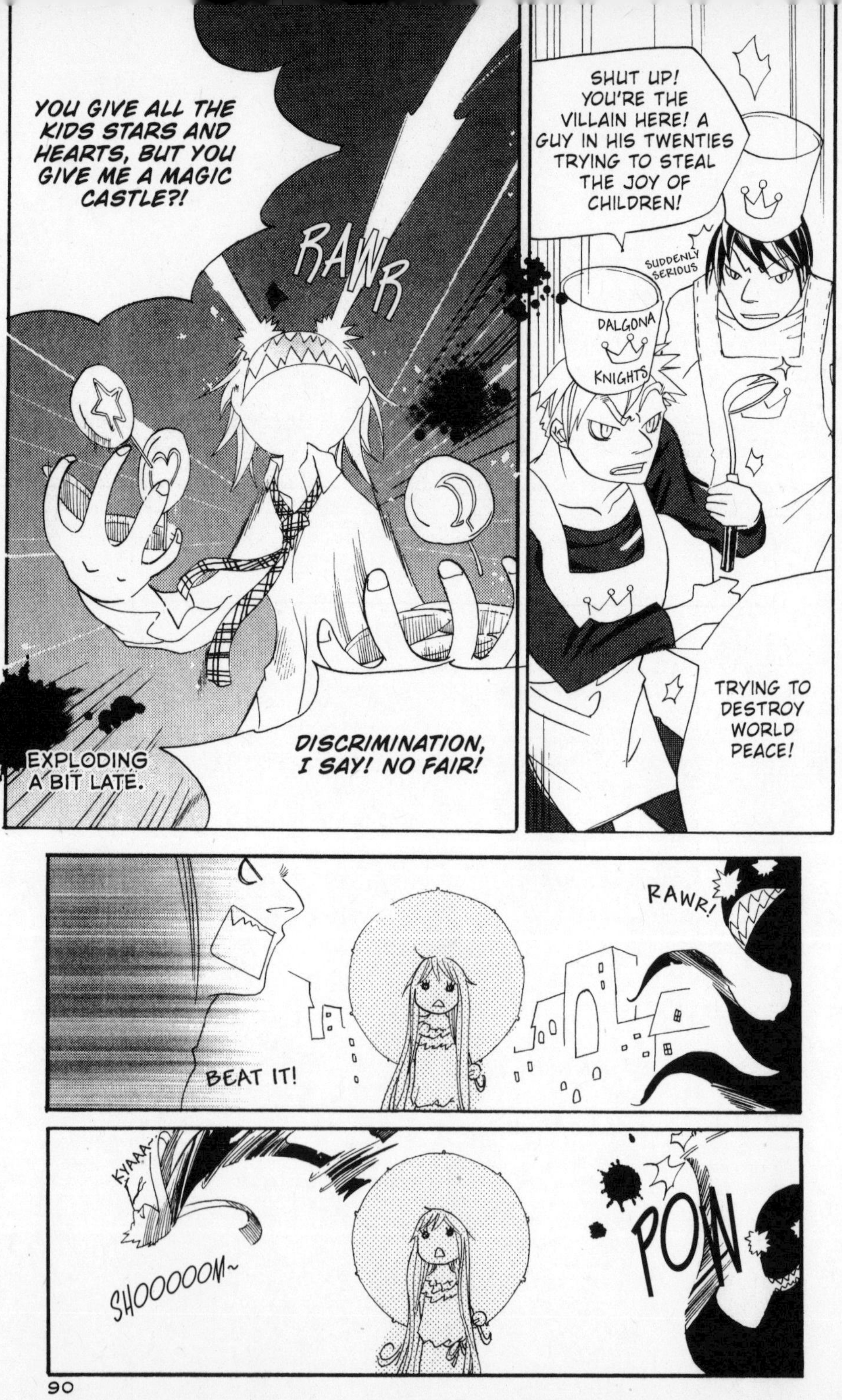
YOU GIVE ALL THE KIDS STARS AND HEARTS, BUT YOU GIVE ME A MAGIC CASTLE?!
RAWR
EXPLODING A BIT LATE.
DISCRIMINATION, I SAY! NO FAIR!
SHUT UP! YOU'RE THE VILLAIN HERE! A GUY IN HIS TWENTIES TRYING TO STEAL THE JOY OF CHILDREN!
SUDDENLY SERIOUS
DALGONA KNIGHTS
TRYING TO DESTROY WORLD PEACE!
RAWR!
BEAT IT!
KYAAA~
SHOOOOOM~
POW

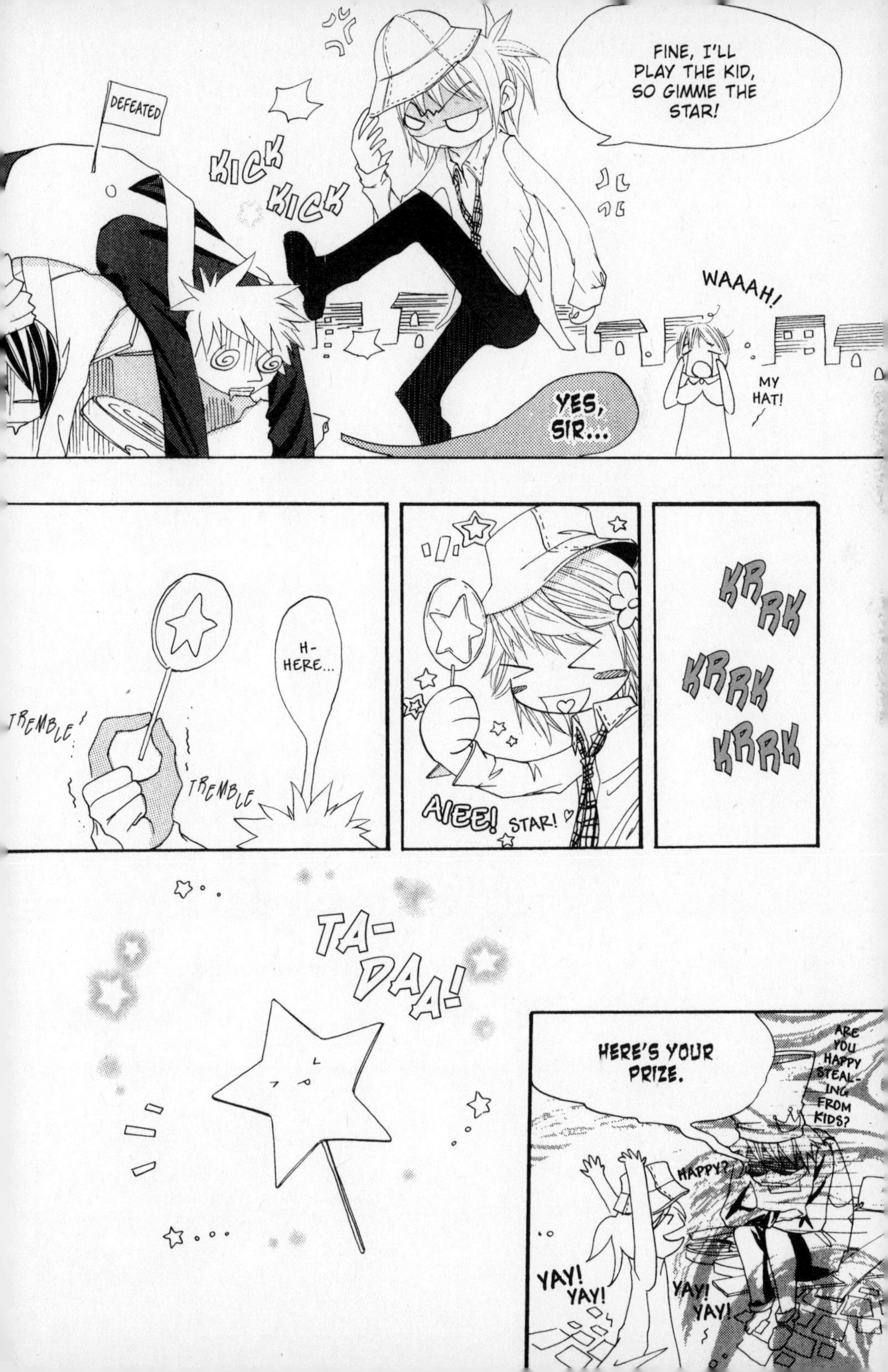
FINE, I'LL PLAY THE KID, SO GIMME THE STAR!
DEFEATED
KICK KICK
YES, SIR...
WAAAH!
MY HAT!
KRRK KRRK KRRK
AIEE! STAR!
H-HERE...
TREMBLE
TREMBLE
TA-DAA!
HERE'S YOUR PRIZE.
ARE YOU HAPPY STEALING FROM KIDS?
HAPPY?
YAY! YAY!
YAY! YAY!

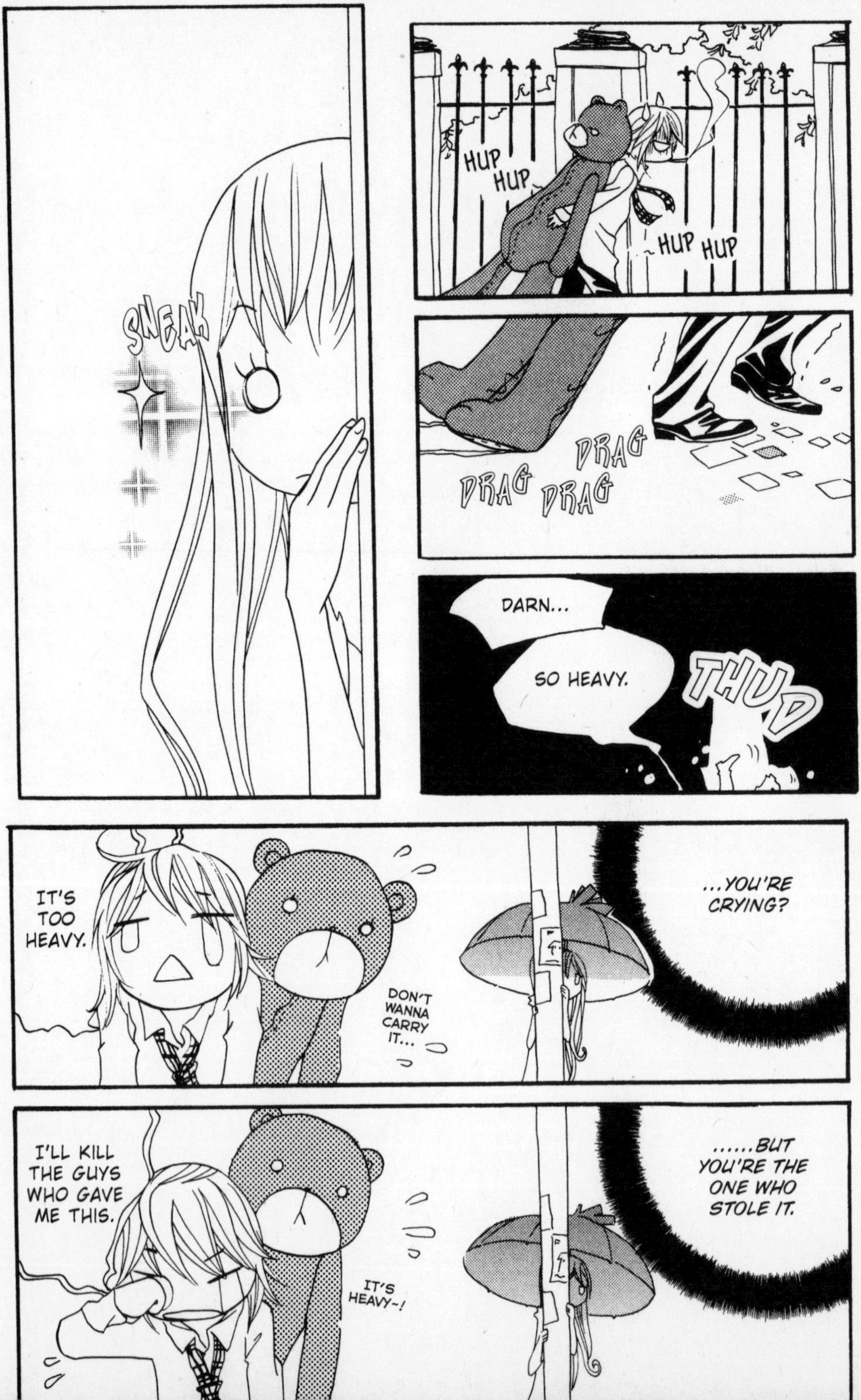
HUP HUP
HUP HUP
DRAG
DRAG
DRAG
DARN...
SO HEAVY.
THUD
SNEAK
...YOU'RE CRYING?
IT'S TOO HEAVY.
DON'T WANNA CARRY IT...
......BUT YOU'RE THE ONE WHO STOLE IT.
I'LL KILL THE GUYS WHO GAVE ME THIS.
IT'S HEAVY~!

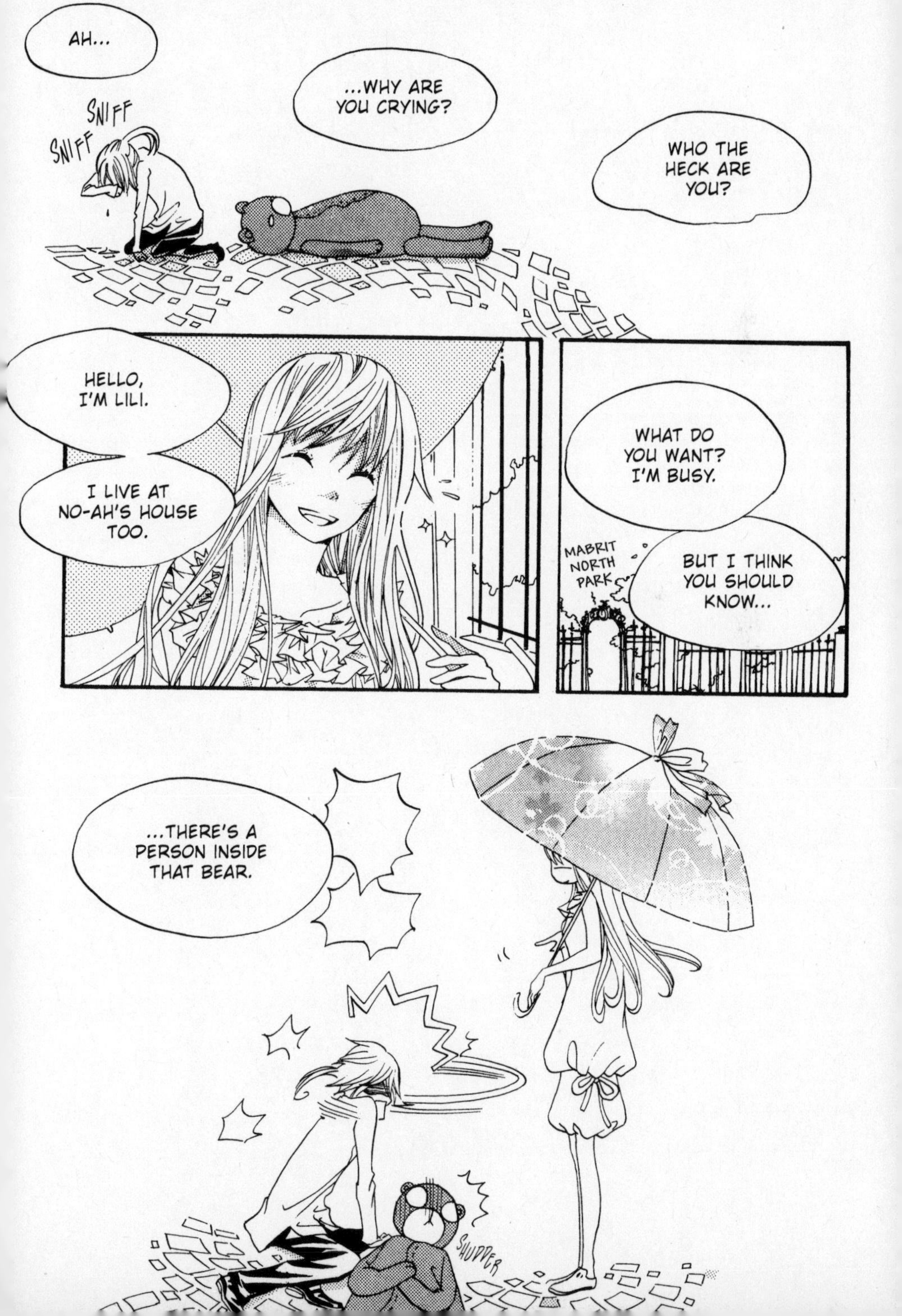
AH...
SNIFF
SNIFF
...WHY ARE YOU CRYING?
WHO THE HECK ARE YOU?
HELLO, I'M LILI.
I LIVE AT NO-AH'S HOUSE TOO.
WHAT DO YOU WANT? I'M BUSY.
MABRIT NORTH PARK
BUT I THINK YOU SHOULD KNOW...
...THERE'S A PERSON INSIDE THAT BEAR.
SHUDDER

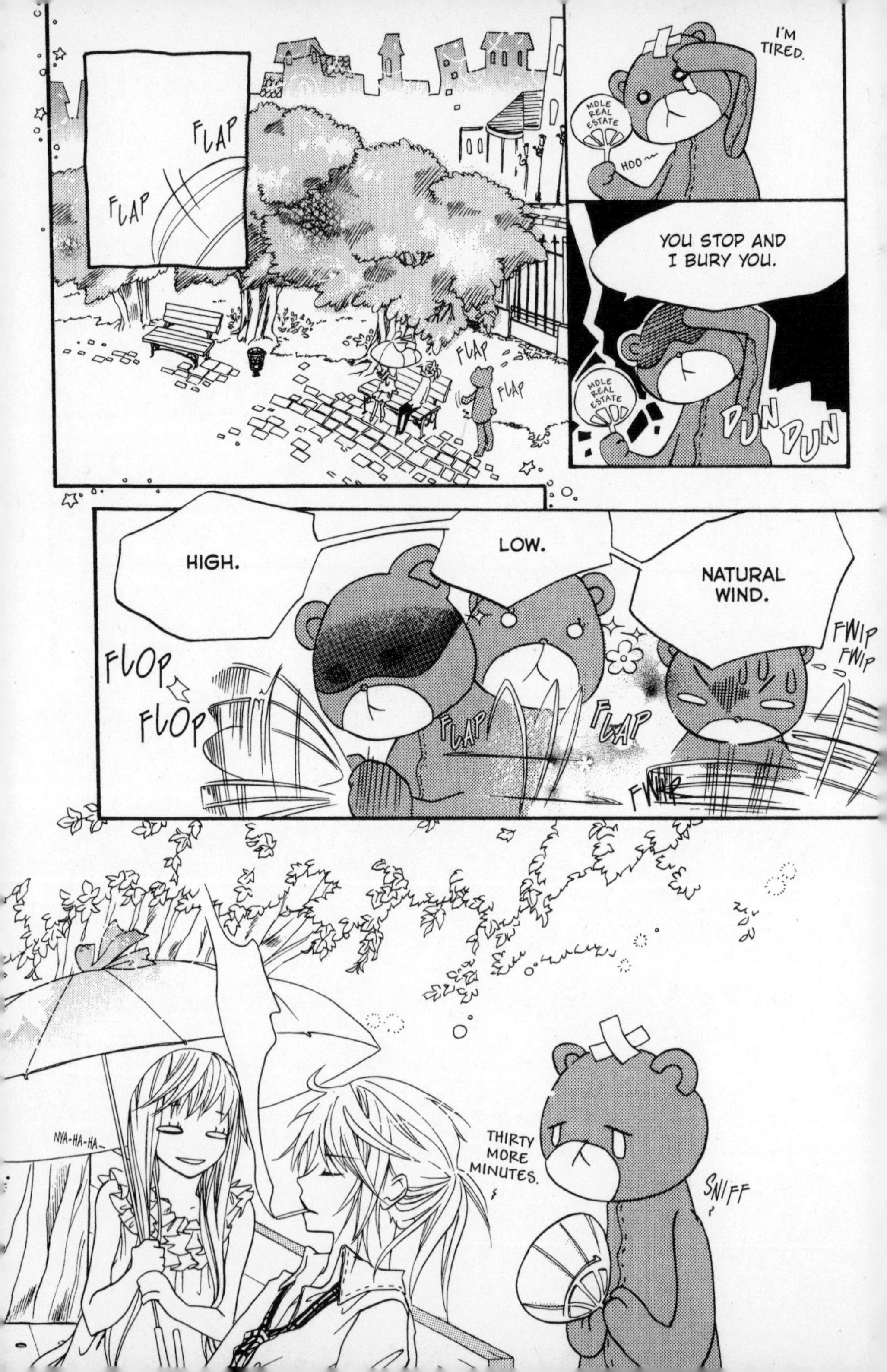
I'M TIRED.
MOLE REAL ESTATE
HOO~
FLAP
FLAP
FLAP
FLAP
YOU STOP AND I BURY YOU.
MOLE REAL ESTATE
DUN DUN
NATURAL WIND.
LOW.
HIGH.
FWIP FWIP
FLAP
FLAP
FLOP FLOP
FWHR
THIRTY MORE MINUTES.
SNIFF
NYA-HA-HA~

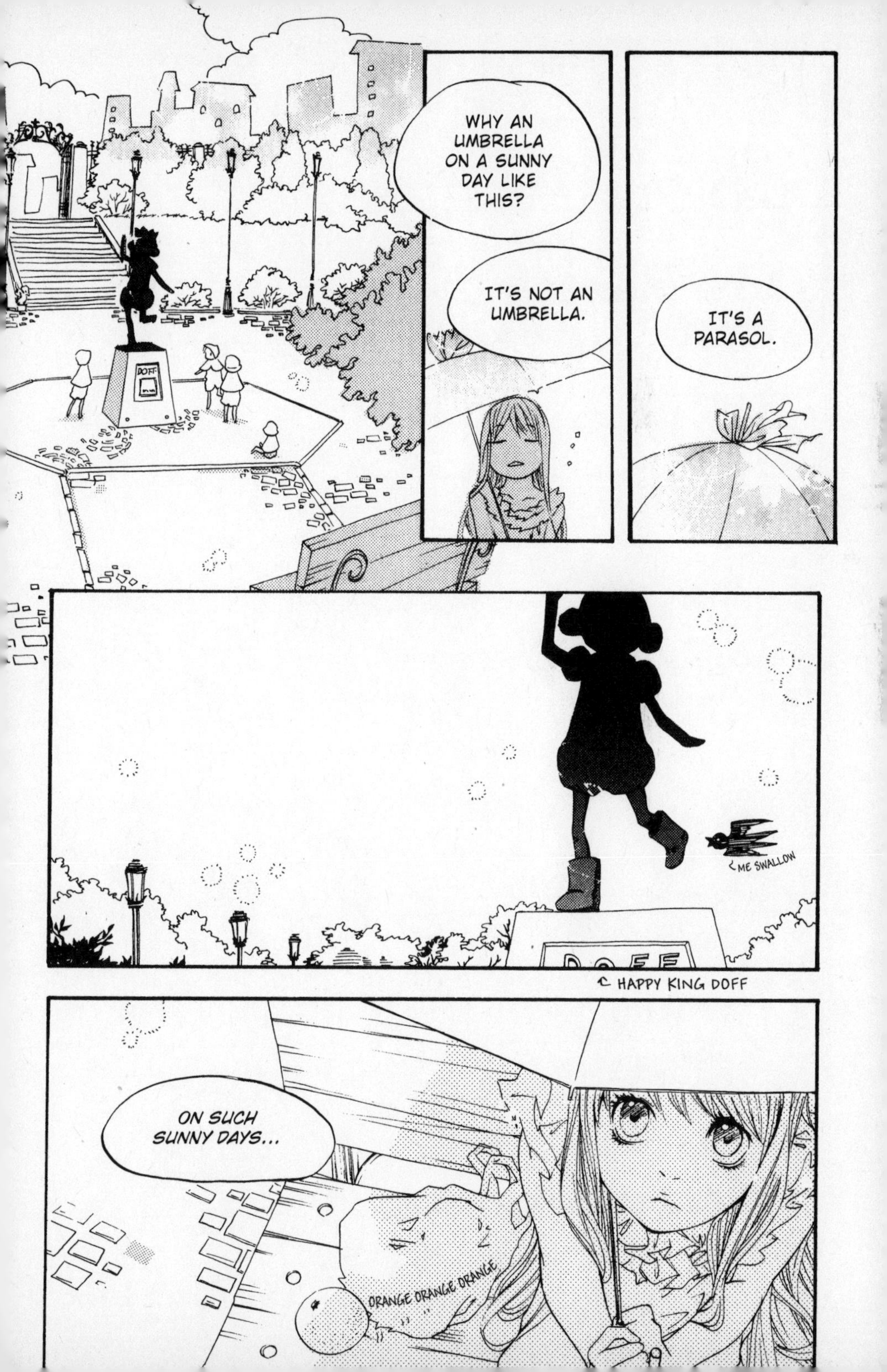
WHY AN UMBRELLA ON A SUNNY DAY LIKE THIS?
IT'S NOT AN UMBRELLA.
IT'S A PARASOL.
DOFF
ME SWALLOW
HAPPY KING DOFF
ON SUCH SUNNY DAYS...
ORANGE ORANGE ORANGE

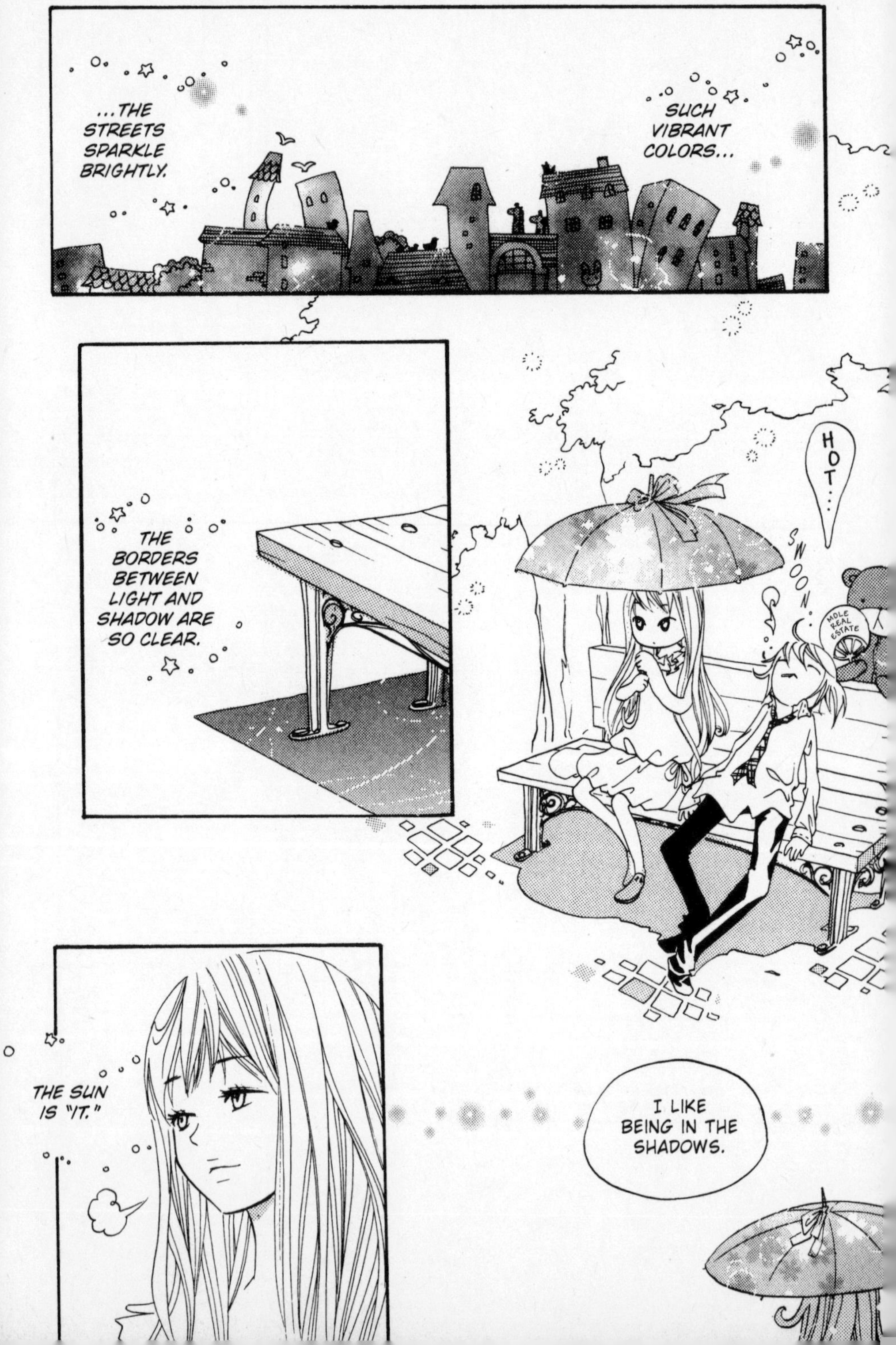
SUCH VIBRANT COLORS...
...THE STREETS SPARKLE BRIGHTLY.
HOT...
SWOON
MOLE REAL ESTATE
THE BORDERS BETWEEN LIGHT AND SHADOW ARE SO CLEAR.
I LIKE BEING IN THE SHADOWS.
THE SUN IS "IT."

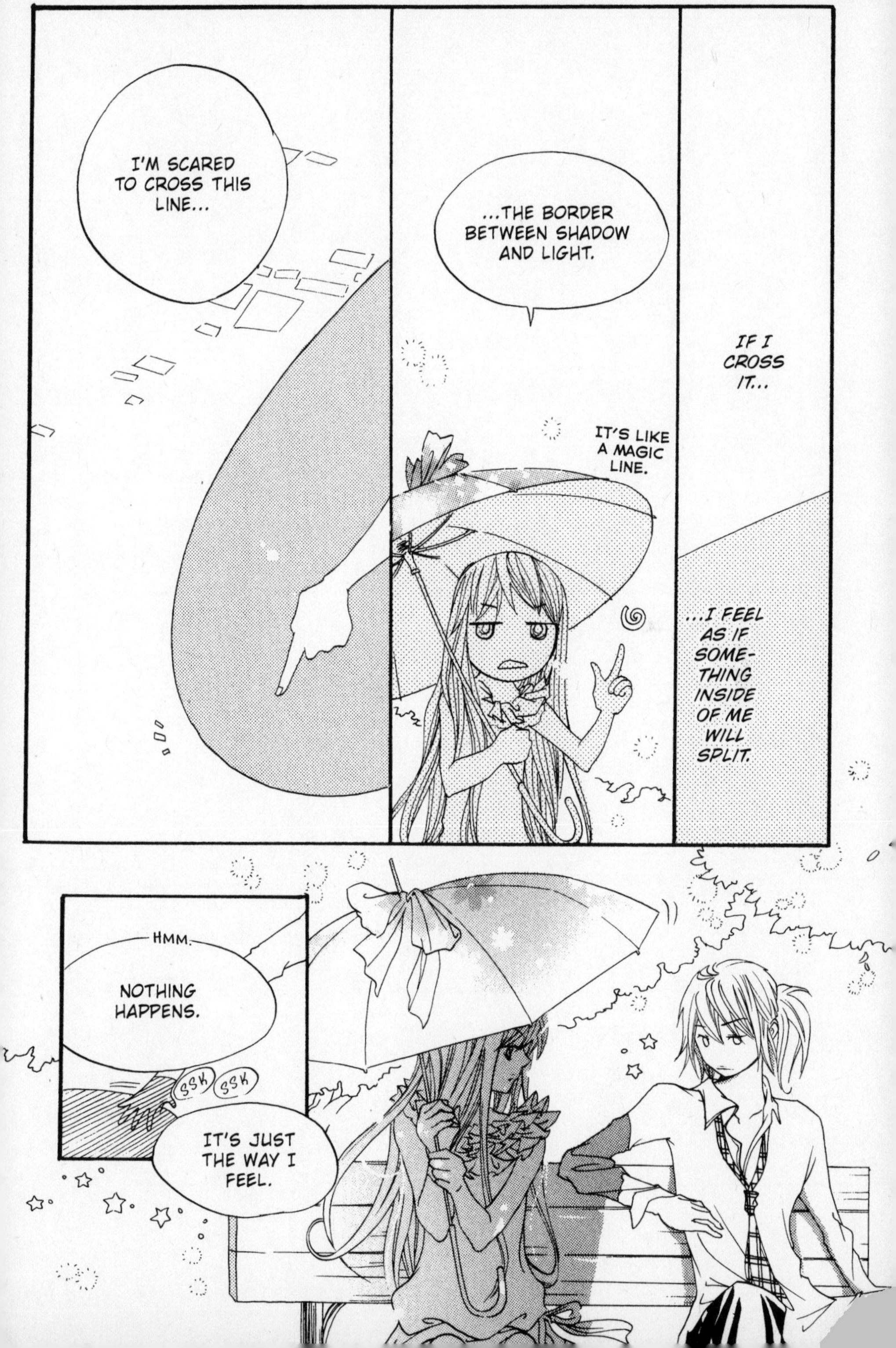
I'M SCARED TO CROSS THIS LINE...
...THE BORDER BETWEEN SHADOW AND LIGHT.
IT'S LIKE A MAGIC LINE.
IF I CROSS IT...
...I FEEL AS IF SOME-THING INSIDE OF ME WILL SPLIT.
HMM.
NOTHING HAPPENS.
SSK SSK
IT'S JUST THE WAY I FEEL.

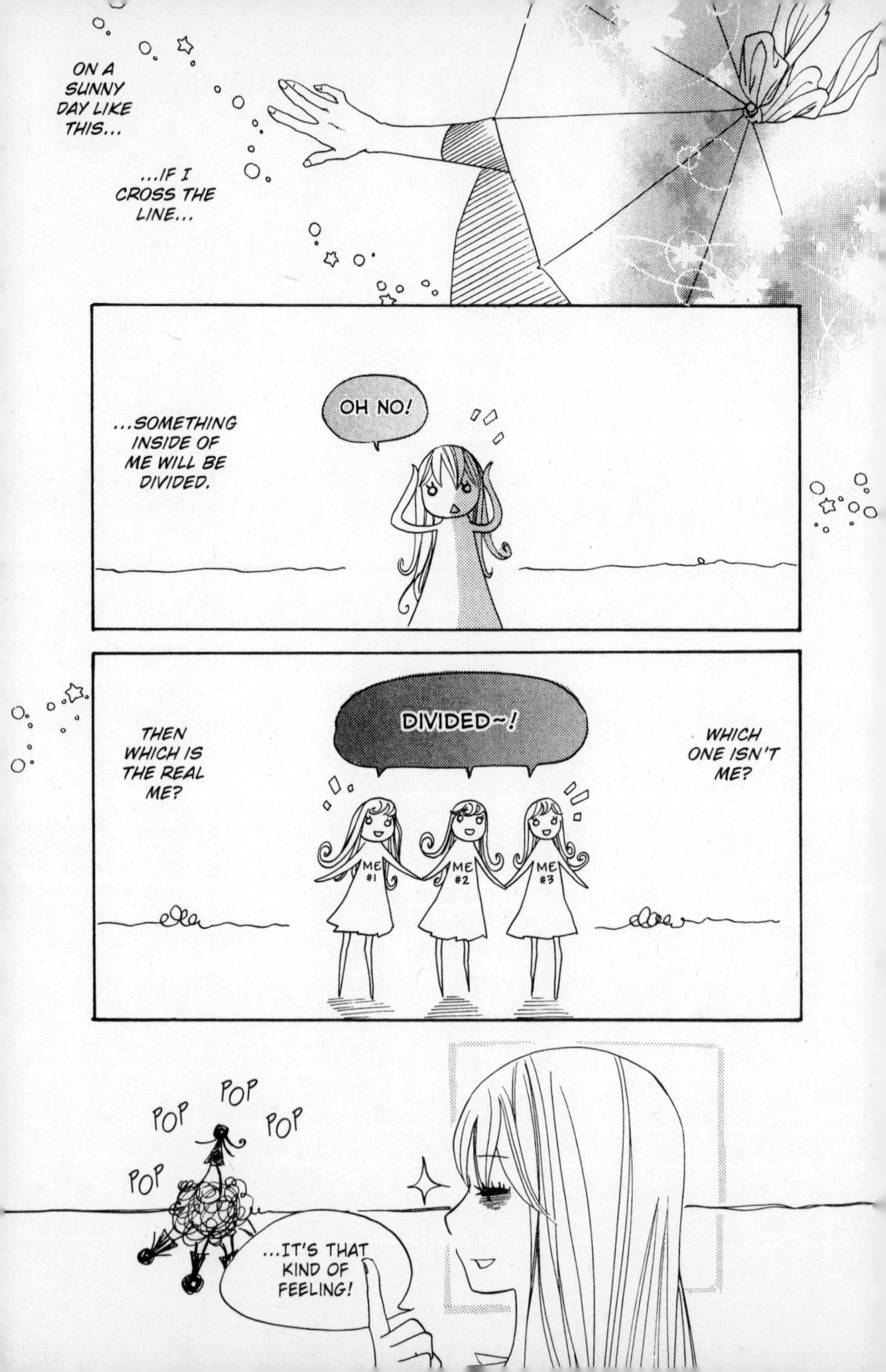
ON A SUNNY DAY LIKE THIS...
...IF I CROSS THE LINE...
...SOMETHING INSIDE OF ME WILL BE DIVIDED.
OH NO!
THEN WHICH IS THE REAL ME?
DIVIDED~!
WHICH ONE ISN'T ME?
ME #1
ME #2
ME #3
POP
POP
POP
POP
...IT'S THAT KIND OF FEELING!

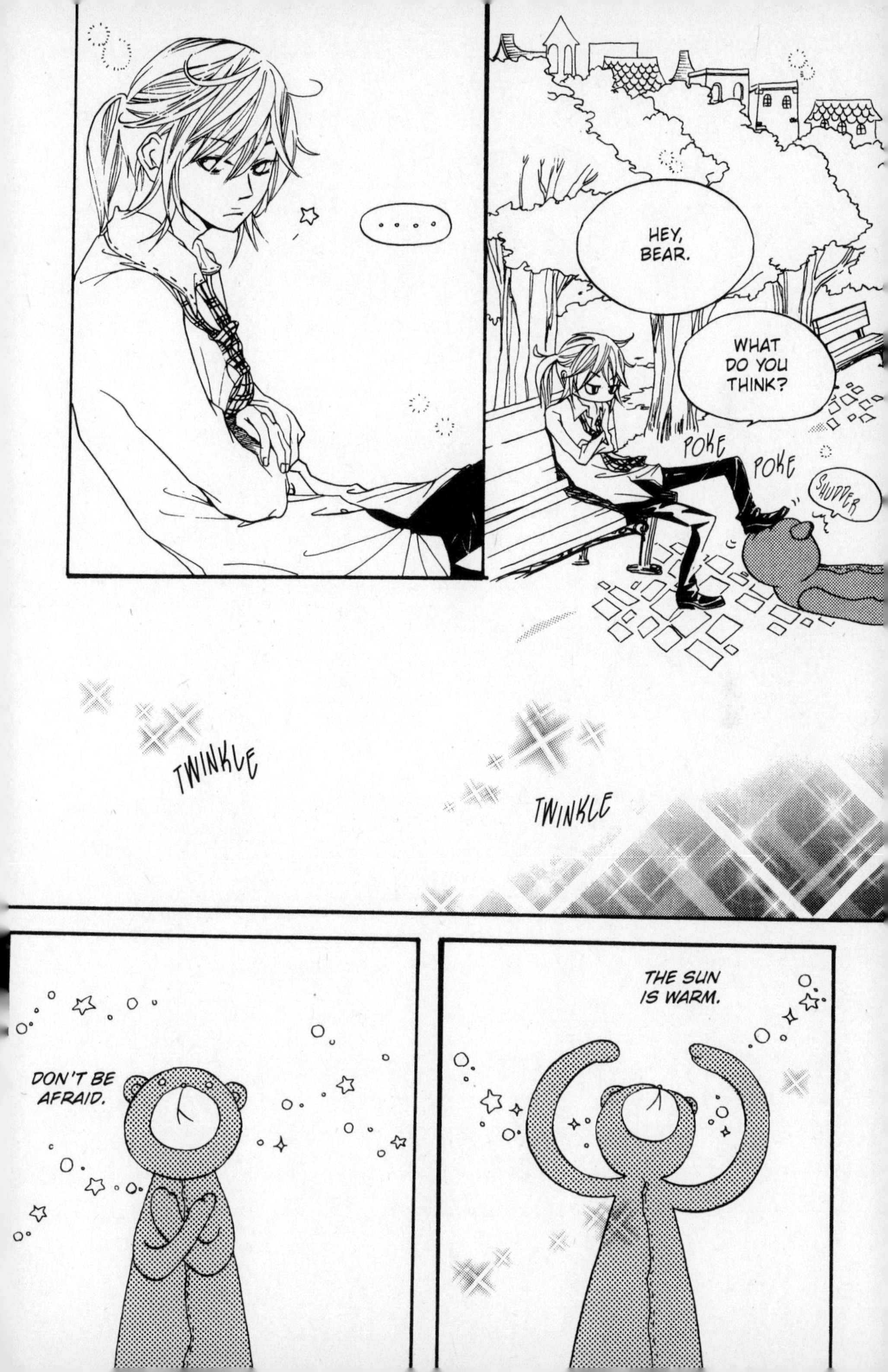
HEY, BEAR.
WHAT DO YOU THINK?
POKE
POKE
SHUDDER
. . . .
TWINKLE
TWINKLE
THE SUN IS WARM.
DON'T BE AFRAID.

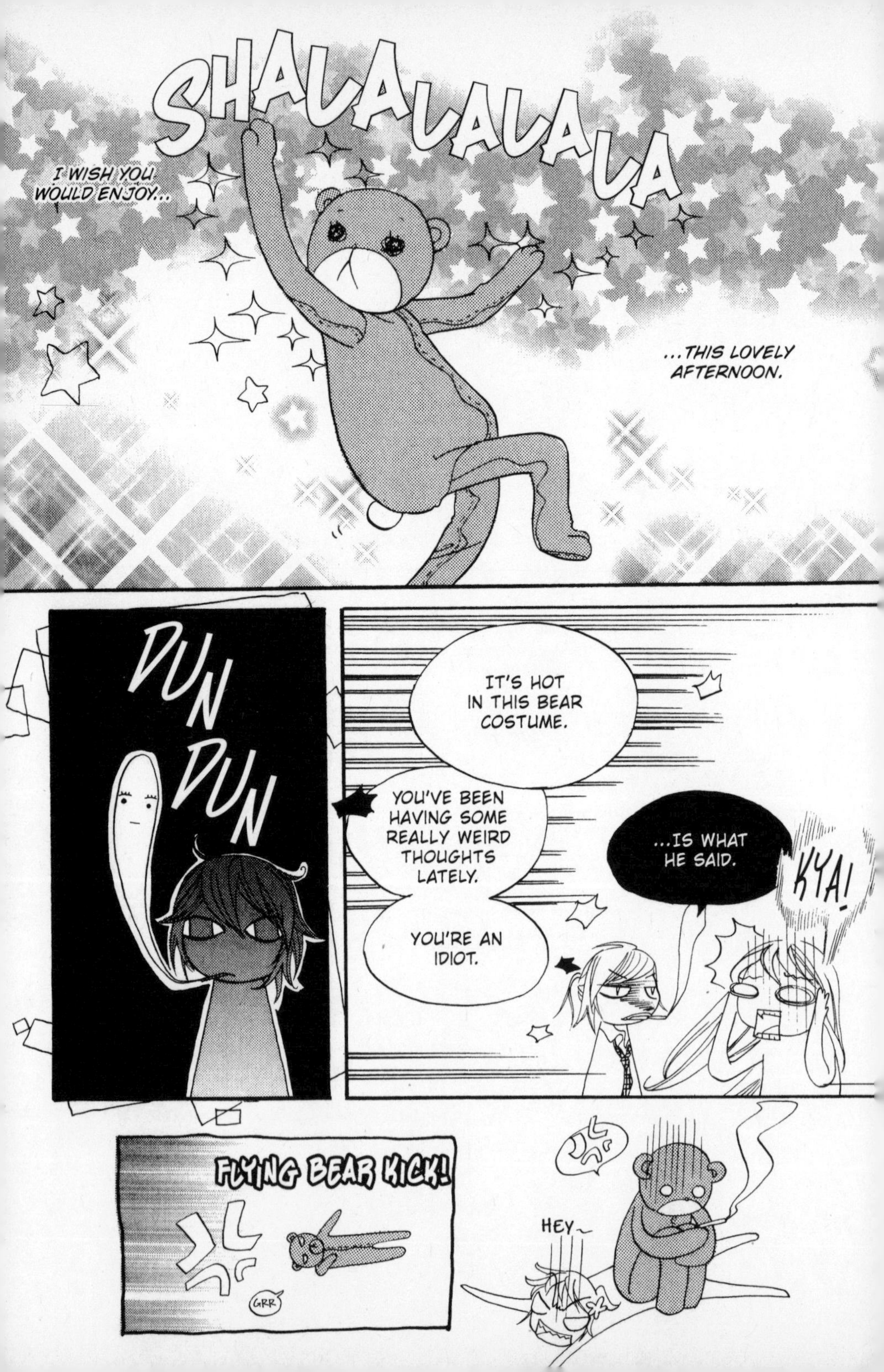
SHALALALALALA
I WISH YOU WOULD ENJOY...
...THIS LOVELY AFTERNOON.
IT'S HOT IN THIS BEAR COSTUME.
YOU'VE BEEN HAVING SOME REALLY WEIRD THOUGHTS LATELY.
YOU'RE AN IDIOT.
...IS WHAT HE SAID.
KYA!
DUN DUN DUN DUN
FLYING BEAR KICK!
GRR
HEY~

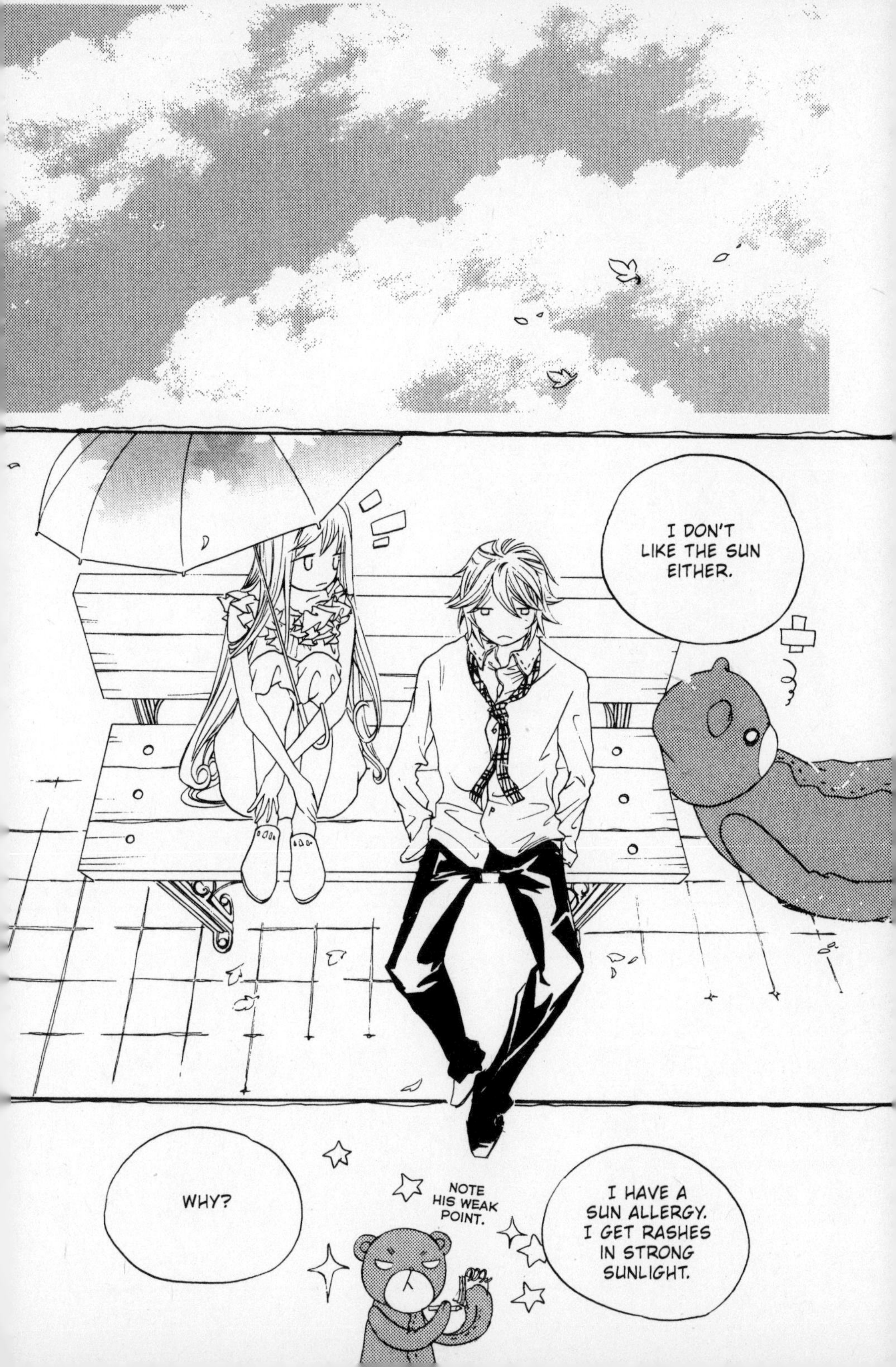
I DON'T LIKE THE SUN EITHER.
WHY?
I HAVE A SUN ALLERGY. I GET RASHES IN STRONG SUNLIGHT.
NOTE HIS WEAK POINT.

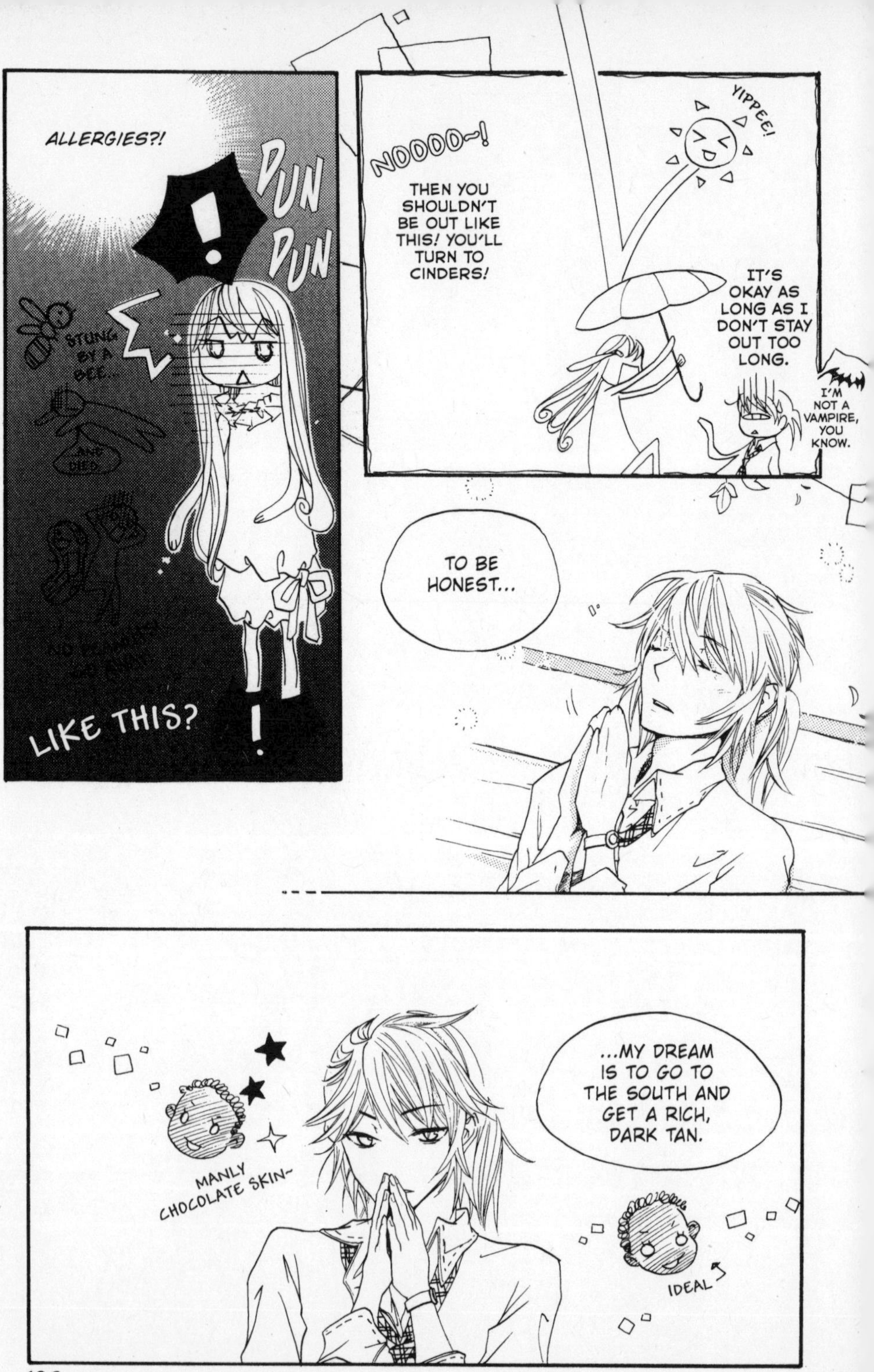
ALLERGIES?!
!
DUN DUN
STUNG BY A BEE...
...AND DIED.
LIKE THIS?
!
NOOOO~!
THEN YOU SHOULDN'T BE OUT LIKE THIS! YOU'LL TURN TO CINDERS!
YIPPEE!
IT'S OKAY AS LONG AS I DON'T STAY OUT TOO LONG.
I'M NOT A VAMPIRE, YOU KNOW.
TO BE HONEST...
...MY DREAM IS TO GO TO THE SOUTH AND GET A RICH, DARK TAN.
MANLY CHOCOLATE SKIN~
IDEAL

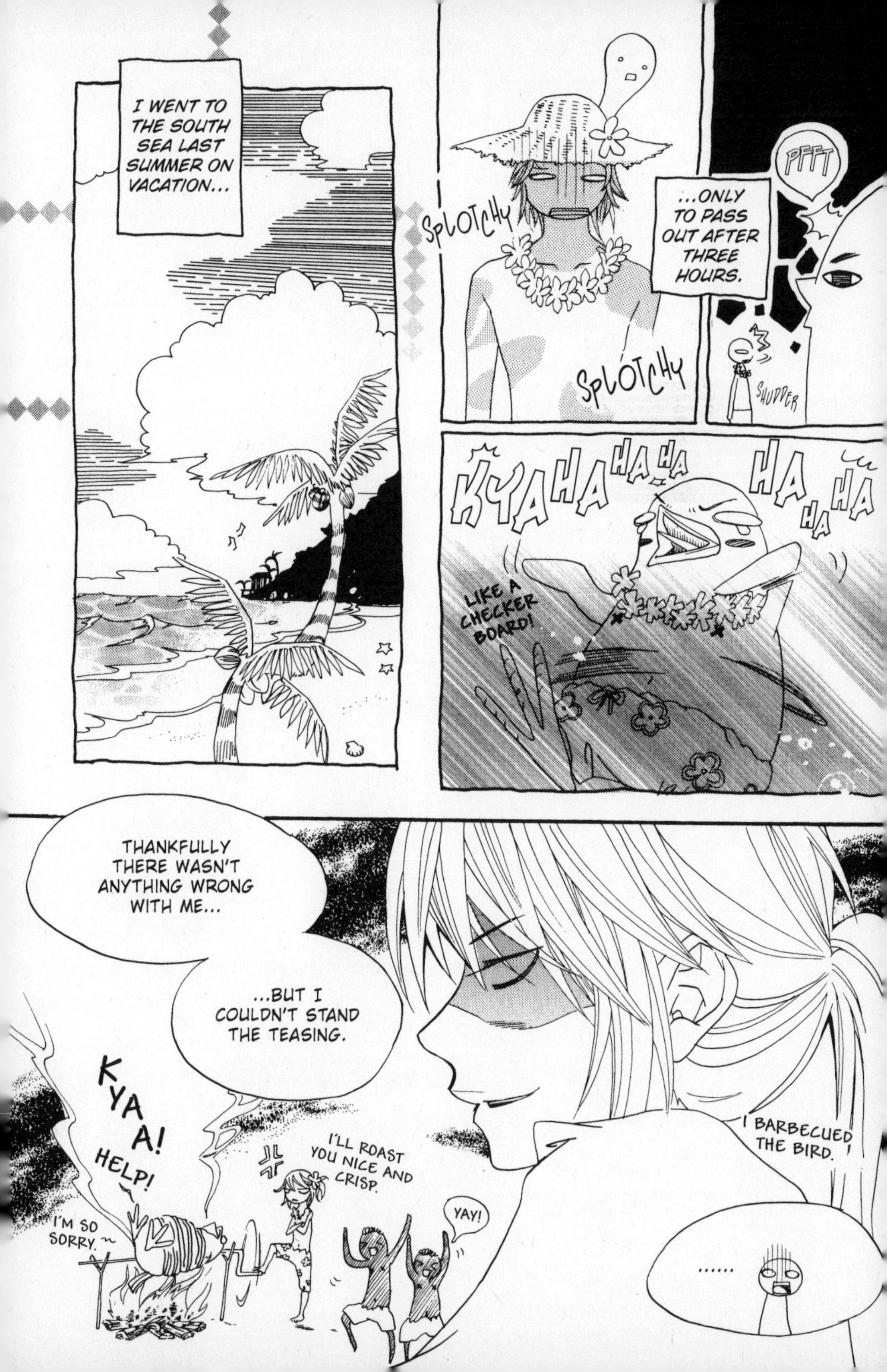

I WENT TO THE SOUTH SEA LAST SUMMER ON VACATION...
SPLOTCHY
SPLOTCHY
...ONLY TO PASS OUT AFTER THREE HOURS.
PFFT
SHUDDER
KYAHAHA HA HA
HA HA HA HA
LIKE A CHECKER BOARD!
THANKFULLY THERE WASN'T ANYTHING WRONG WITH ME...
...BUT I COULDN'T STAND THE TEASING.
KYAA! HELP!
I'M SO SORRY.
I'LL ROAST YOU NICE AND CRISP.
YAY!
I BARBECUED THE BIRD.
......

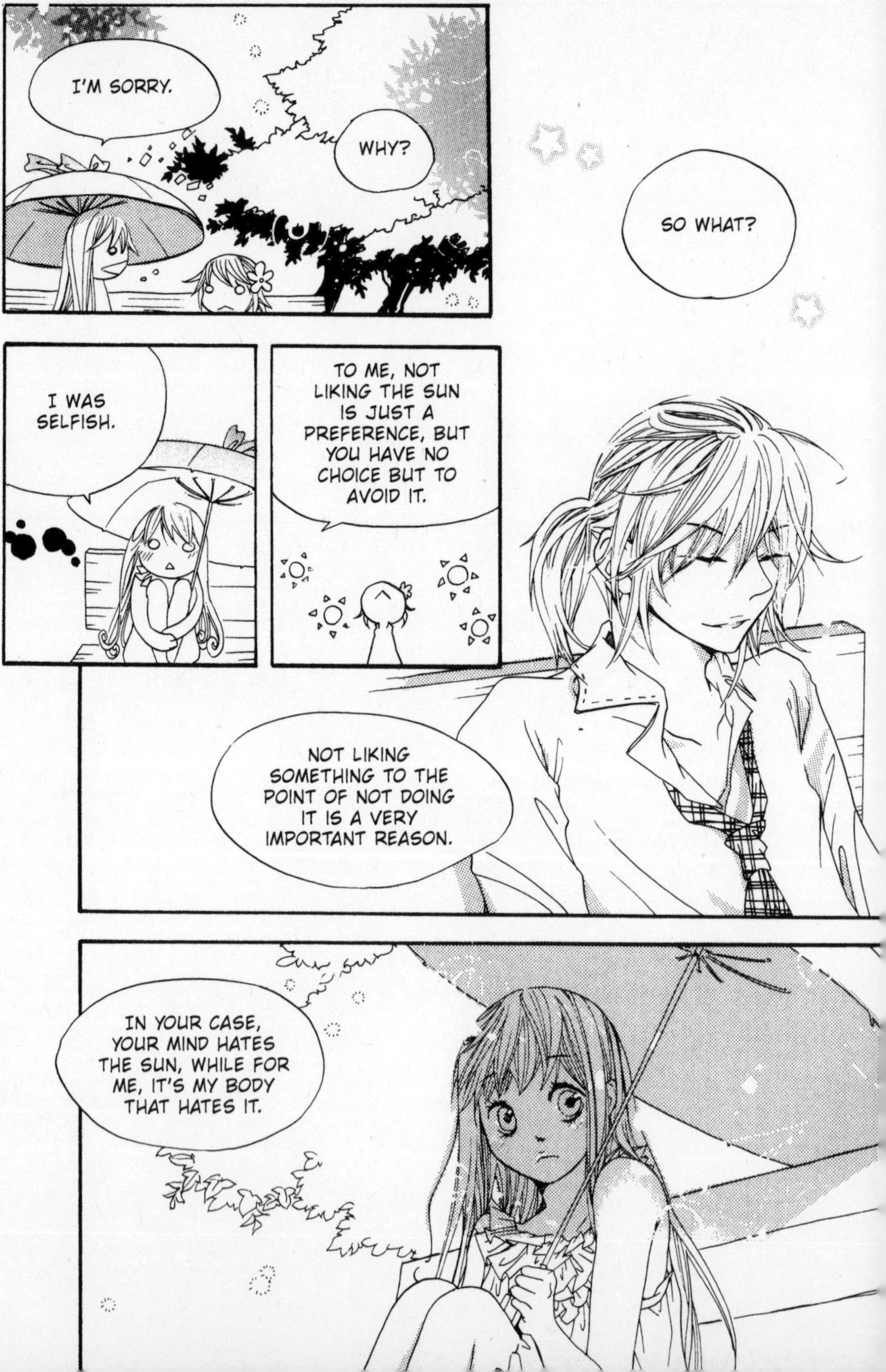
I'M SORRY.
WHY?
I WAS SELFISH.
TO ME, NOT LIKING THE SUN IS JUST A PREFERENCE, BUT YOU HAVE NO CHOICE BUT TO AVOID IT.
SO WHAT?
NOT LIKING SOMETHING TO THE POINT OF NOT DOING IT IS A VERY IMPORTANT REASON.
IN YOUR CASE, YOUR MIND HATES THE SUN, WHILE FOR ME, IT'S MY BODY THAT HATES IT.

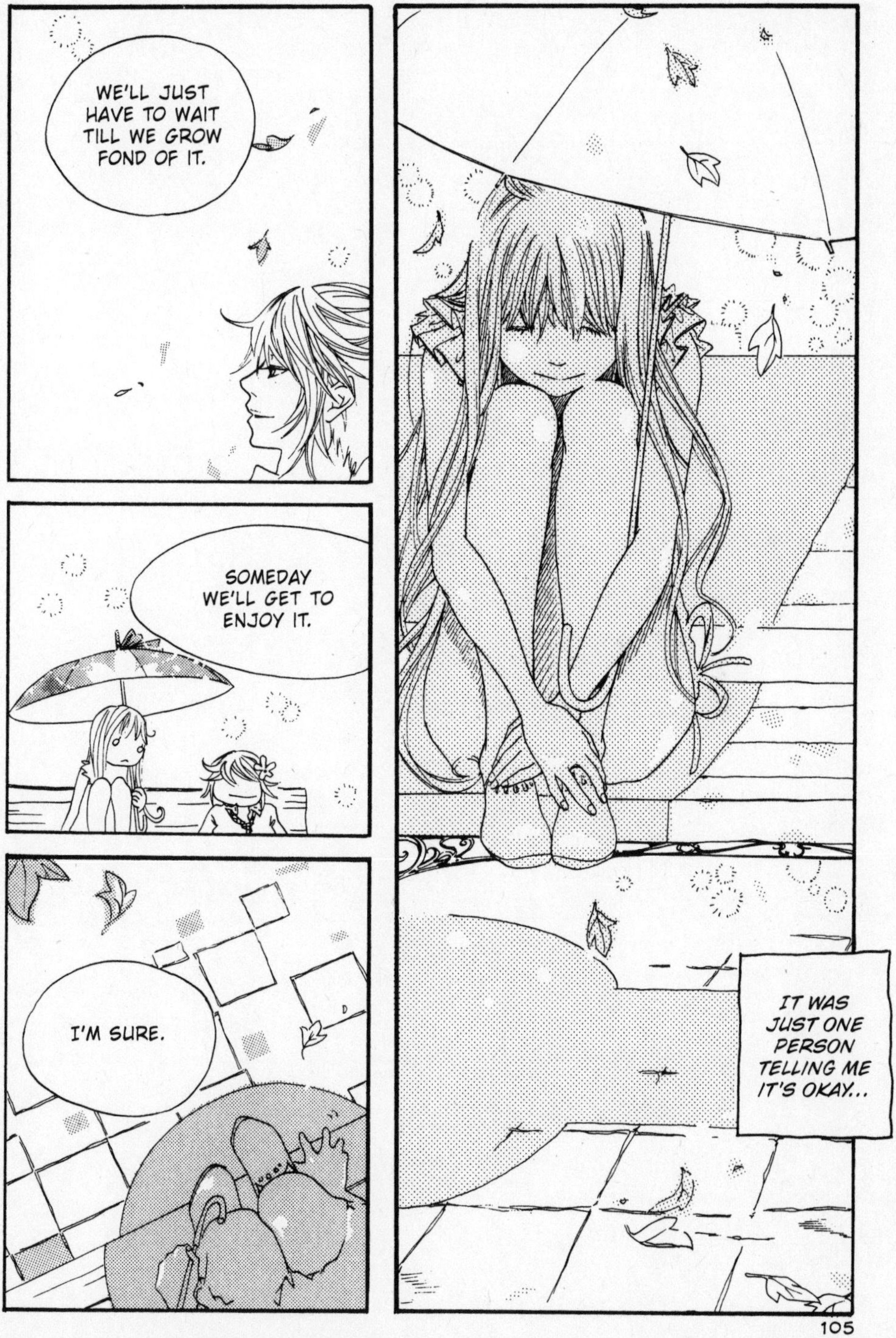
WE'LL JUST HAVE TO WAIT TILL WE GROW FOND OF IT.
SOMEDAY WE'LL GET TO ENJOY IT.
I'M SURE.
IT WAS JUST ONE PERSON TELLING ME IT'S OKAY...

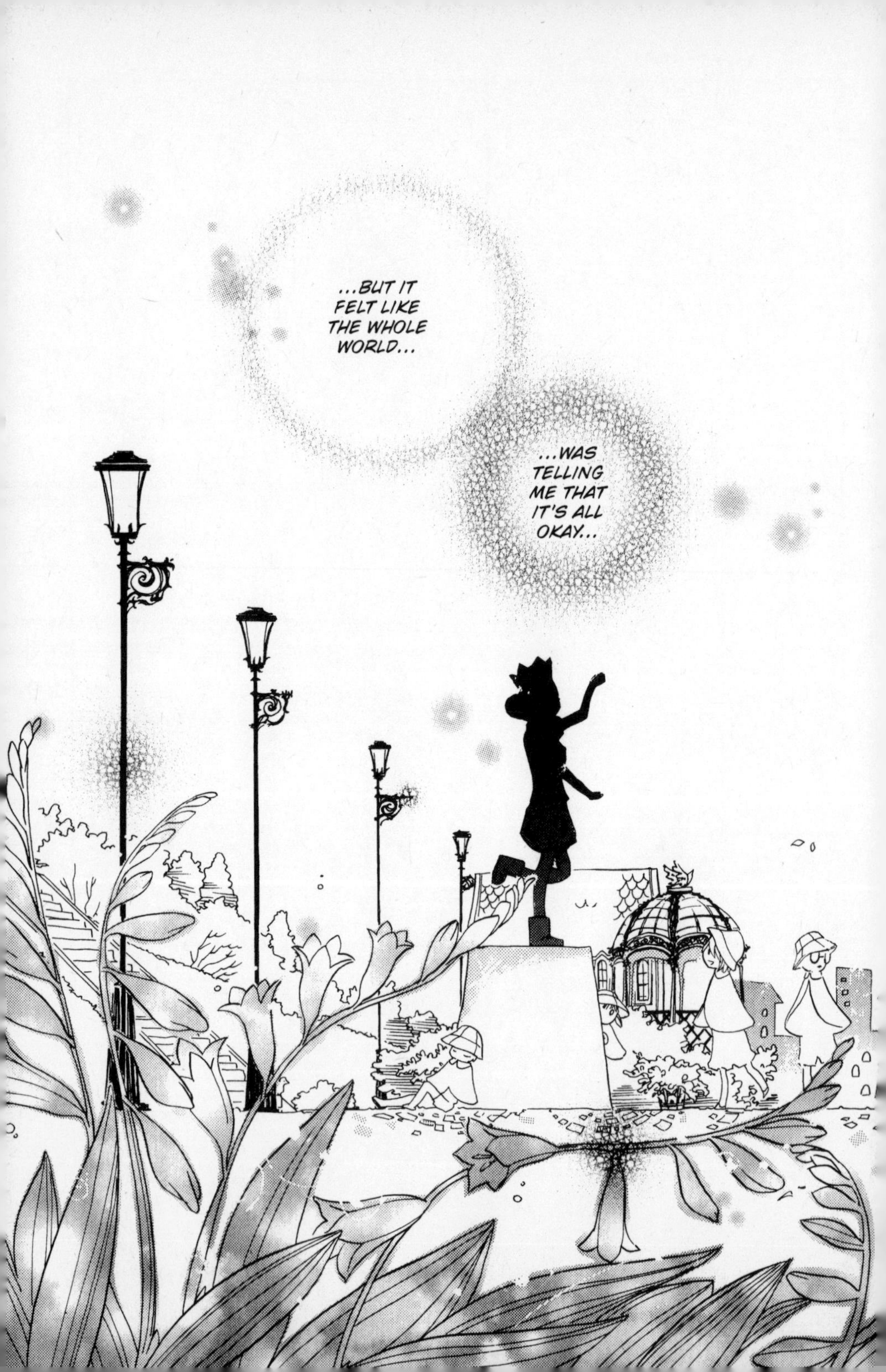
...BUT IT FELT LIKE THE WHOLE WORLD...
...WAS TELLING ME THAT IT'S ALL OKAY...

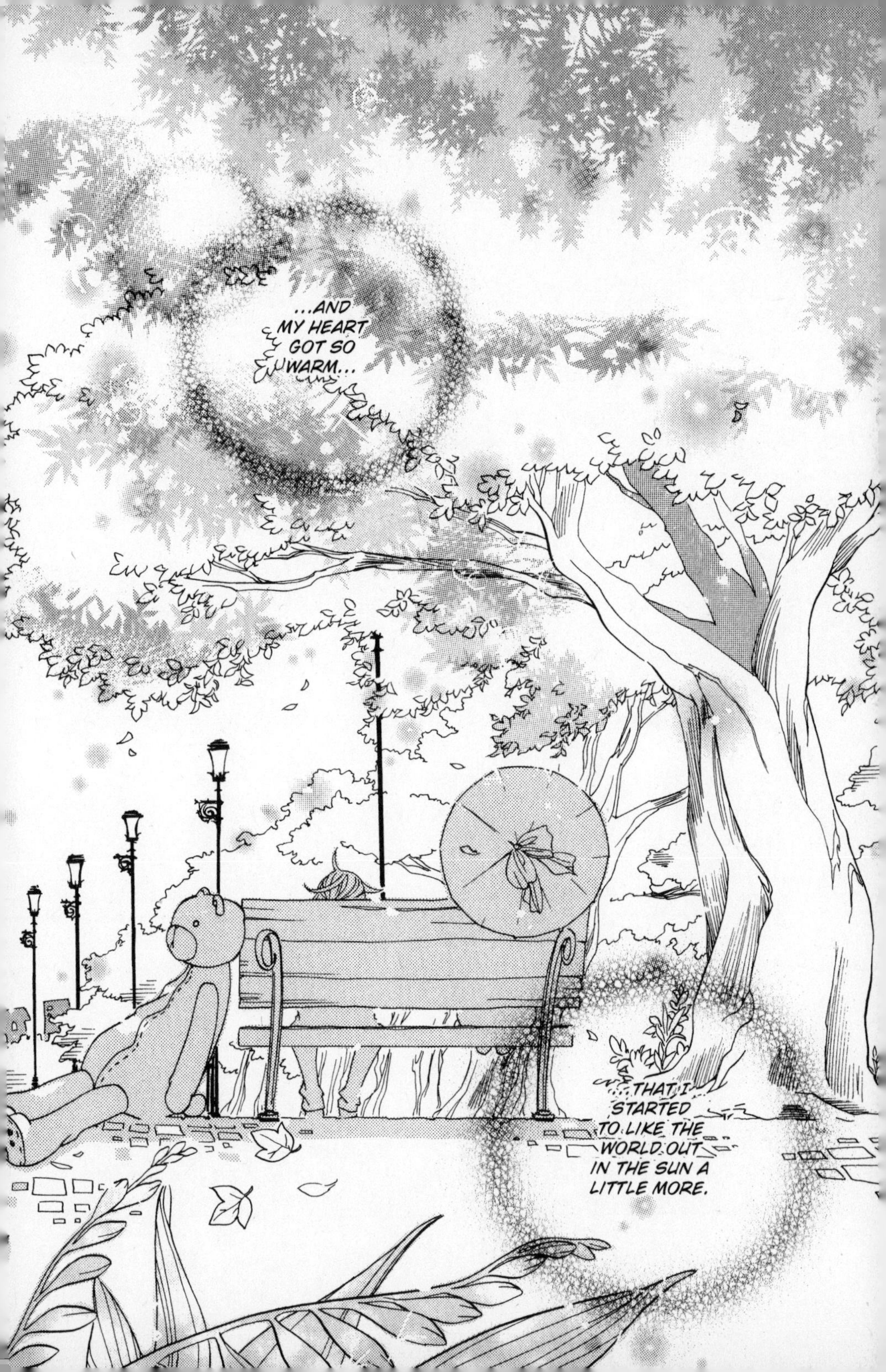
...AND MY HEART GOT SO WARM...
...THAT I STARTED TO LIKE THE WORLD OUT IN THE SUN A LITTLE MORE.

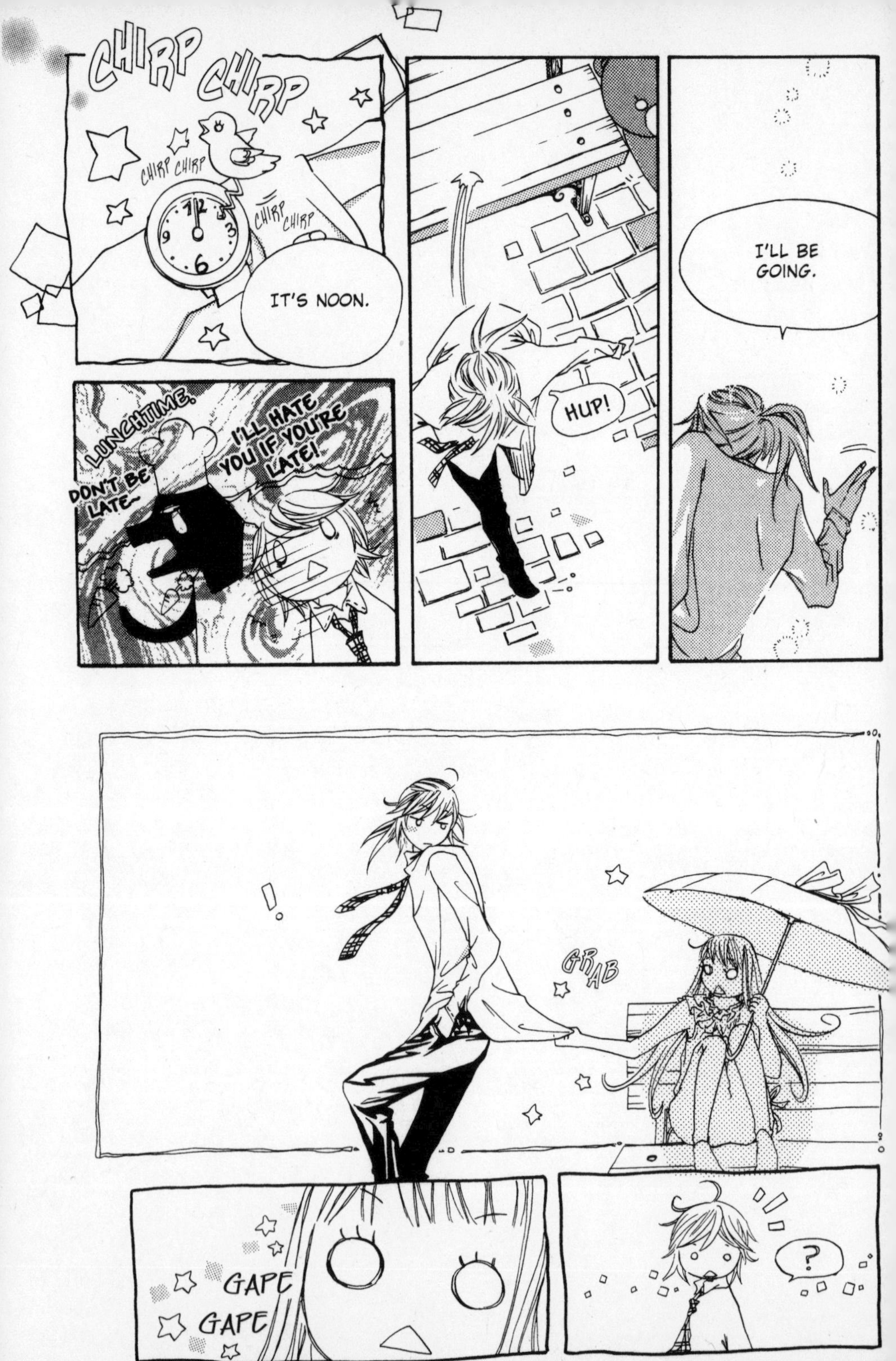
CHIRP CHIRP
CHIRP CHIRP
CHIRP CHIRP
IT'S NOON.
LUNCHTIME.
DON'T BE LATE~
I'LL HATE YOU IF YOU'RE LATE!
HUP!
I'LL BE GOING.
!
GRAB
GAPE
GAPE
?

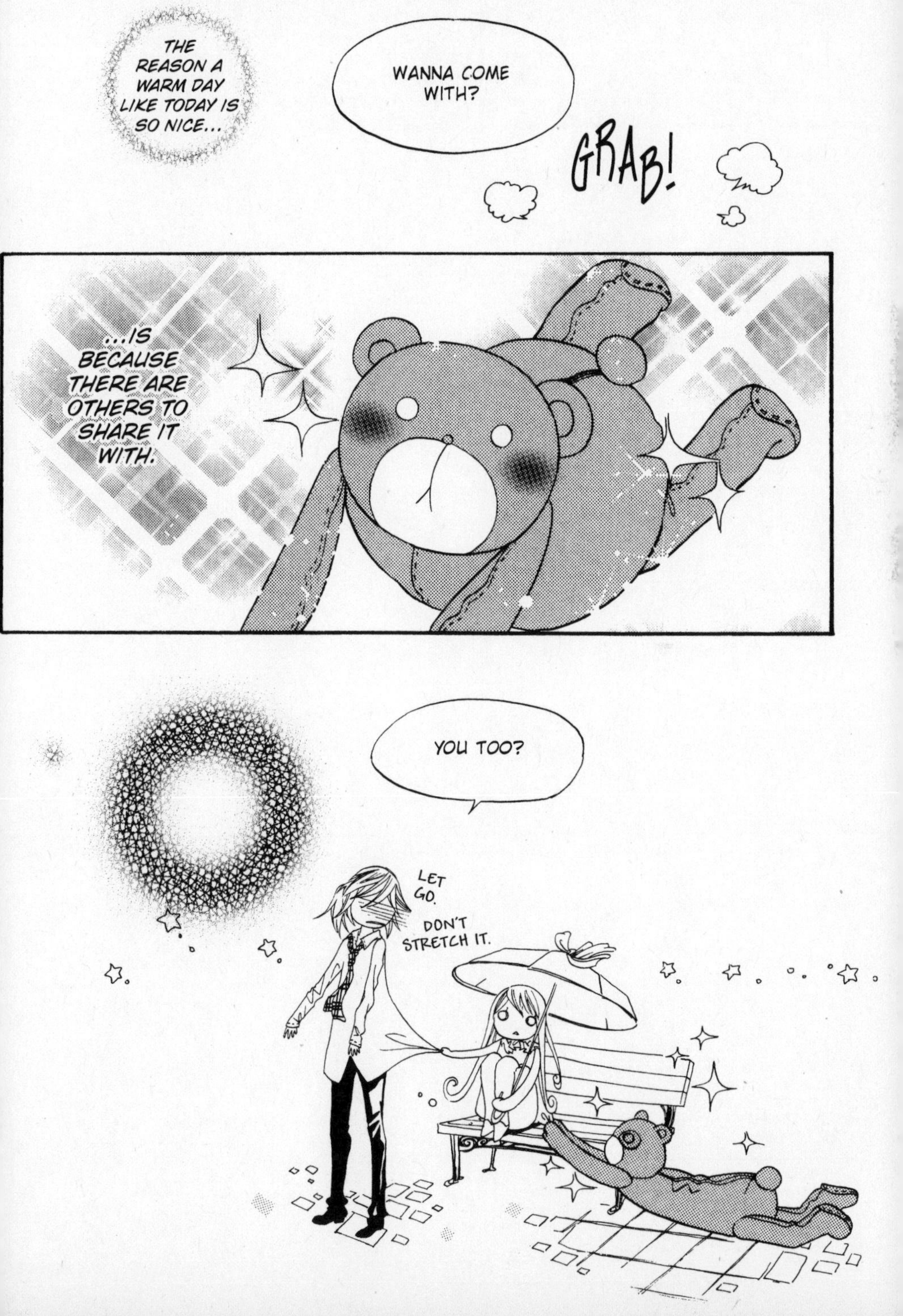
WANNA COME WITH?
GRAB!
THE REASON A WARM DAY LIKE TODAY IS SO NICE...
...IS BECAUSE THERE ARE OTHERS TO SHARE IT WITH.
YOU TOO?
LET GO.
DON'T STRETCH IT.

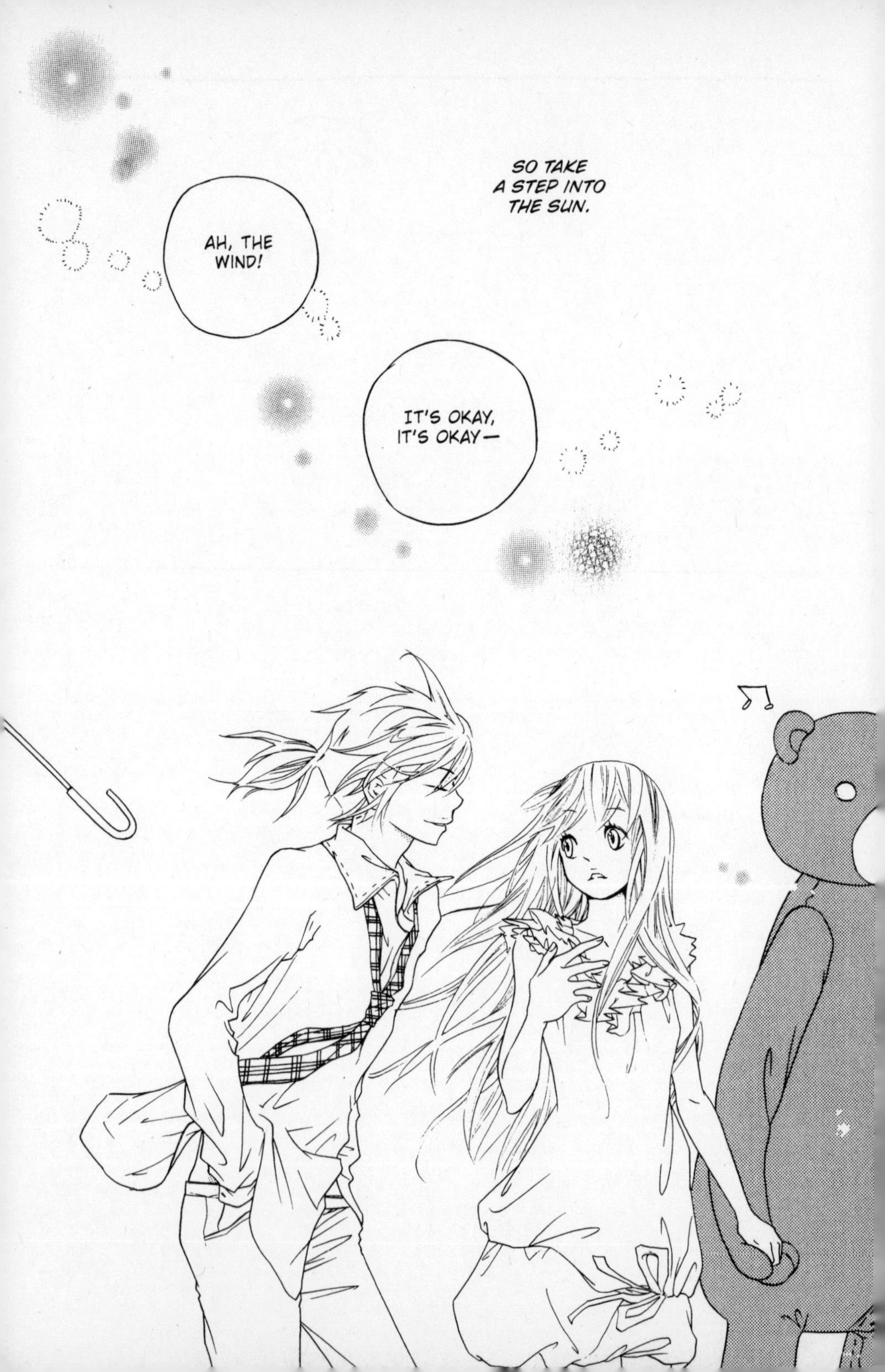
SO TAKE A STEP INTO THE SUN.
AH, THE WIND!
IT'S OKAY, IT'S OKAY—

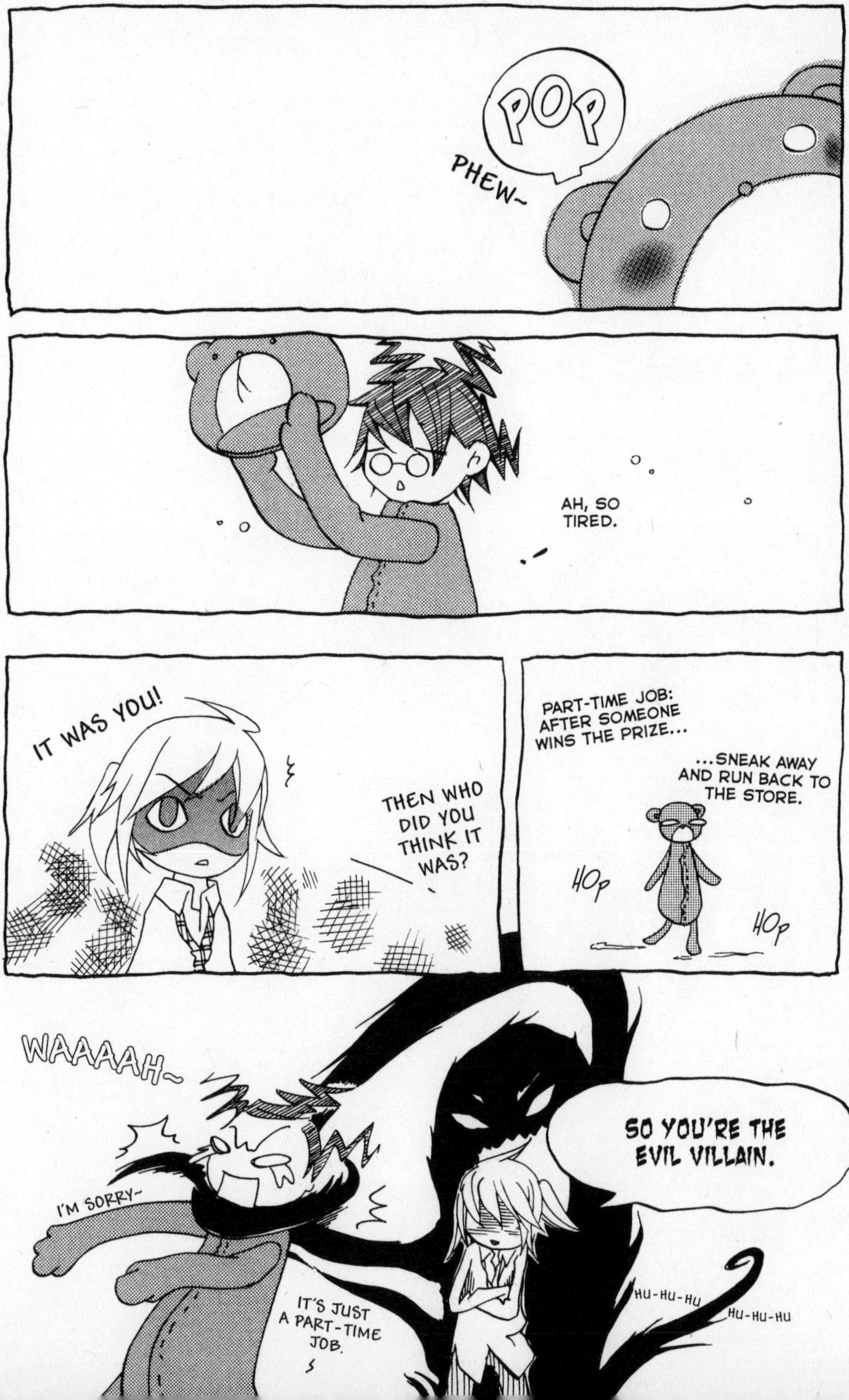
POP
PHEW~
AH, SO TIRED.
IT WAS YOU!
THEN WHO DID YOU THINK IT WAS?
PART-TIME JOB: AFTER SOMEONE WINS THE PRIZE...
...SNEAK AWAY AND RUN BACK TO THE STORE.
HOP
HOP
WAAAAH~
SO YOU'RE THE EVIL VILLAIN.
I'M SORRY~
IT'S JUST A PART-TIME JOB.
HU-HU-HU
HU-HU-HU

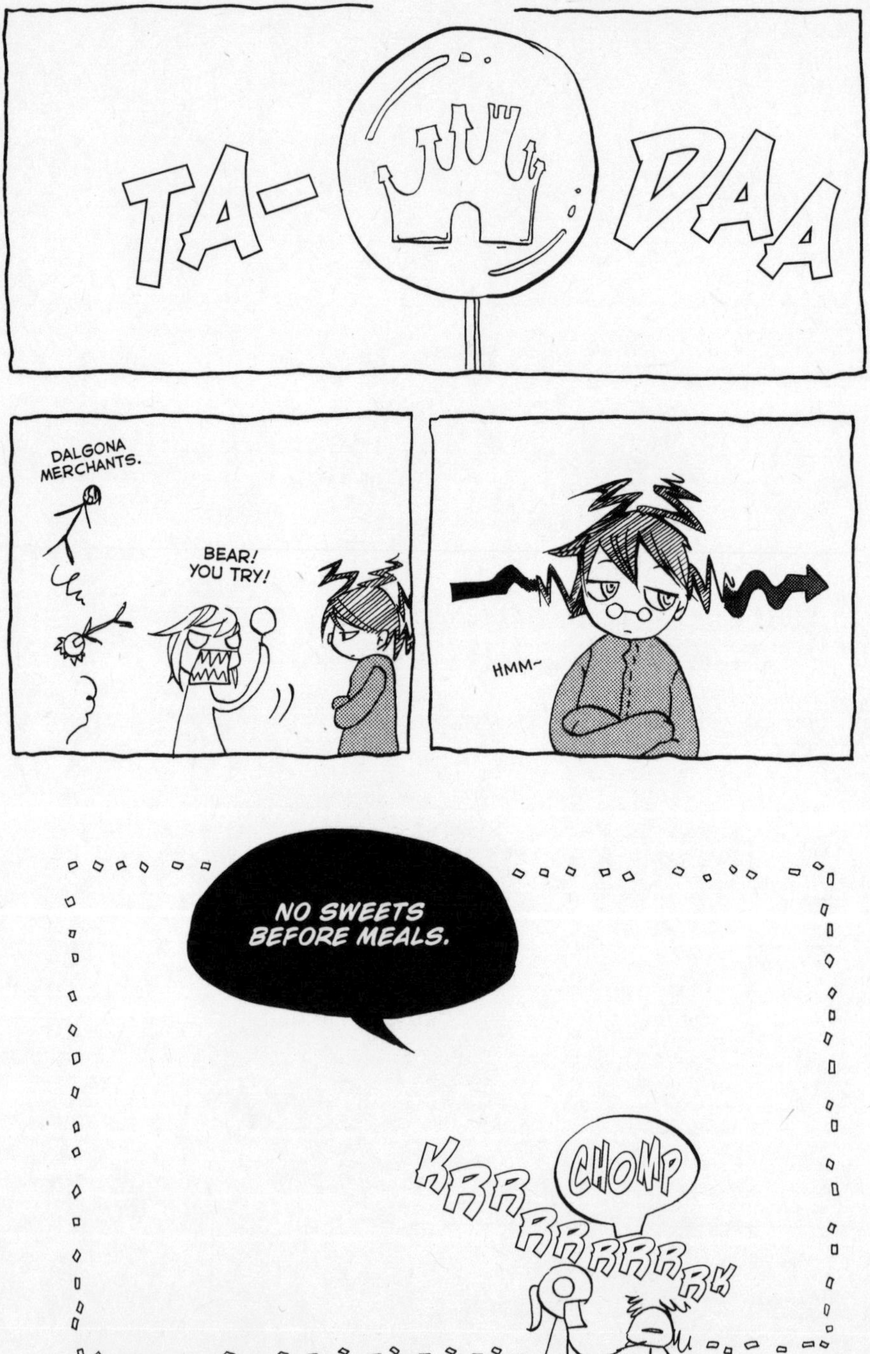
TA-DAA
DALGONA MERCHANTS.
BEAR! YOU TRY!
HMM~
NO SWEETS BEFORE MEALS.
KRRRRRRRRRK
CHOMP

END OF DAY 27

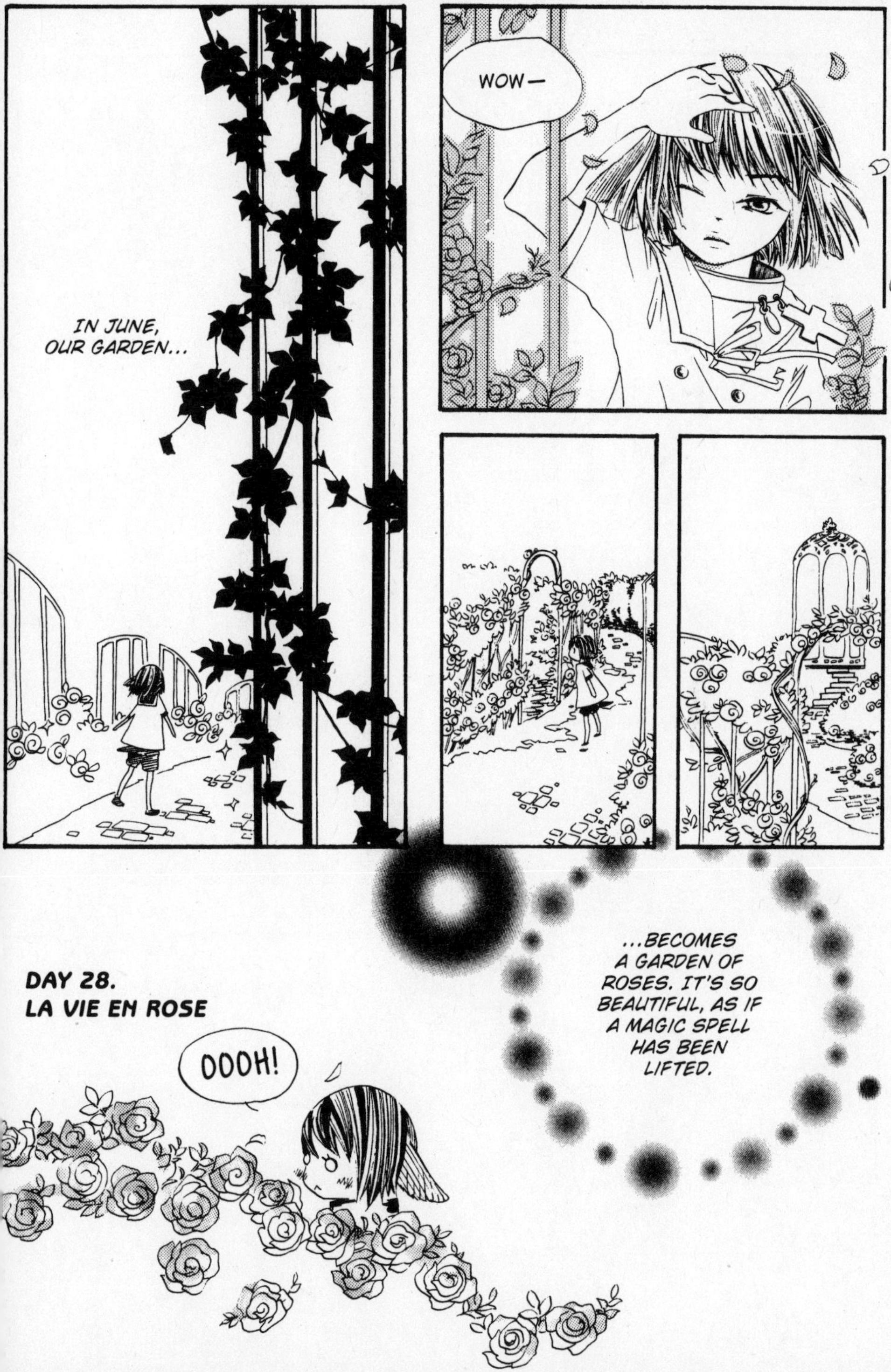
IN JUNE, OUR GARDEN...
WOW—
...BECOMES A GARDEN OF ROSES. IT'S SO BEAUTIFUL, AS IF A MAGIC SPELL HAS BEEN LIFTED.
DAY 28.
LA VIE EN ROSE
OOOH!

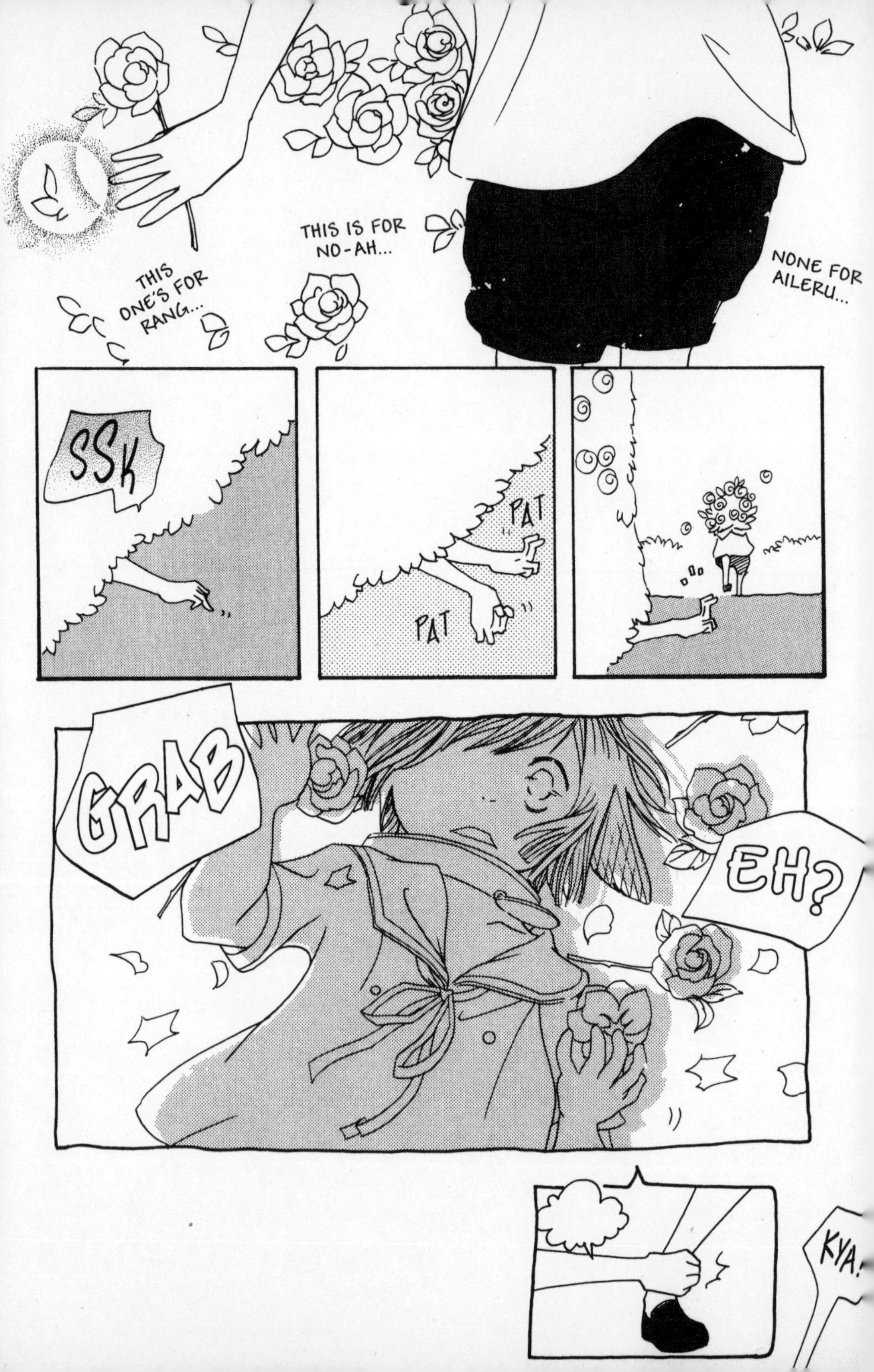
NONE FOR AILERU...
THIS IS FOR NO-AH...
THIS ONE'S FOR RANG...
SSK
PAT
PAT
EH?
GRAB
KYA!

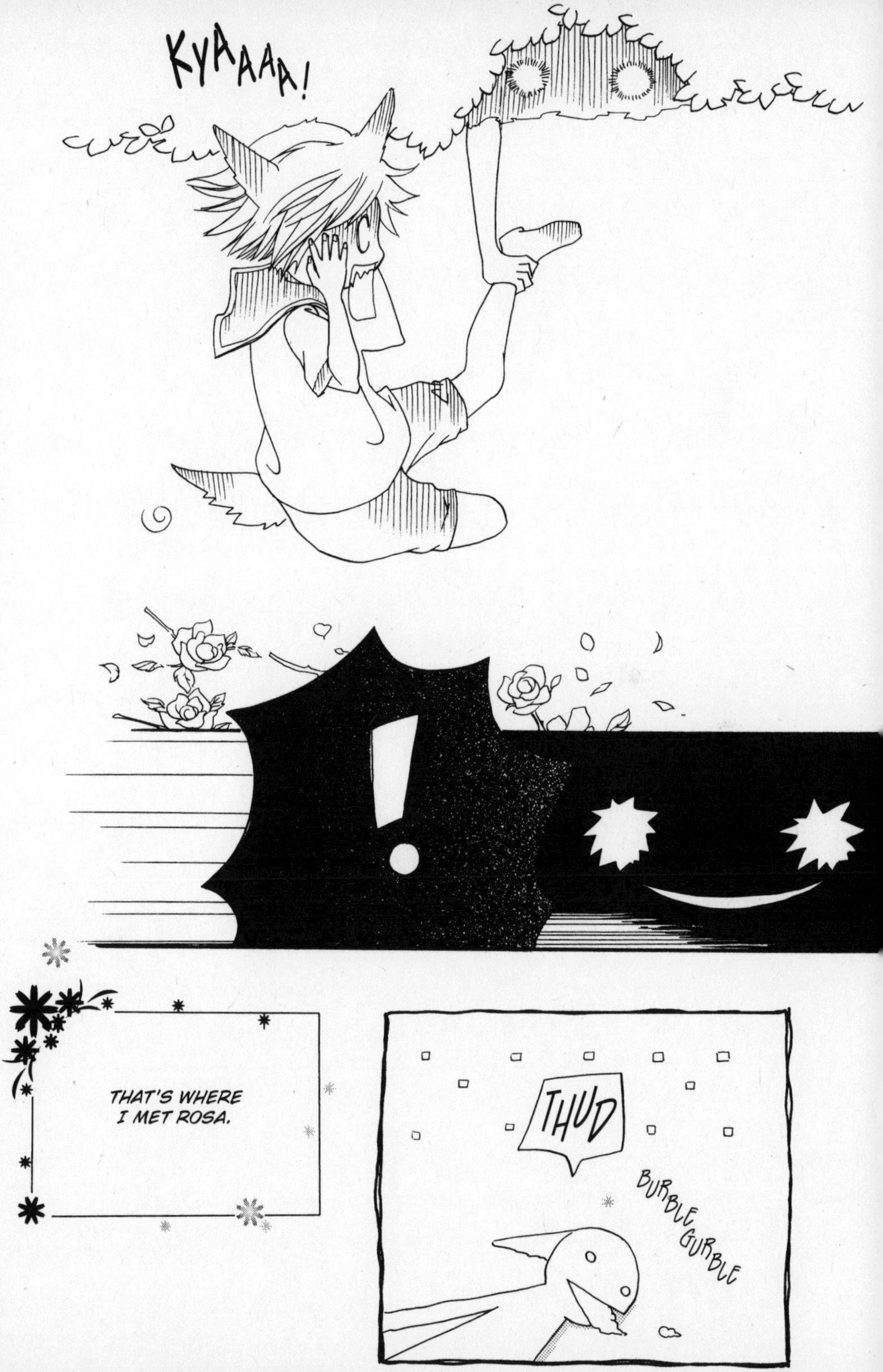
KYAAAA!
!
THAT'S WHERE I MET ROSA.
THUD
BURBLE GURBLE

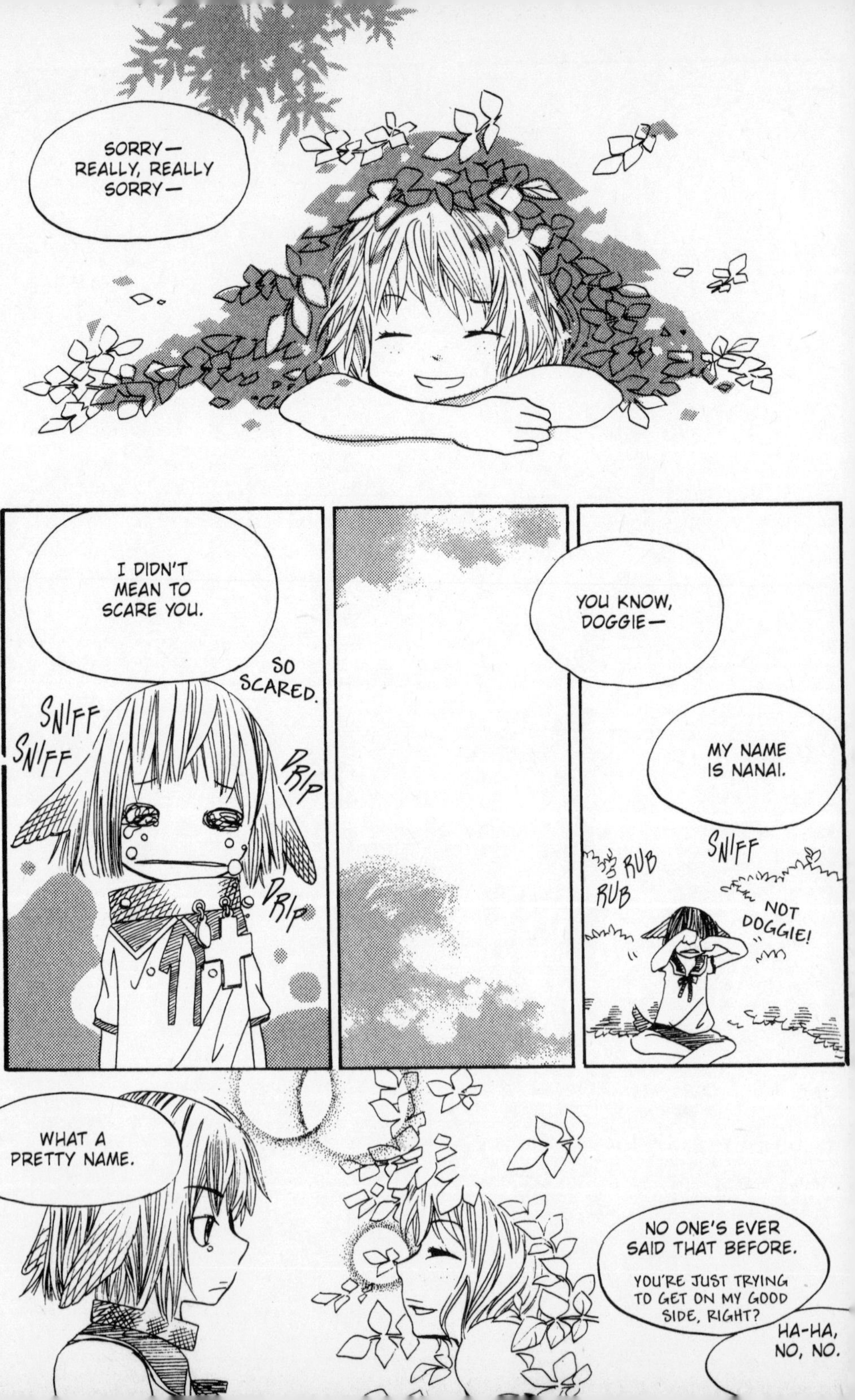
SORRY—
REALLY, REALLY
SORRY—
I DIDN'T
MEAN TO
SCARE YOU.
SO
SCARED.
SNIFF
SNIFF
DRIP
DRIP
YOU KNOW,
DOGGIE—
MY NAME
IS NANAI.
SNIFF
RUB
RUB
NOT
DOGGIE!
WHAT A
PRETTY NAME.
NO ONE'S EVER
SAID THAT BEFORE.
YOU'RE JUST TRYING
TO GET ON MY GOOD
SIDE, RIGHT?
HA-HA,
NO, NO.

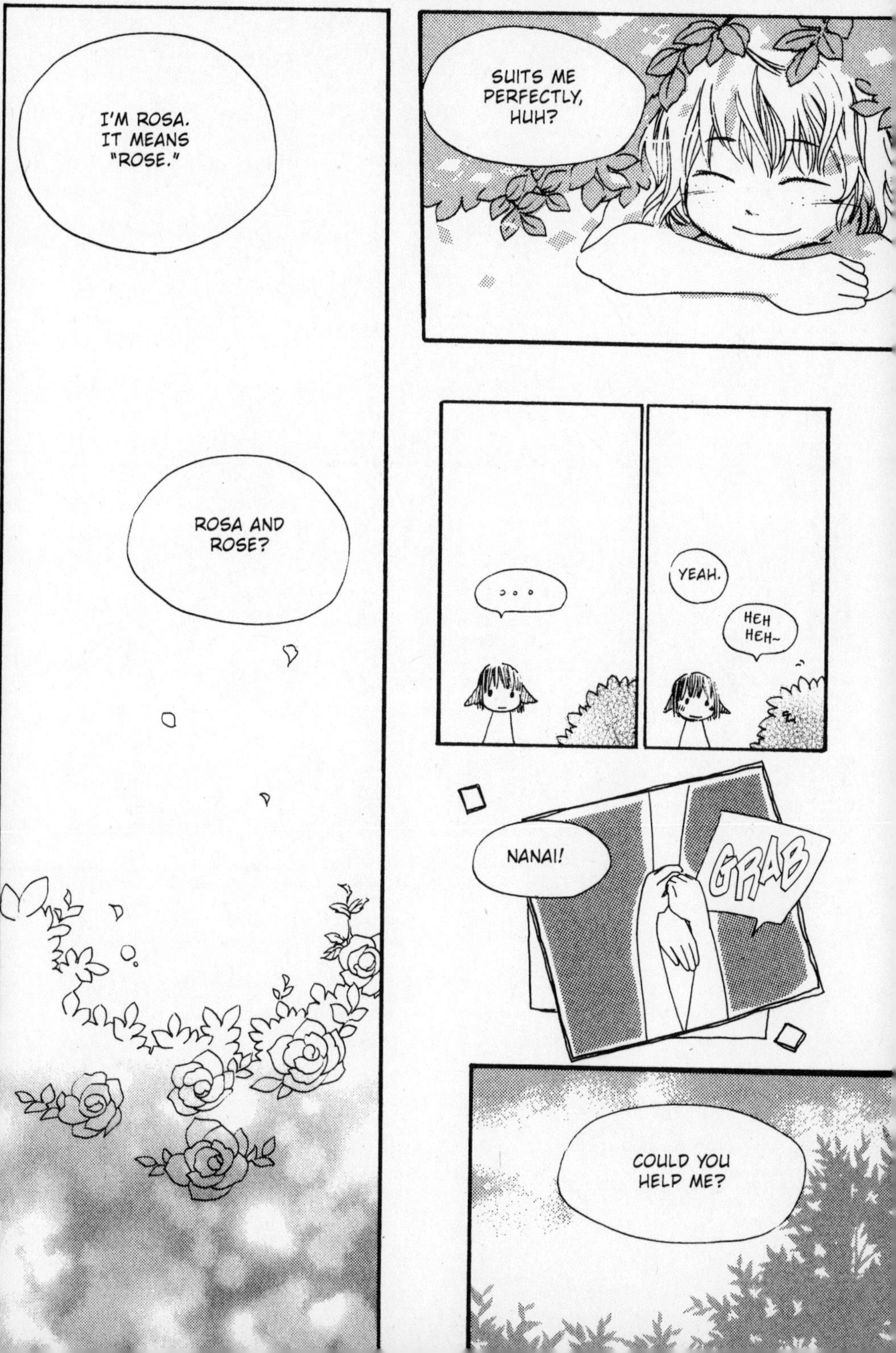
I'M ROSA. IT MEANS "ROSE."
SUITS ME PERFECTLY, HUH?
ROSA AND ROSE?
...
YEAH.
HEH HEH~
NANAI!
GRAB
COULD YOU HELP ME?

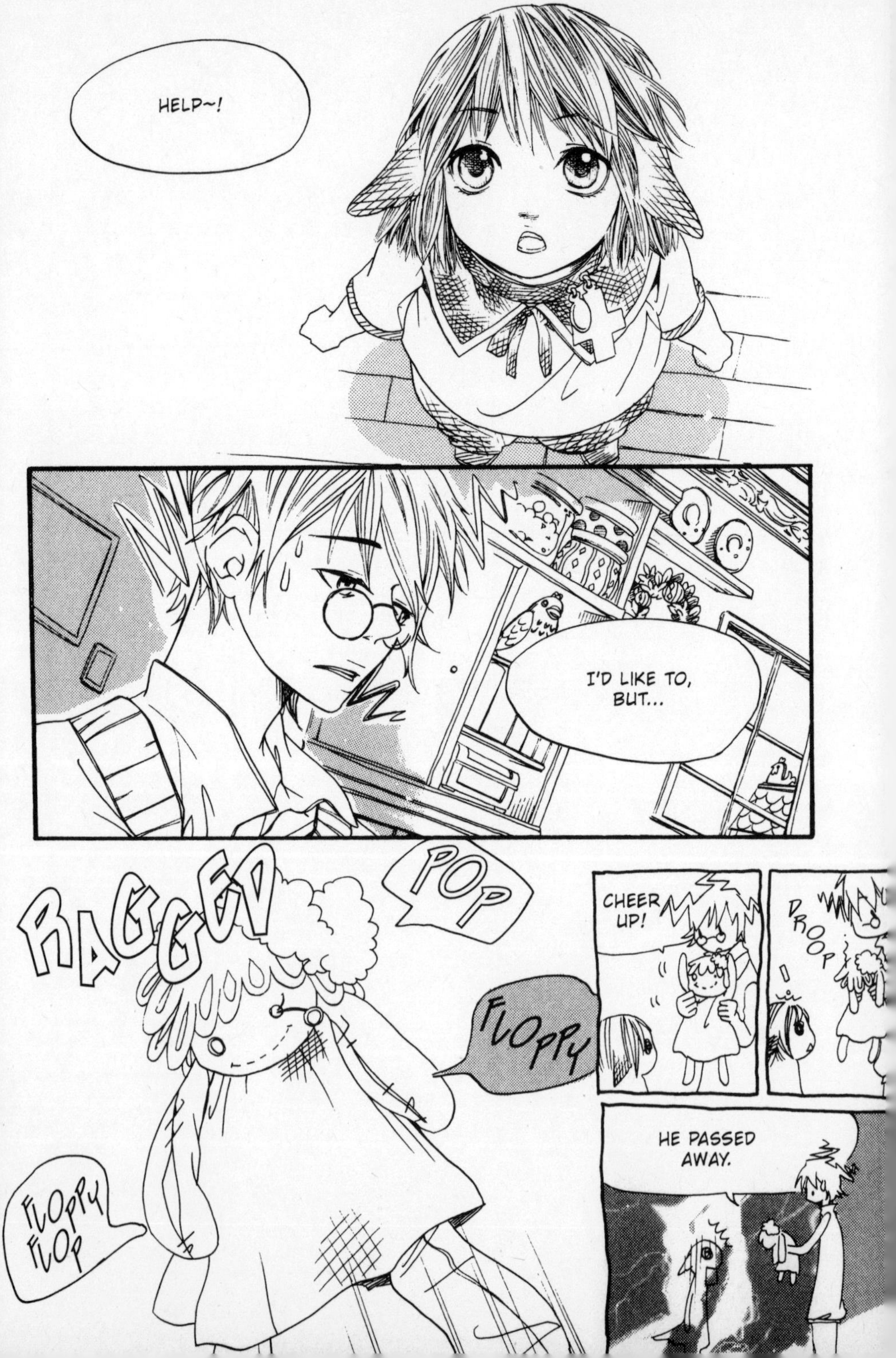
HELP~!
I'D LIKE TO, BUT...
RAGGED
POP
FLOPPY
FLOPPY FLOP
CHEER UP!
DROOP
HE PASSED AWAY.

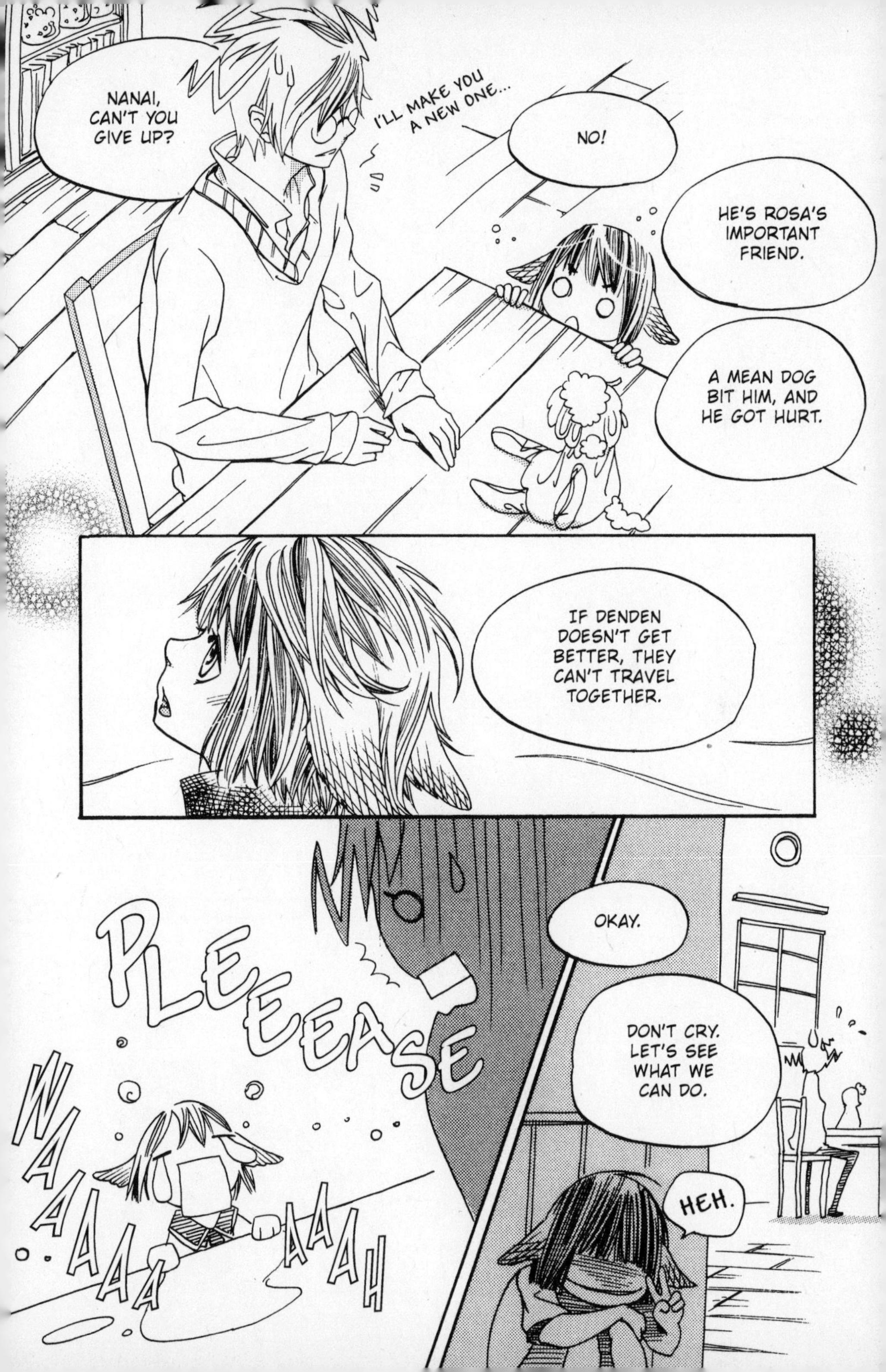
NANAI, CAN'T YOU GIVE UP?
I'LL MAKE YOU A NEW ONE...
NO!
HE'S ROSA'S IMPORTANT FRIEND.
A MEAN DOG BIT HIM, AND HE GOT HURT.
IF DENDEN DOESN'T GET BETTER, THEY CAN'T TRAVEL TOGETHER.
PLEEEASE
WAAAAAAAAAH
OKAY.
DON'T CRY. LET'S SEE WHAT WE CAN DO.
HEH.

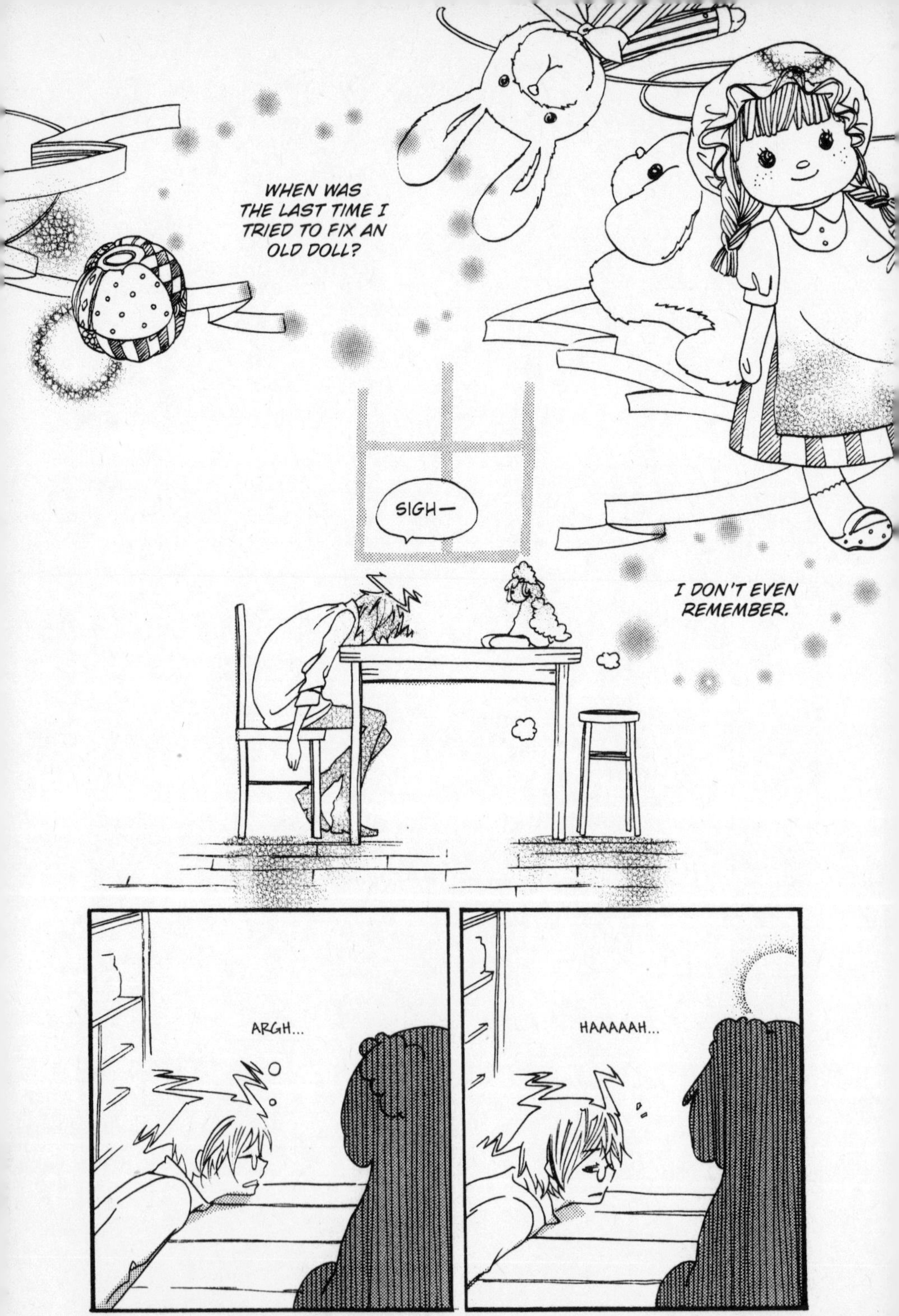

WHEN WAS THE LAST TIME I TRIED TO FIX AN OLD DOLL?
SIGH—
I DON'T EVEN REMEMBER.
ARGH...
HAAAAAH...

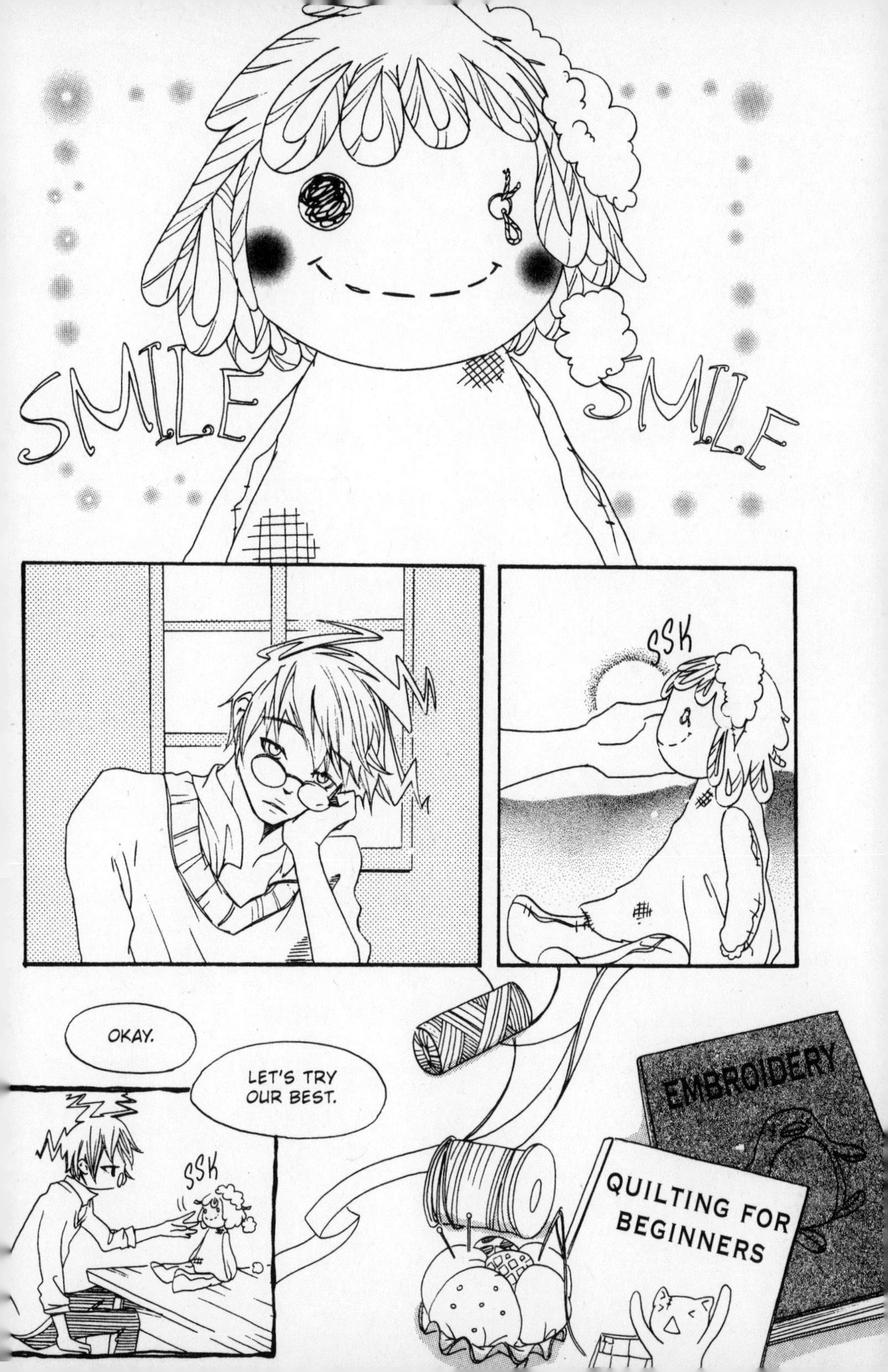
SMILE
SMILE
SSK
OKAY.
LET'S TRY OUR BEST.
SSK
EMBROIDERY
QUILTING FOR BEGINNERS

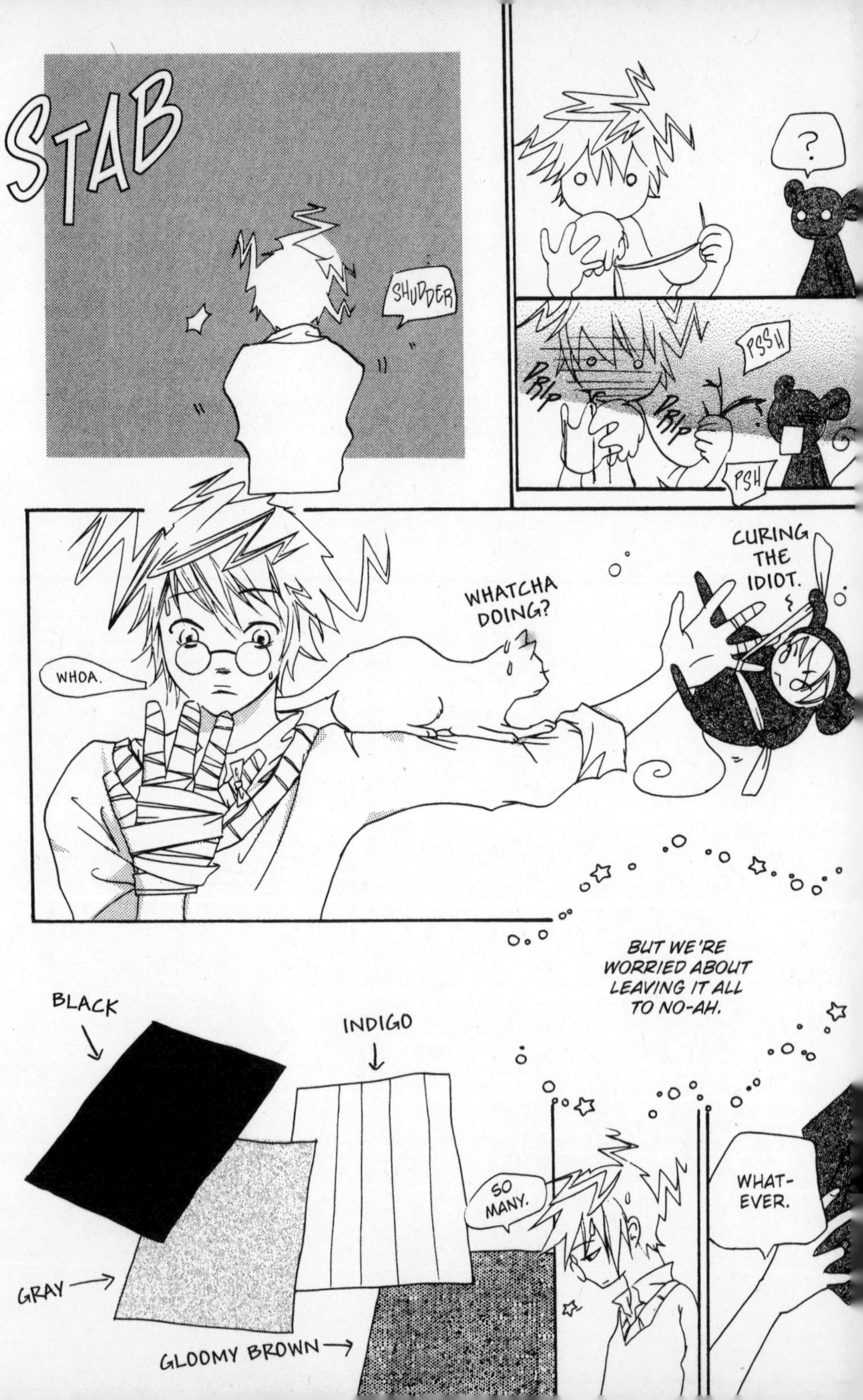
STAB
SHUDDER
?
DRIP
DRIP
PSSH
PSH
CURING THE IDIOT.
WHATCHA DOING?
WHOA.
BUT WE'RE WORRIED ABOUT LEAVING IT ALL TO NO-AH.
WHAT-EVER.
SO MANY.
INDIGO
BLACK
GRAY
GLOOMY BROWN

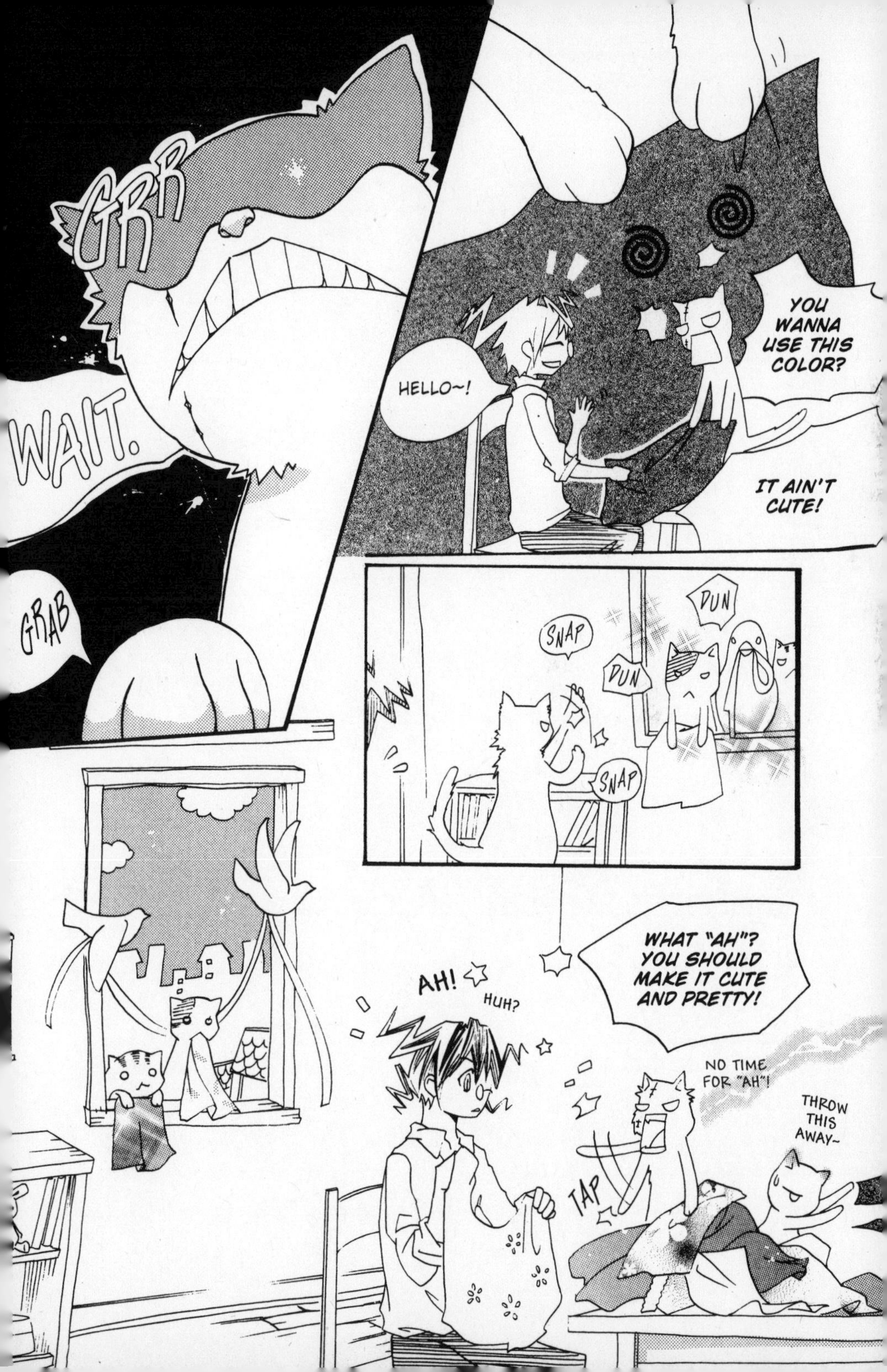
GRR
WAIT.
GRAB
YOU WANNA USE THIS COLOR?
HELLO~!
IT AIN'T CUTE!
DUN
SNAP
DUN
SNAP
WHAT "AH"? YOU SHOULD MAKE IT CUTE AND PRETTY!
AH!
HUH?
NO TIME FOR "AH"!
THROW THIS AWAY~
TAP

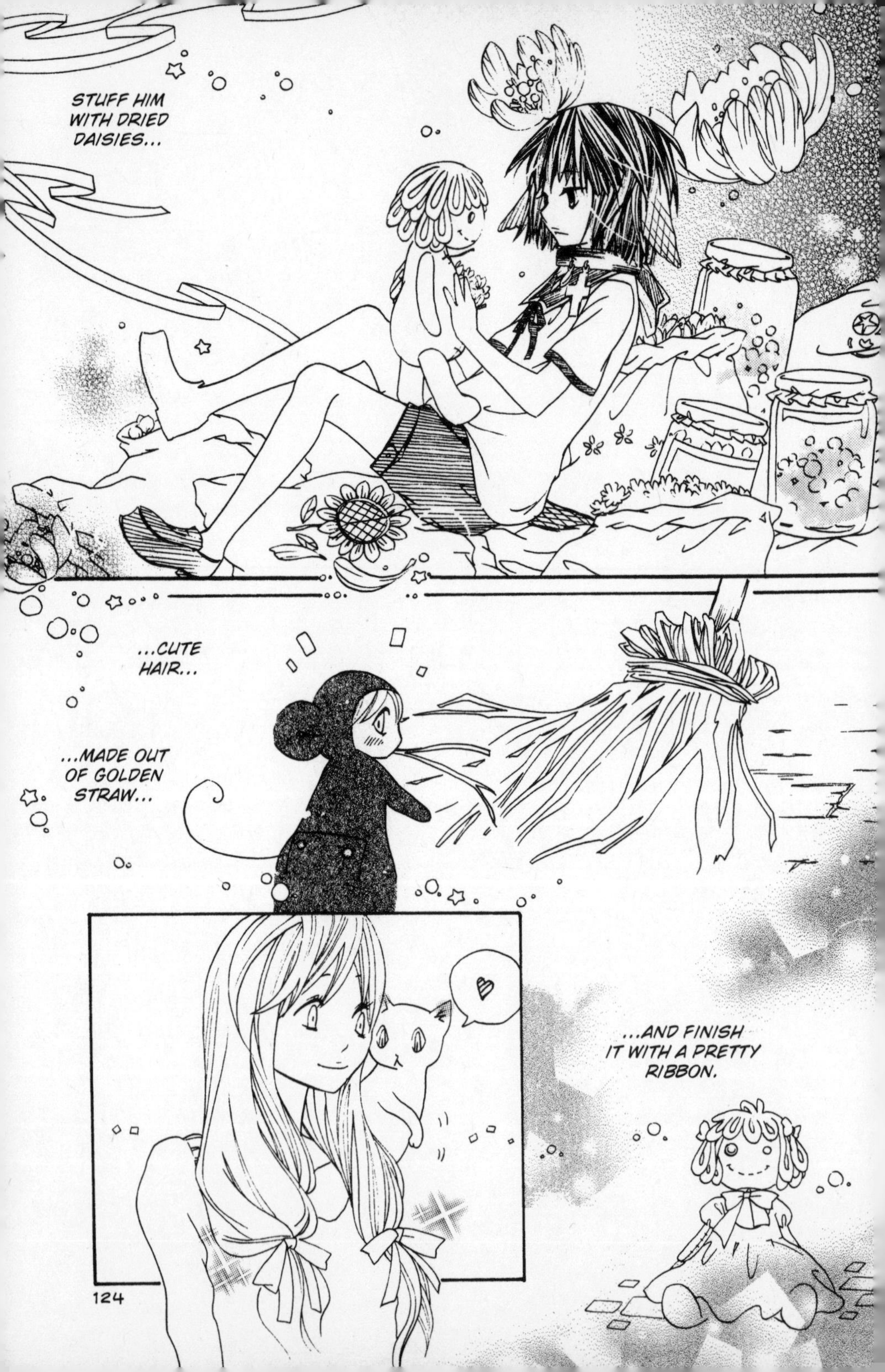
STUFF HIM WITH DRIED DAISIES...
...CUTE HAIR...
...MADE OUT OF GOLDEN STRAW...
...AND FINISH IT WITH A PRETTY RIBBON.

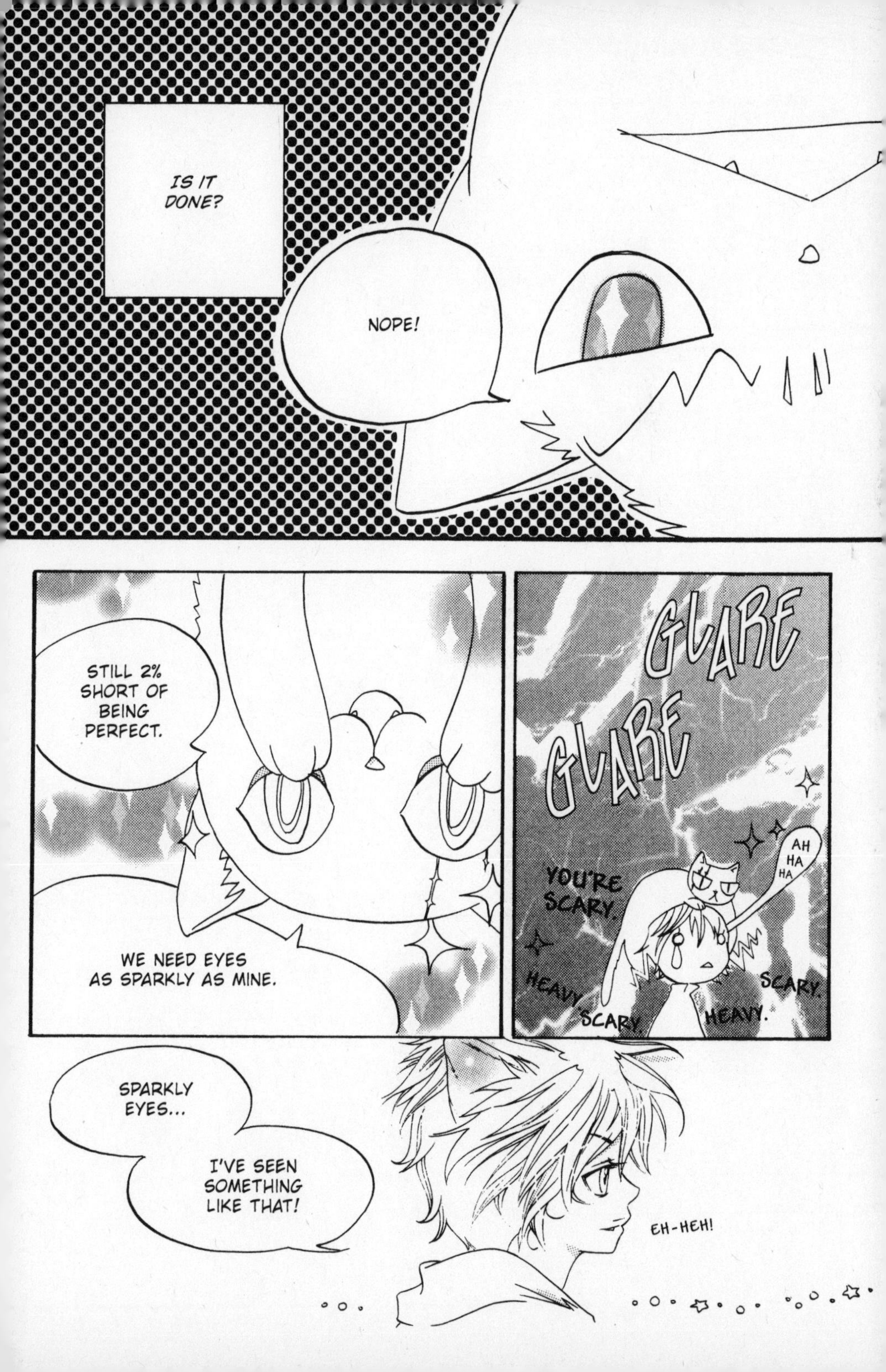
IS IT DONE?
NOPE!
STILL 2% SHORT OF BEING PERFECT.
WE NEED EYES AS SPARKLY AS MINE.
GLARE GLARE
AH HA HA
YOU'RE SCARY.
HEAVY SCARY. HEAVY. SCARY.
SPARKLY EYES...
I'VE SEEN SOMETHING LIKE THAT!
EH-HEH!

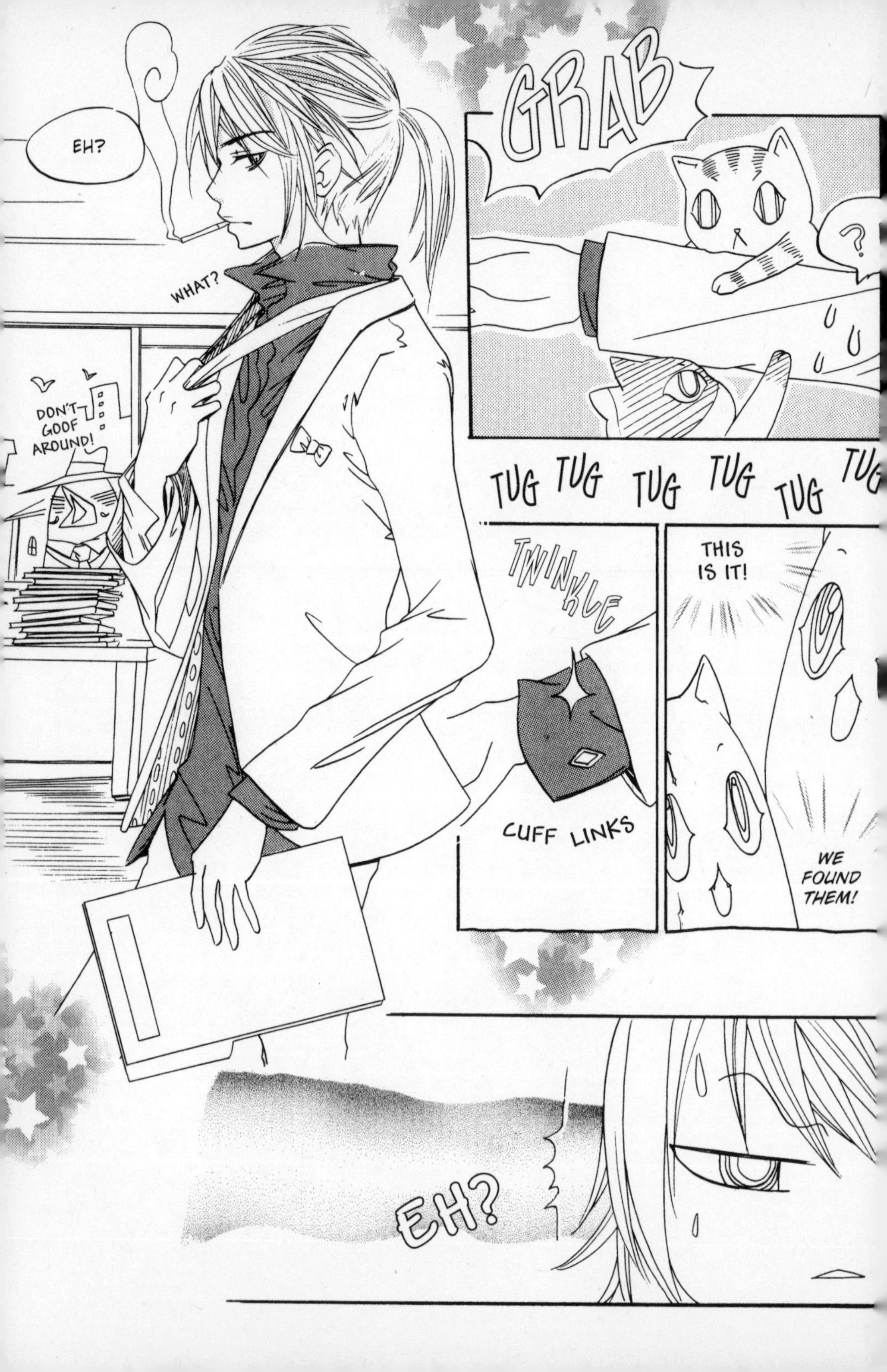
GRAB
?
TUG TUG TUG TUG TUG TUG
THIS IS IT!
WE FOUND THEM!
TWINKLE
CUFF LINKS
EH?
WHAT?
DON'T GOOF AROUND!
EH?

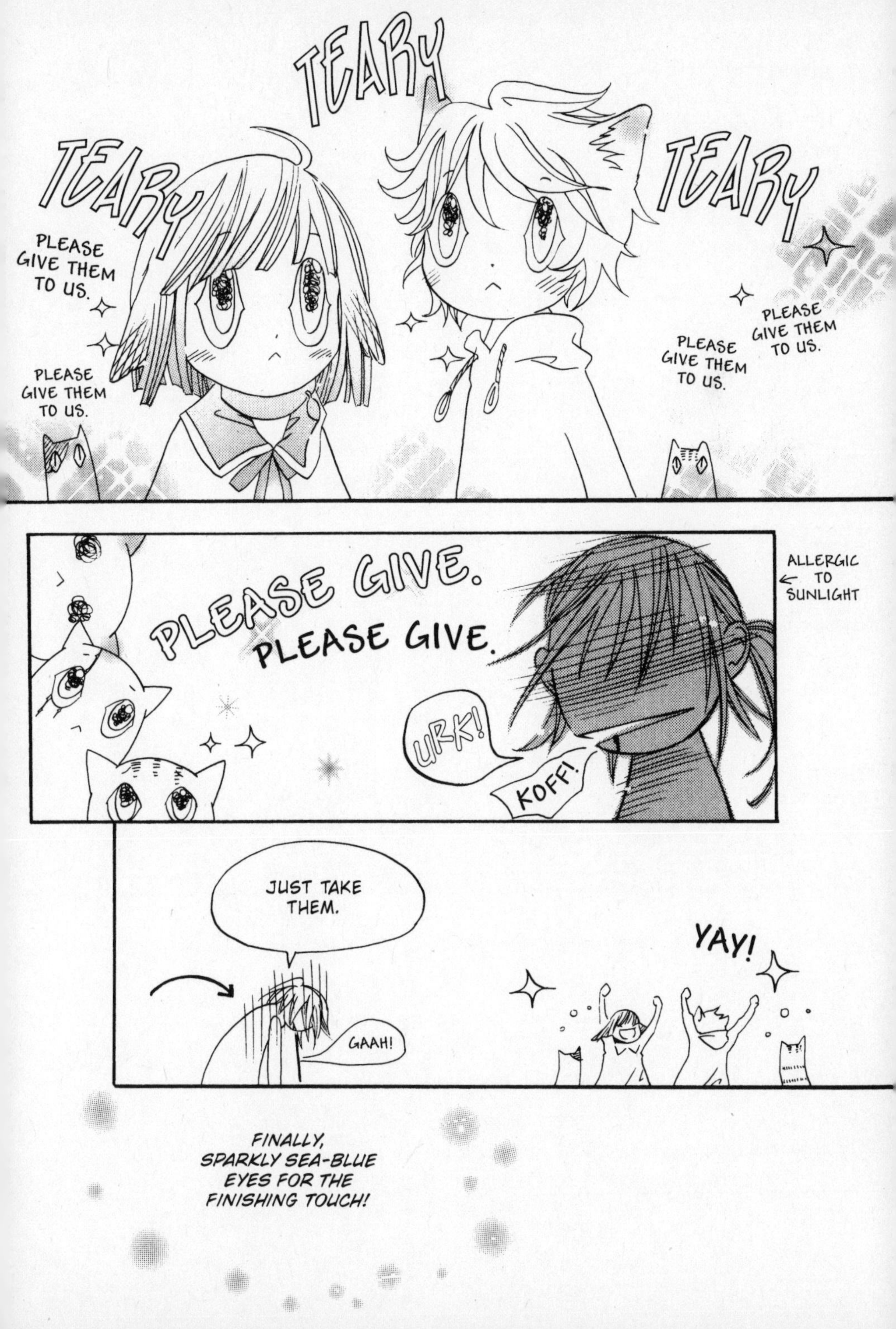
TEARY
TEARY
TEARY
PLEASE GIVE THEM TO US.
PLEASE GIVE THEM TO US.
PLEASE GIVE THEM TO US.
PLEASE GIVE THEM TO US.
ALLERGIC TO SUNLIGHT
PLEASE GIVE.
PLEASE GIVE.
URK!
KOFF!
YAY!
JUST TAKE THEM.
GAAH!
FINALLY, SPARKLY SEA-BLUE EYES FOR THE FINISHING TOUCH!

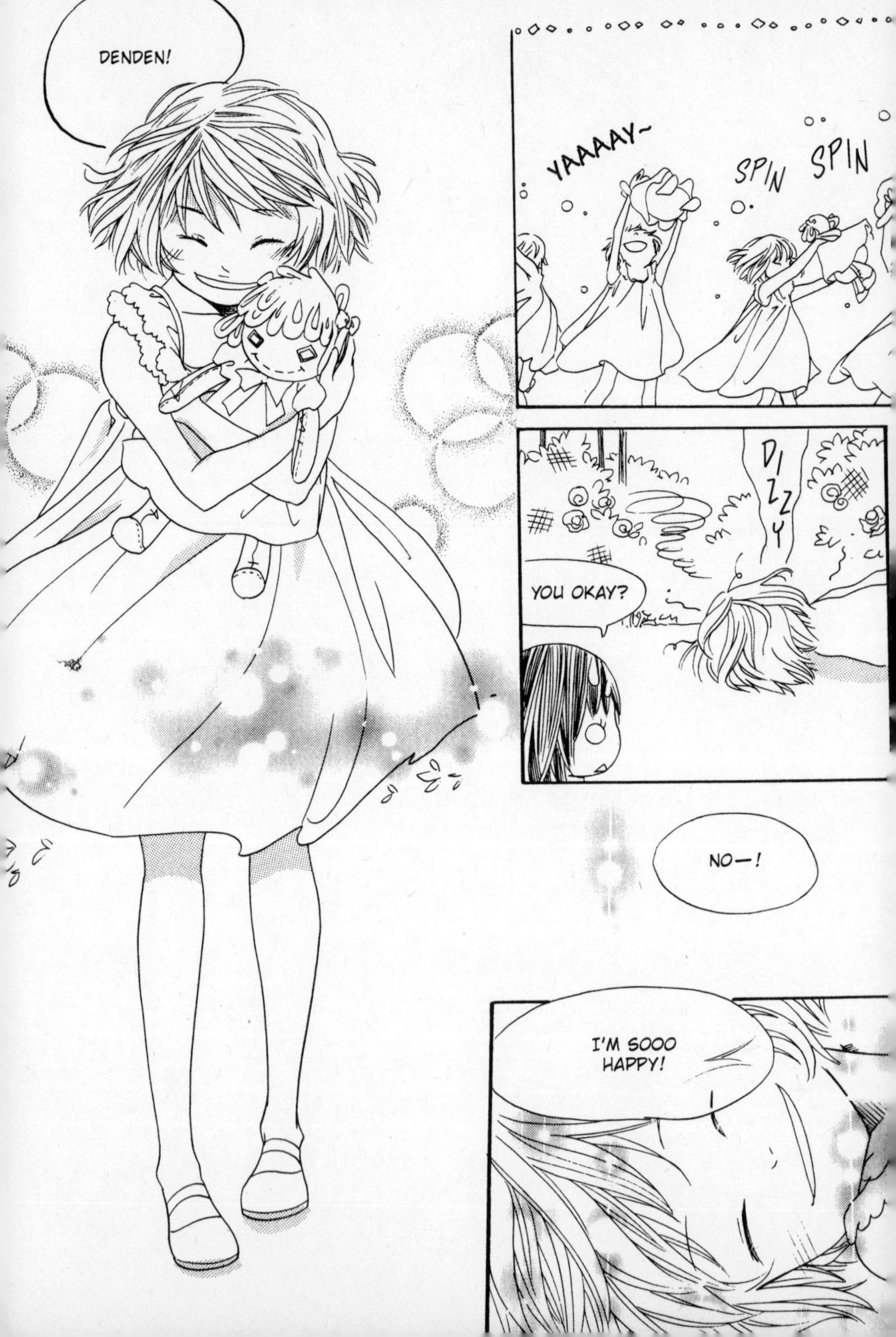
SPIN SPIN
YAAAAY~
DIZZY
YOU OKAY?
NO—!
I'M SOOO HAPPY!
DENDEN!

ME TOO.

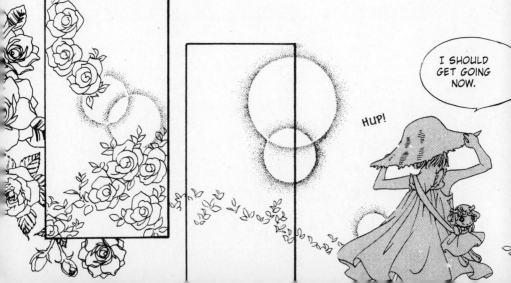

HUP!

I SHOULD GET GOING NOW.

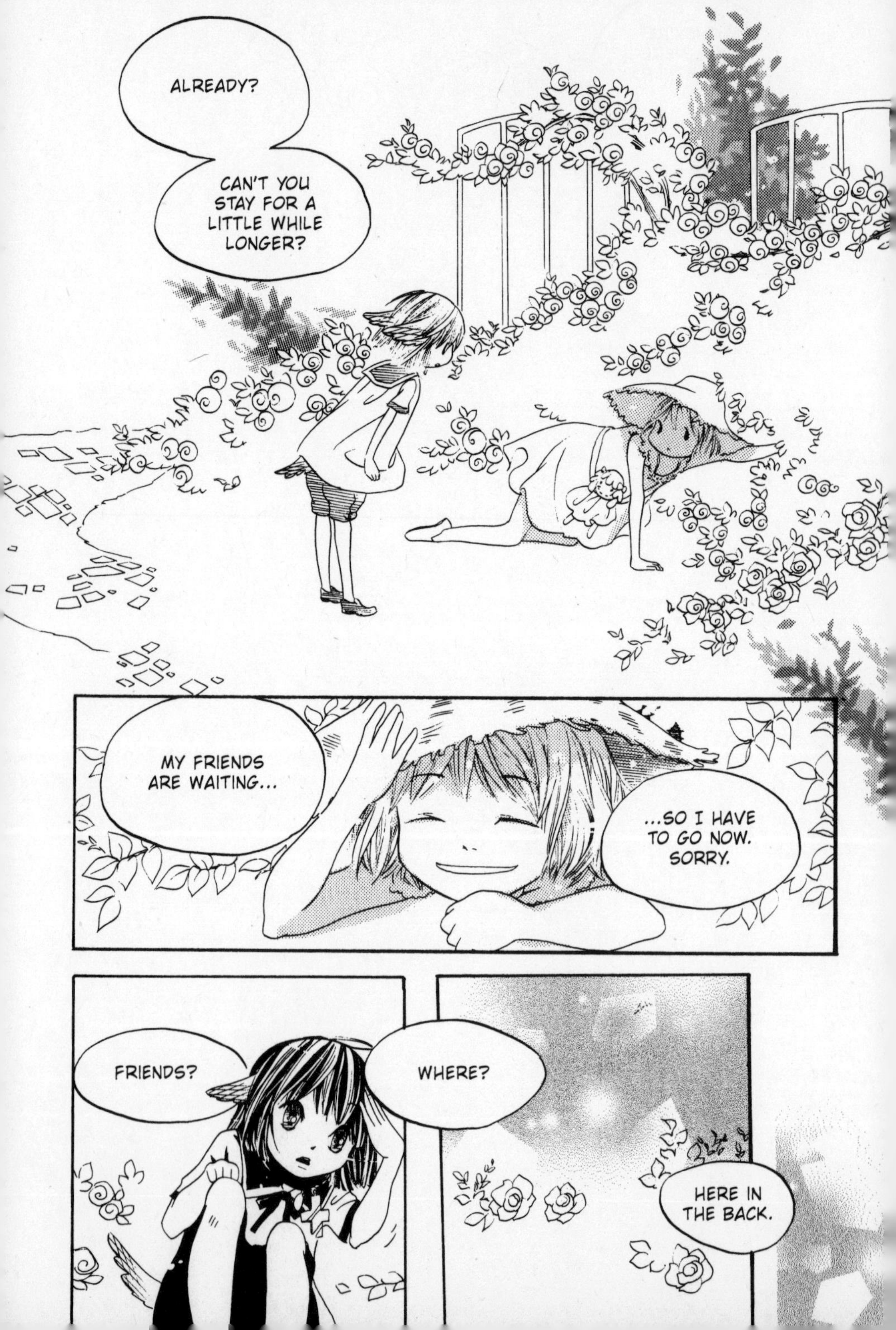
ALREADY?
CAN'T YOU STAY FOR A LITTLE WHILE LONGER?
MY FRIENDS ARE WAITING...
...SO I HAVE TO GO NOW. SORRY.
FRIENDS?
WHERE?
HERE IN THE BACK.

THEY'RE
ALL HERE
TOGETHER.

I CAN'T
REALLY SEE
WITH THE SUN
IN MY EYES...

?

HEY—

RUSTLE

RUSTLE

LET ME
COME TOO!

ROSA!

ROSA—

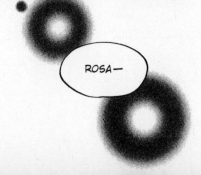

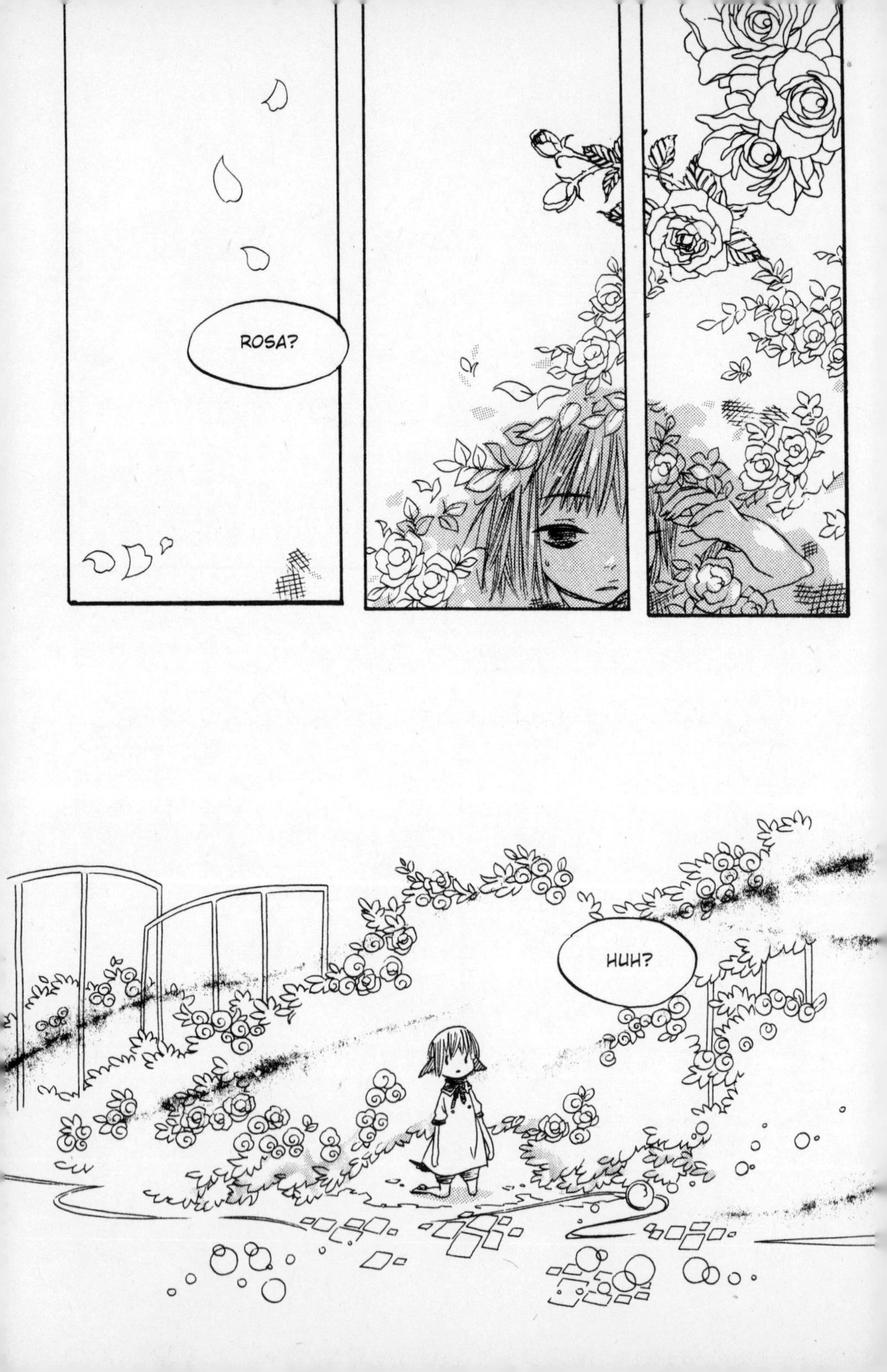
ROSA?
HUH?

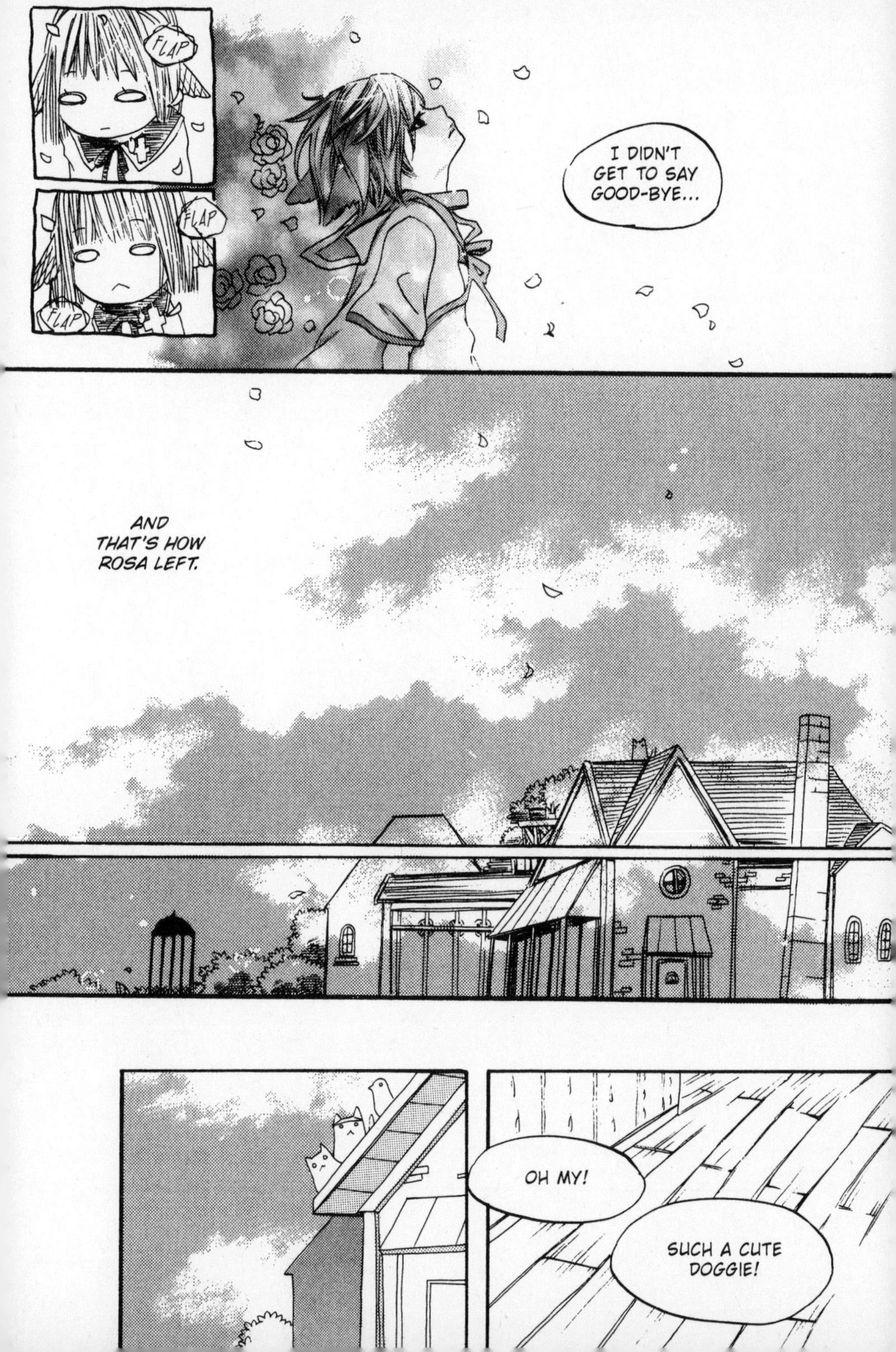
FLAP
FLAP
FLAP
I DIDN'T GET TO SAY GOOD-BYE...
AND THAT'S HOW ROSA LEFT.
OH MY!
SUCH A CUTE DOGGIE!

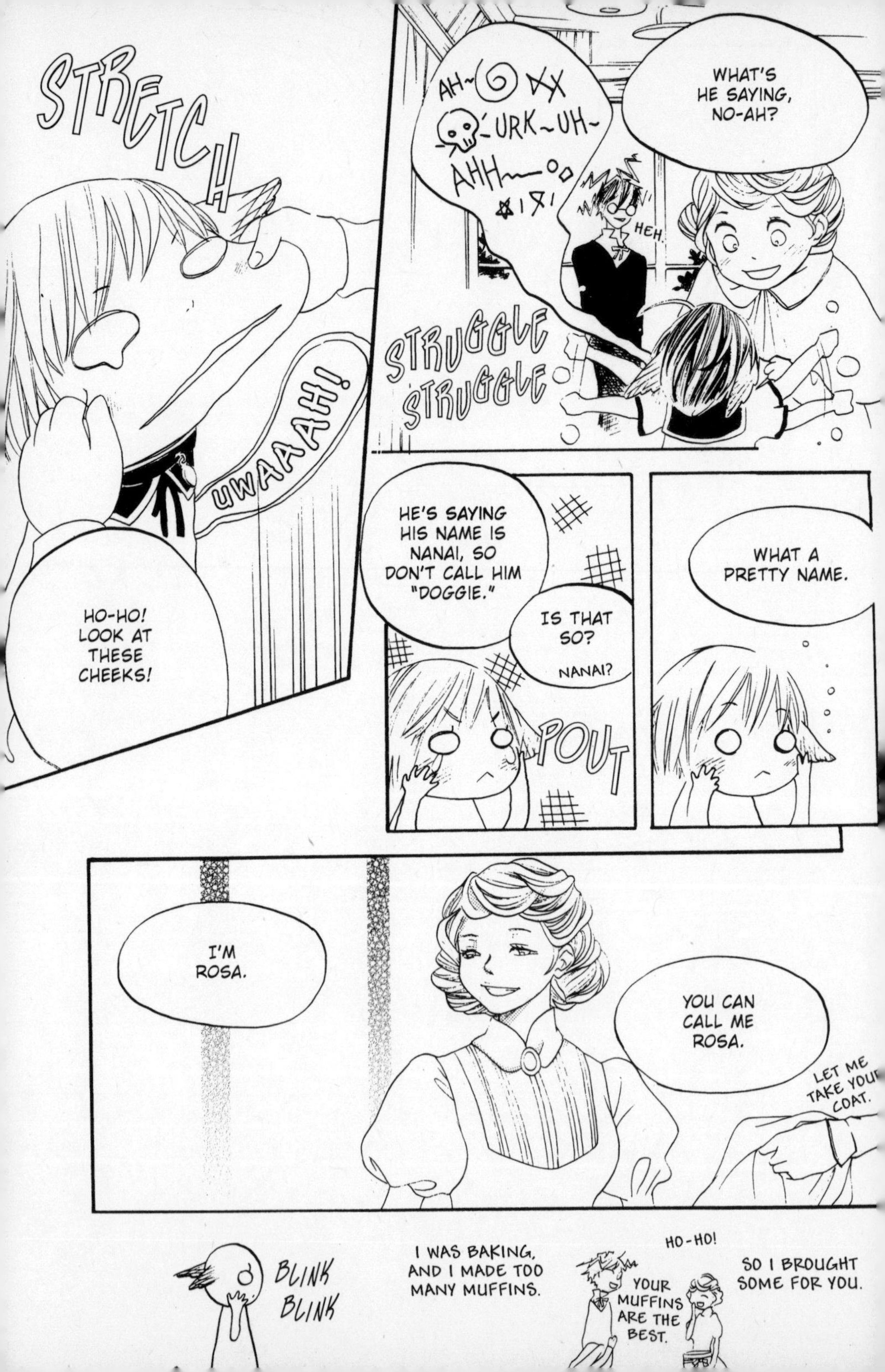

STRETCH
UWAAAAH!
HO-HO! LOOK AT THESE CHEEKS!
WHAT'S HE SAYING, NO-AH?
AH~ XX ~URK~UH~ AHH~
HEH.
STRUGGLE STRUGGLE
HE'S SAYING HIS NAME IS NANAI, SO DON'T CALL HIM "DOGGIE."
IS THAT SO?
NANAI?
POUT
WHAT A PRETTY NAME.
I'M ROSA.
YOU CAN CALL ME ROSA.
LET ME TAKE YOUR COAT.
BLINK BLINK
I WAS BAKING, AND I MADE TOO MANY MUFFINS.
HO-HO!
YOUR MUFFINS ARE THE BEST.
SO I BROUGHT SOME FOR YOU.

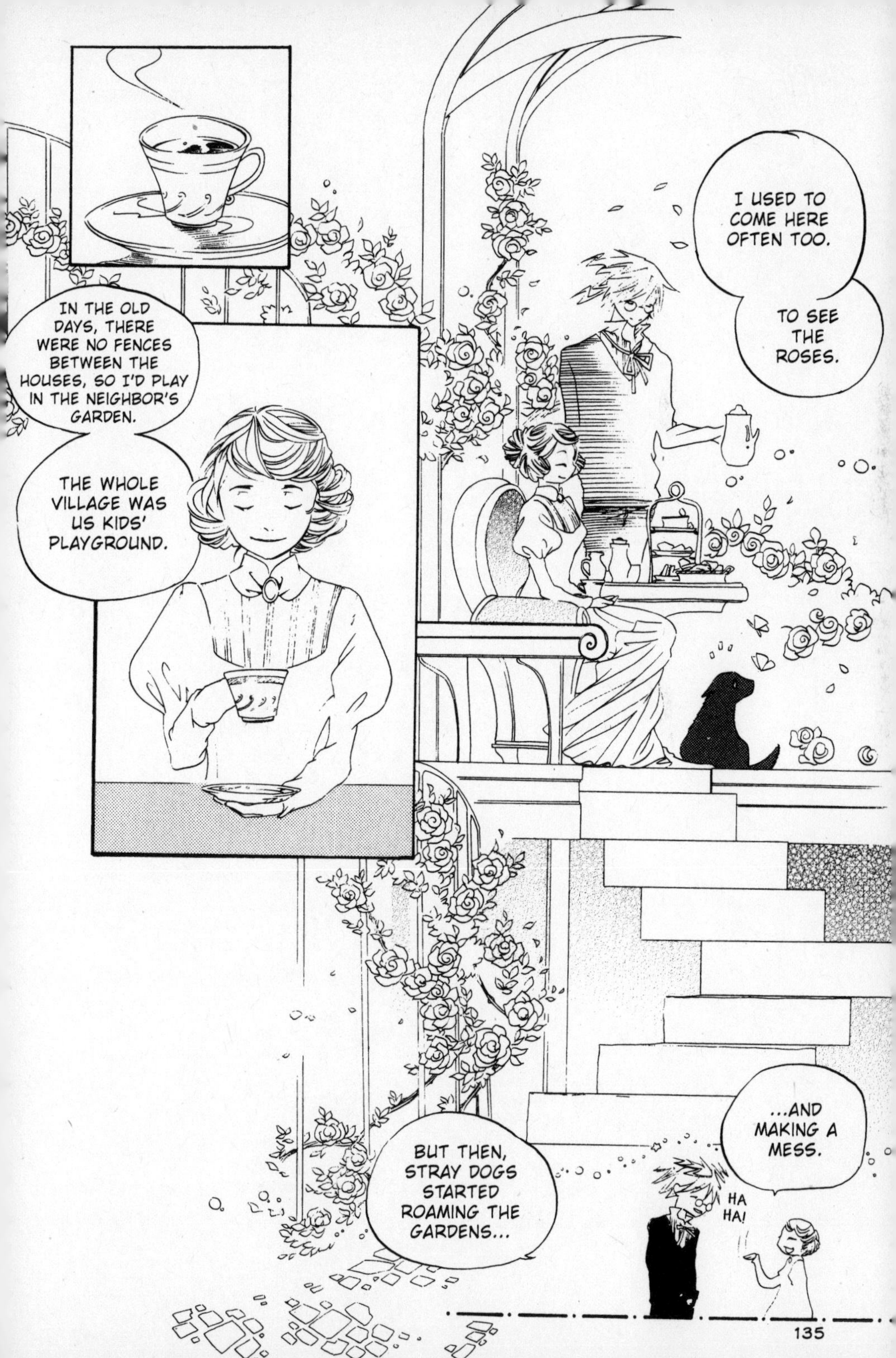

IN THE OLD DAYS, THERE WERE NO FENCES BETWEEN THE HOUSES, SO I'D PLAY IN THE NEIGHBOR'S GARDEN.
THE WHOLE VILLAGE WAS US KIDS' PLAYGROUND.
I USED TO COME HERE OFTEN TOO.
TO SEE THE ROSES.
BUT THEN, STRAY DOGS STARTED ROAMING THE GARDENS...
...AND MAKING A MESS.
HA HA!

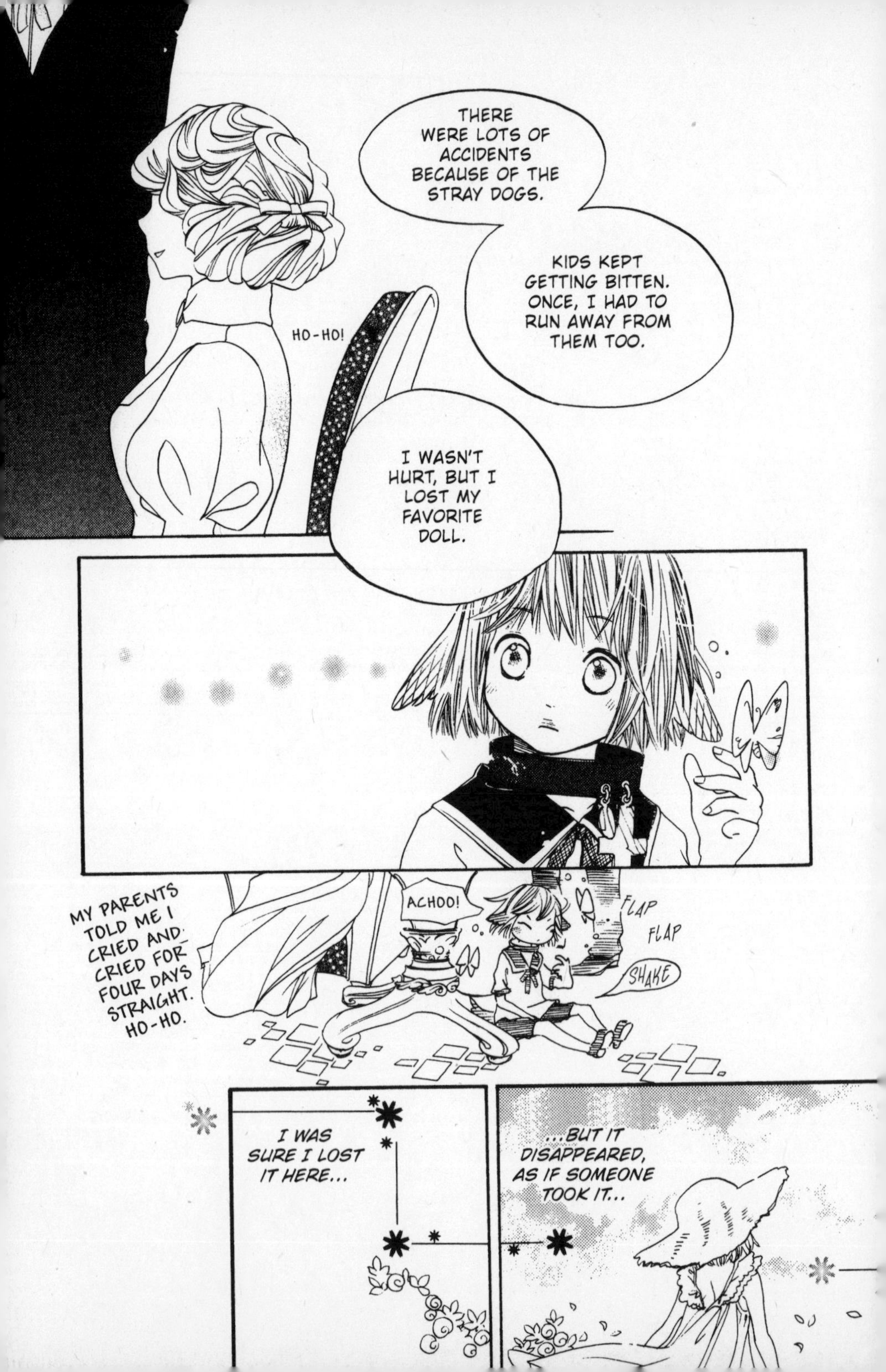
THERE WERE LOTS OF ACCIDENTS BECAUSE OF THE STRAY DOGS.
KIDS KEPT GETTING BITTEN. ONCE, I HAD TO RUN AWAY FROM THEM TOO.
HO-HO!
I WASN'T HURT, BUT I LOST MY FAVORITE DOLL.
ACHOO!
FLAP
FLAP
SHAKE
MY PARENTS TOLD ME I CRIED AND CRIED FOR FOUR DAYS STRAIGHT. HO-HO.
I WAS SURE I LOST IT HERE...
...BUT IT DISAPPEARED, AS IF SOMEONE TOOK IT...

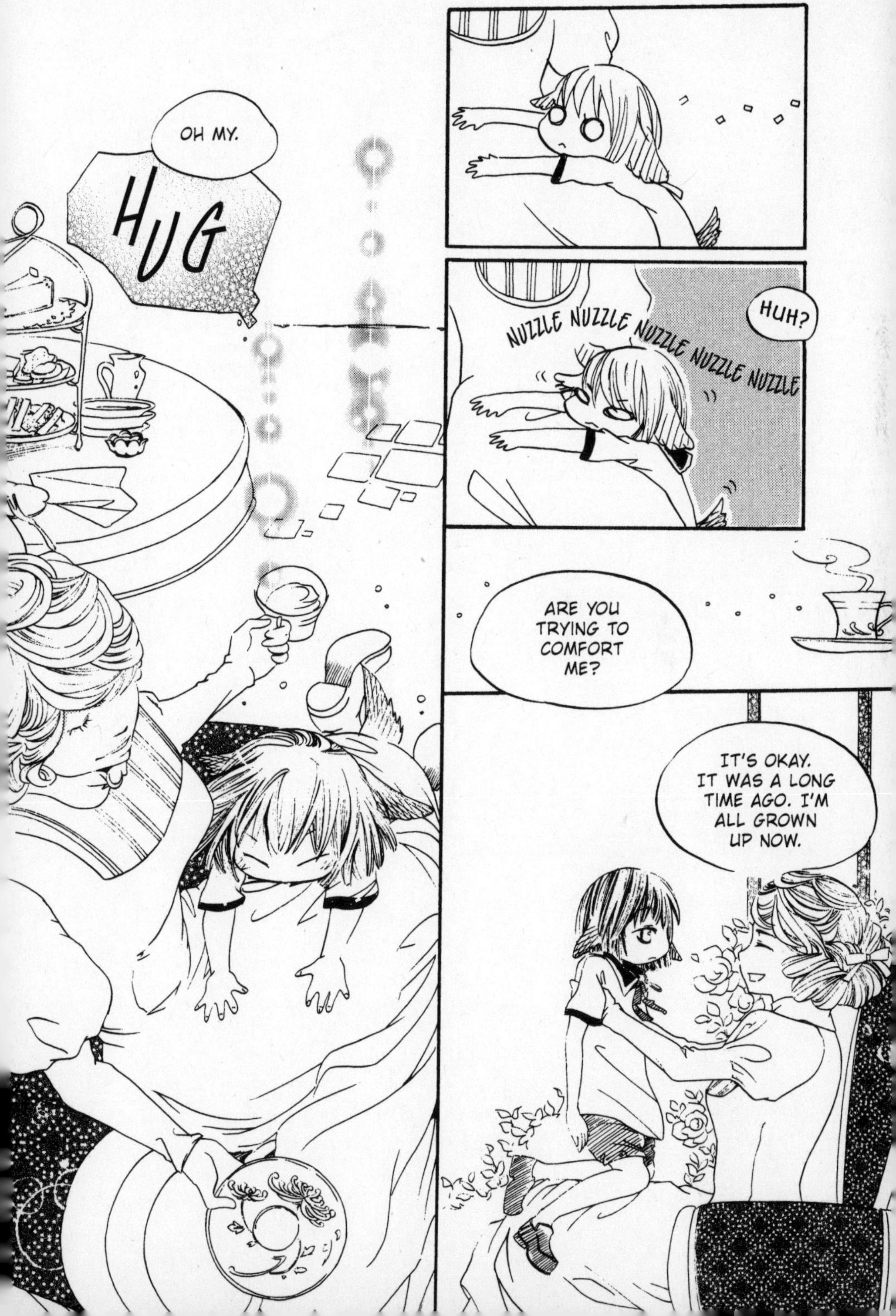
HUG
OH MY.
NUZZLE NUZZLE NUZZLE NUZZLE NUZZLE
HUH?
ARE YOU TRYING TO COMFORT ME?
IT'S OKAY. IT WAS A LONG TIME AGO. I'M ALL GROWN UP NOW.

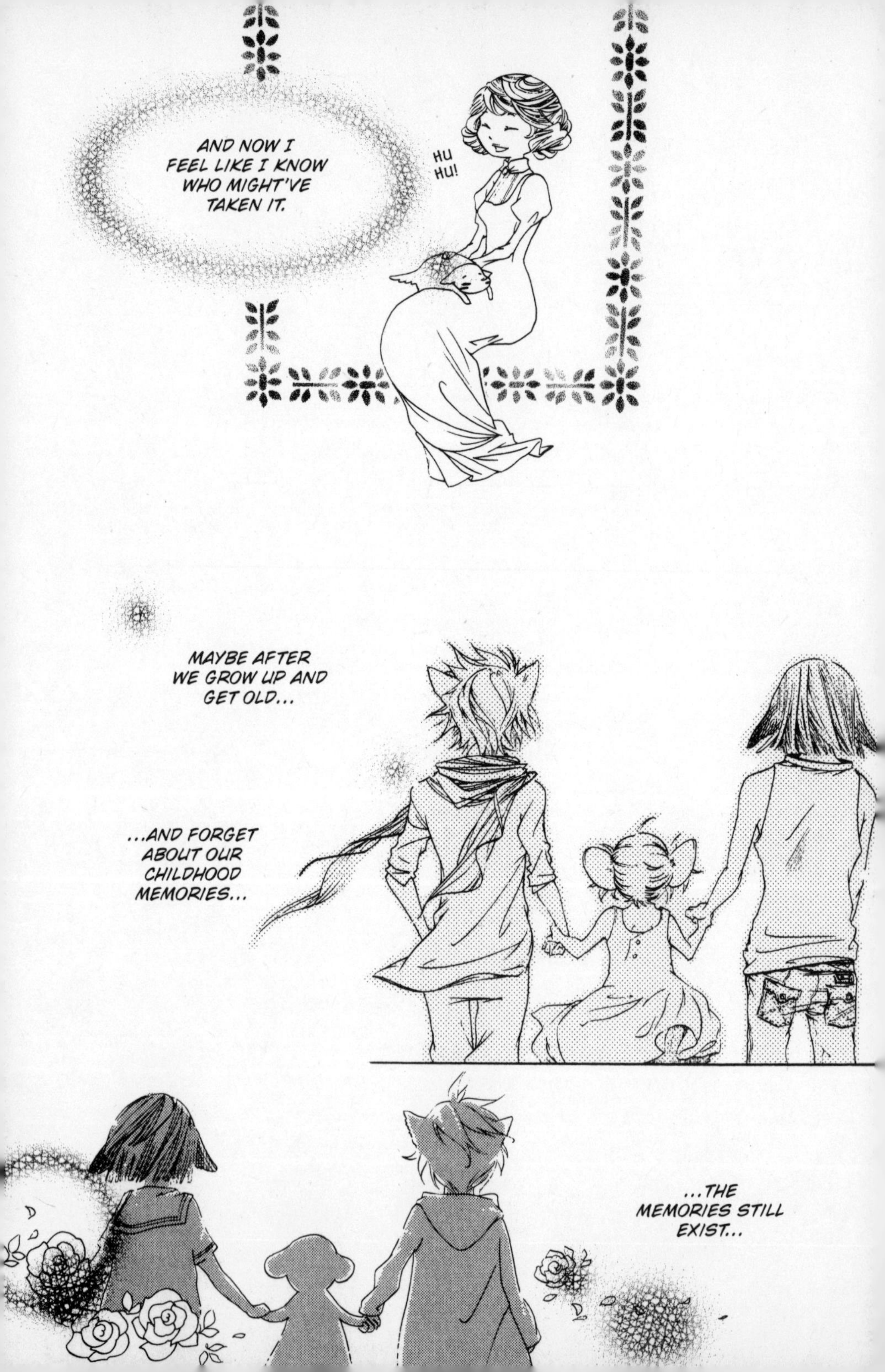
HU HU!
AND NOW I FEEL LIKE I KNOW WHO MIGHT'VE TAKEN IT.
MAYBE AFTER WE GROW UP AND GET OLD...
...AND FORGET ABOUT OUR CHILDHOOD MEMORIES...
...THE MEMORIES STILL EXIST...

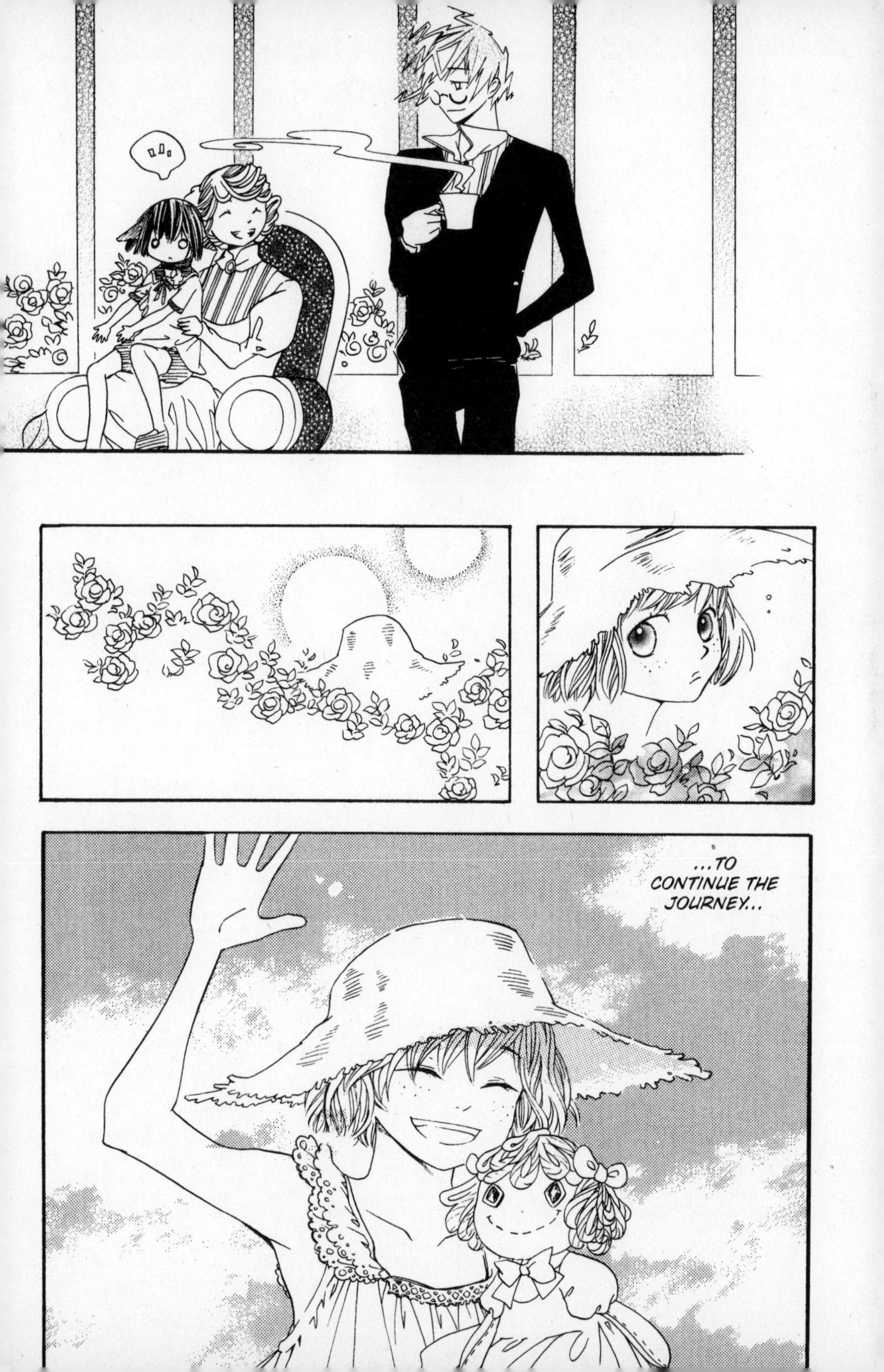
...TO
CONTINUE THE
JOURNEY...

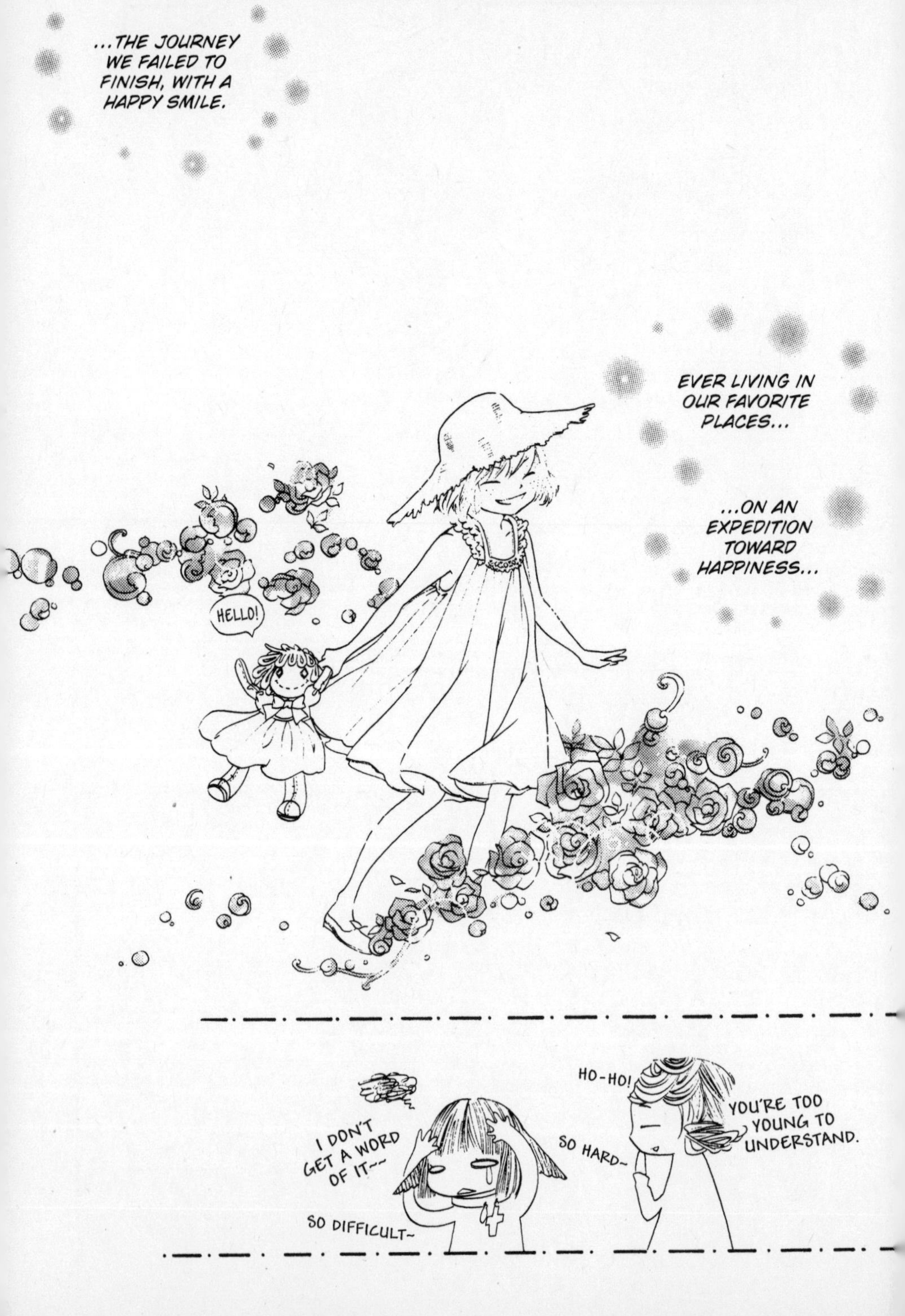
...THE JOURNEY WE FAILED TO FINISH, WITH A HAPPY SMILE.
EVER LIVING IN OUR FAVORITE PLACES...
...ON AN EXPEDITION TOWARD HAPPINESS...
HELLO!
HO-HO!
YOU'RE TOO YOUNG TO UNDERSTAND.
SO HARD~
I DON'T GET A WORD OF IT~~
SO DIFFICULT~

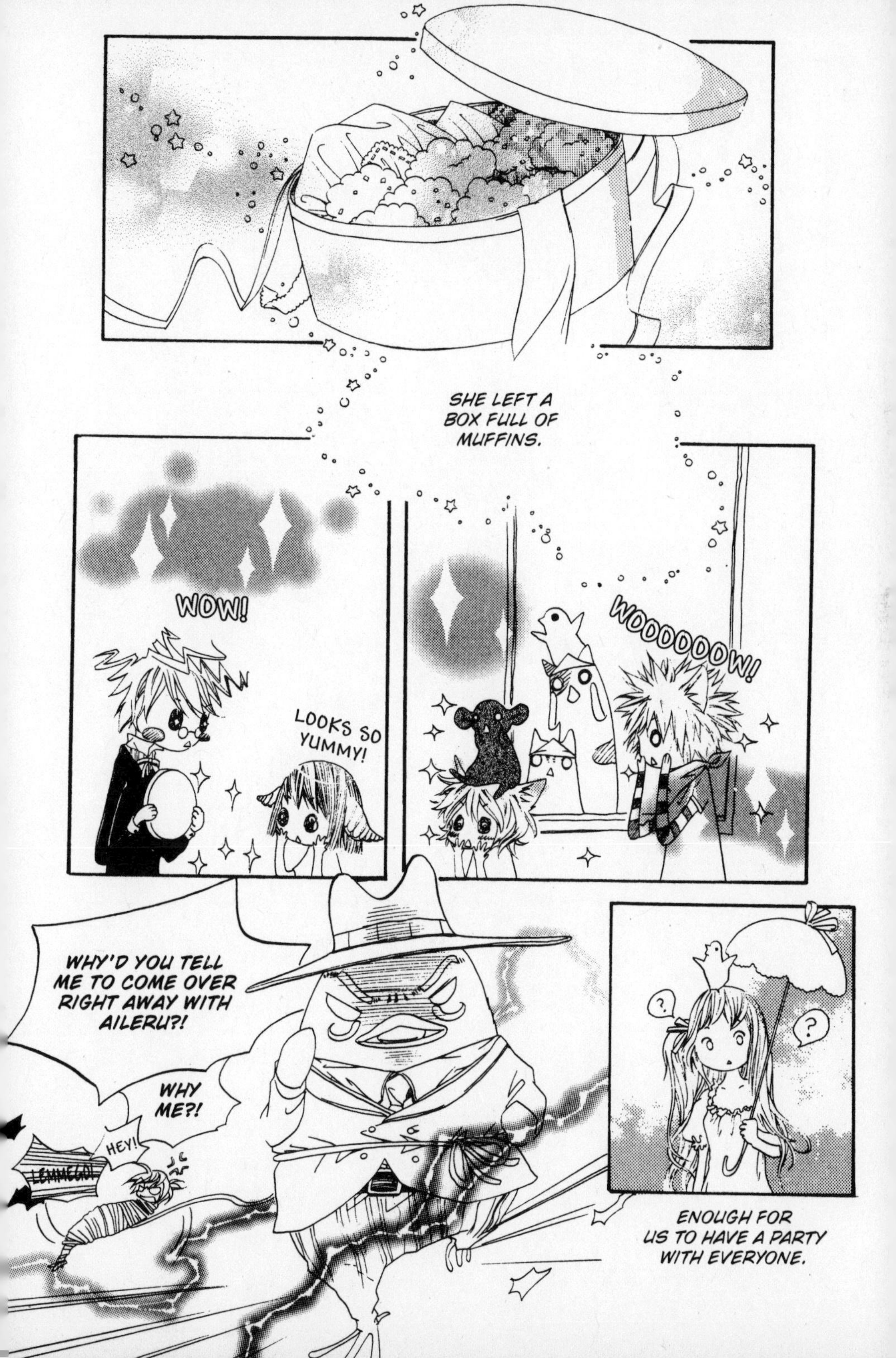
SHE LEFT A BOX FULL OF MUFFINS.
WOOOOOOOW!
WOW!
LOOKS SO YUMMY!
ENOUGH FOR US TO HAVE A PARTY WITH EVERYONE.
WHY'D YOU TELL ME TO COME OVER RIGHT AWAY WITH AILERU?!
WHY ME?!
HEY!
LEMMEGO!

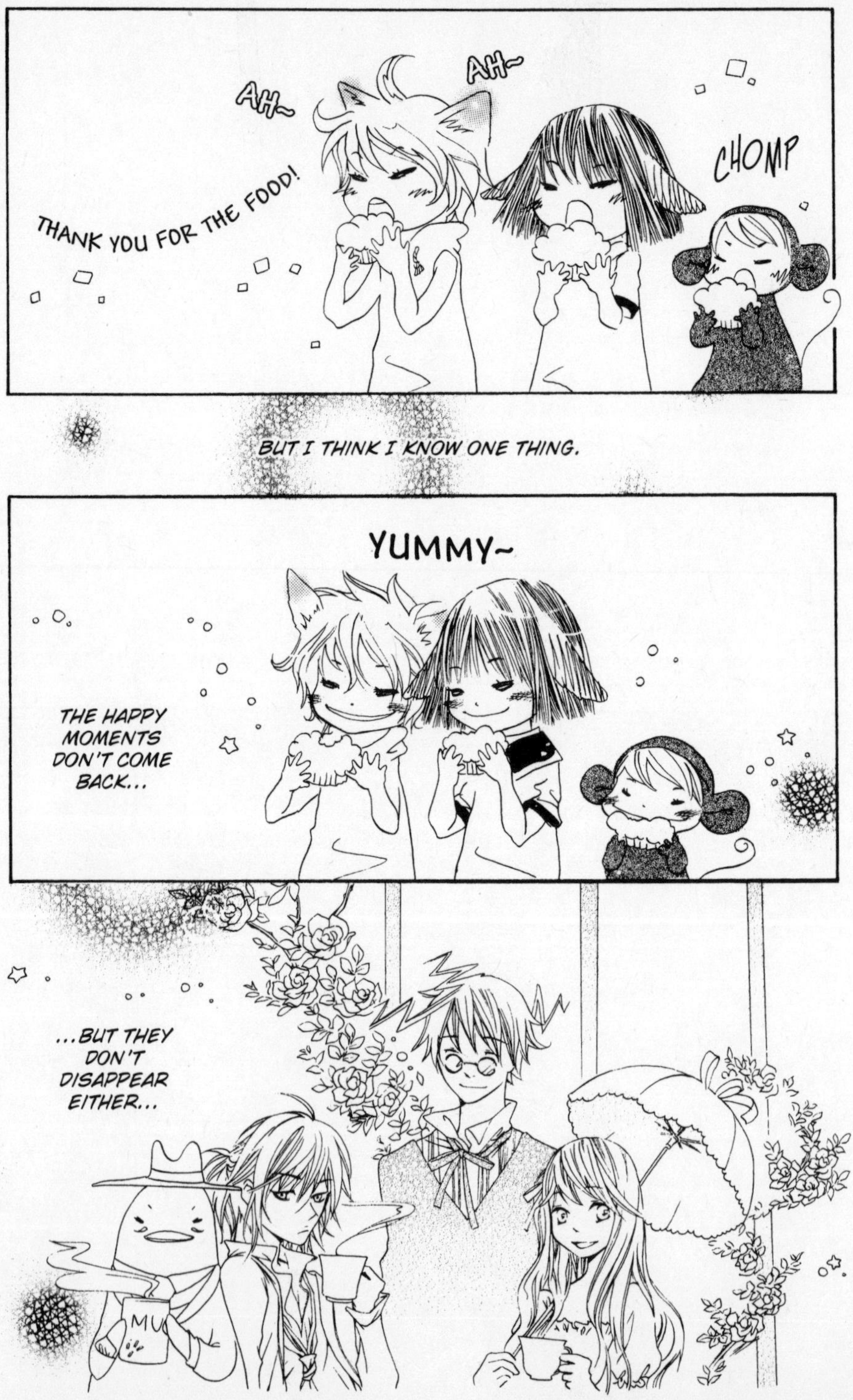
AH~
AH~
CHOMP
THANK YOU FOR THE FOOD!
BUT I THINK I KNOW ONE THING.
YUMMY~
THE HAPPY MOMENTS DON'T COME BACK...
...BUT THEY DON'T DISAPPEAR EITHER...
MU

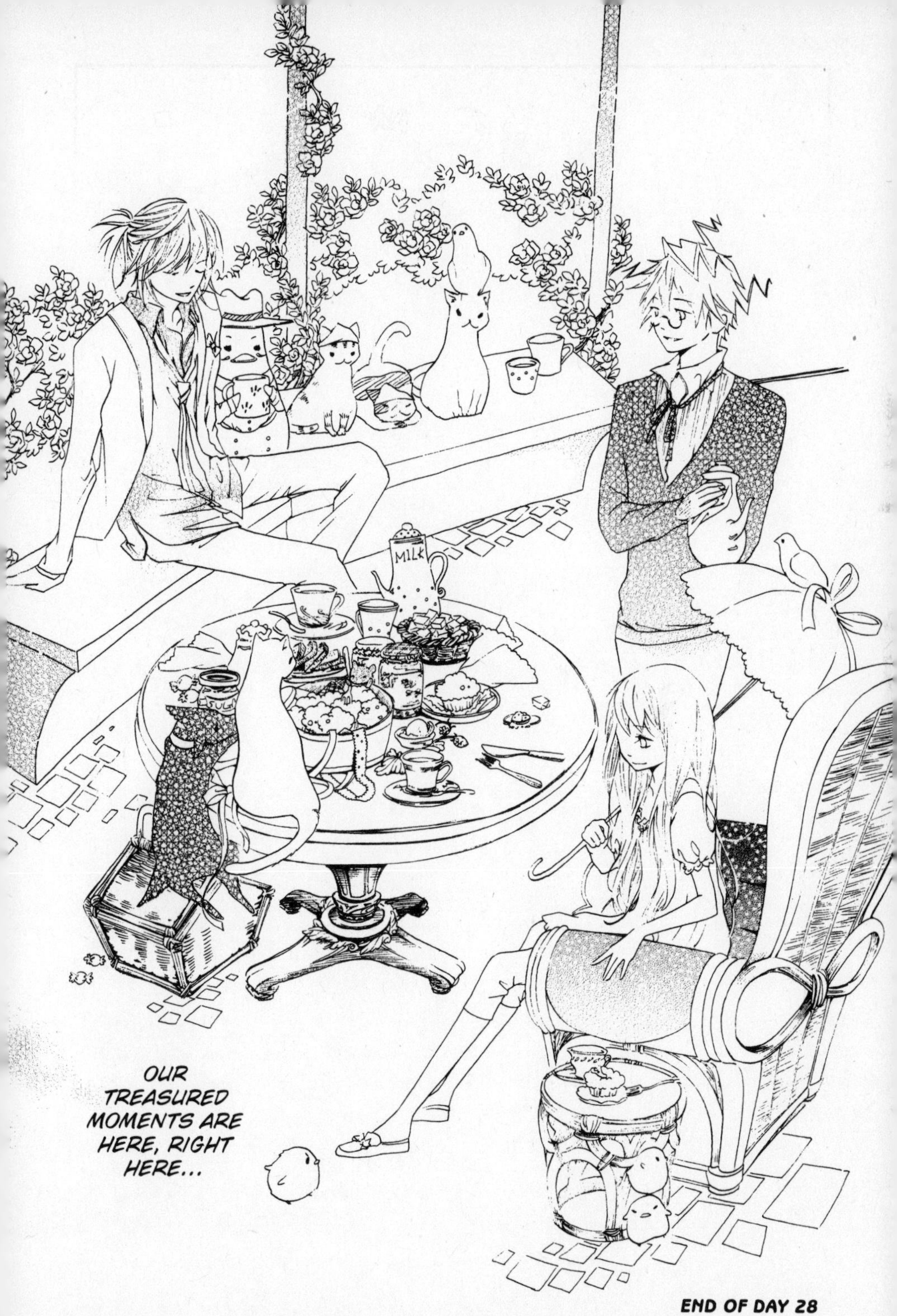
MILK
OUR TREASURED MOMENTS ARE HERE, RIGHT HERE...

END OF DAY 28

OUTFIT SWAP 1

OUTFIT SWAP 2

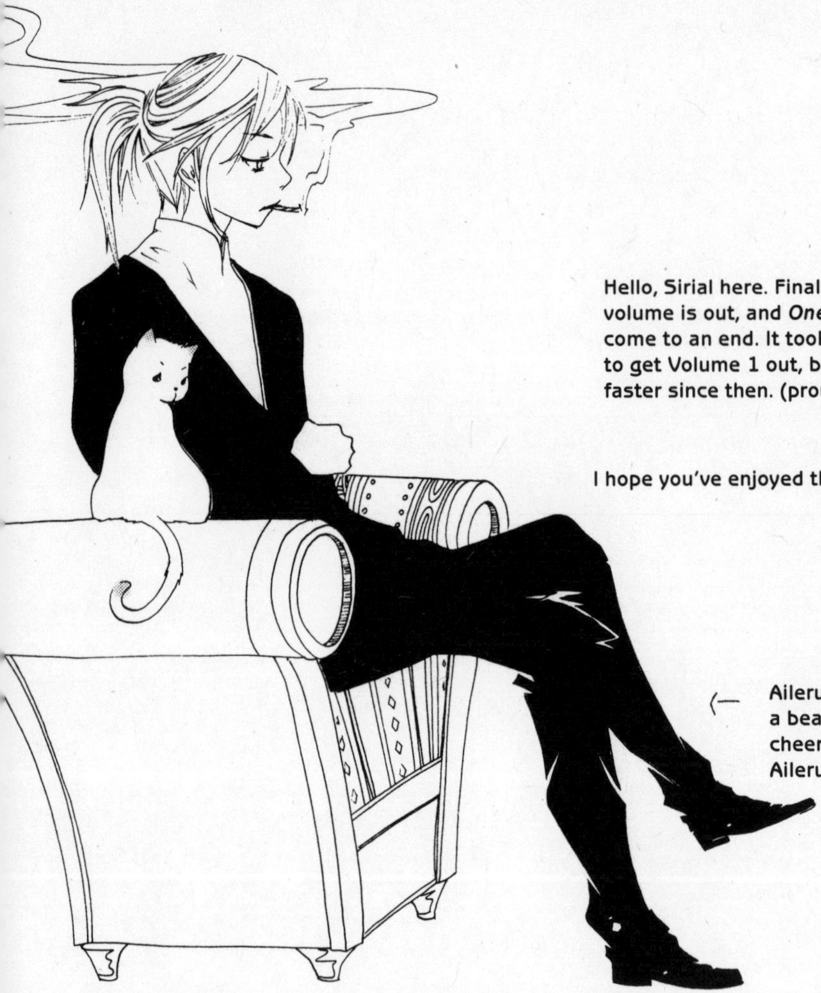

Hello, Sirial here. Finally the third volume is out, and *One Fine Day* has come to an end. It took a long time to get Volume 1 out, but I've gotten faster since then. (proud)

I hope you've enjoyed the books!

← Aileru is something of a beauty. My friend cheered for this pair: Aileru-Guru. (Pfft!)

Official couple #1. Will Nanai ever be able to confess his feelings to Rang?

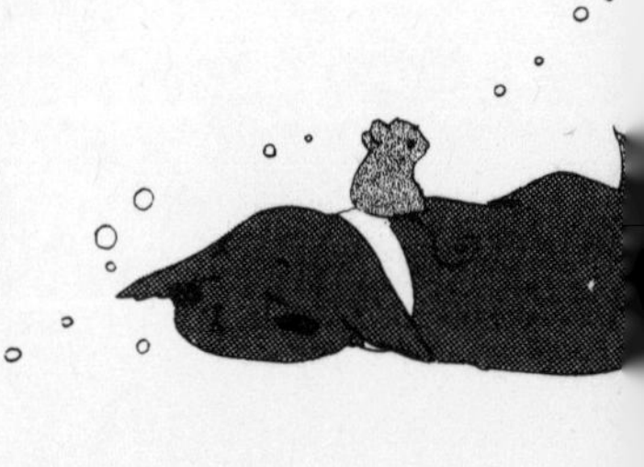

Confession time.

I made a lot of mistakes, but when I asked my friend, she said that Rang's size differences were the most shocking. So I drew them all! Original size, middle size that appears now and then, small size that fits in No-Ah's hand, and the size of a three-year-old. It really is shocking! She was supposed to be a mouse but became a little girl who transforms instead.

Sorry—

It wasn't on purpose. At least you didn't get fat—

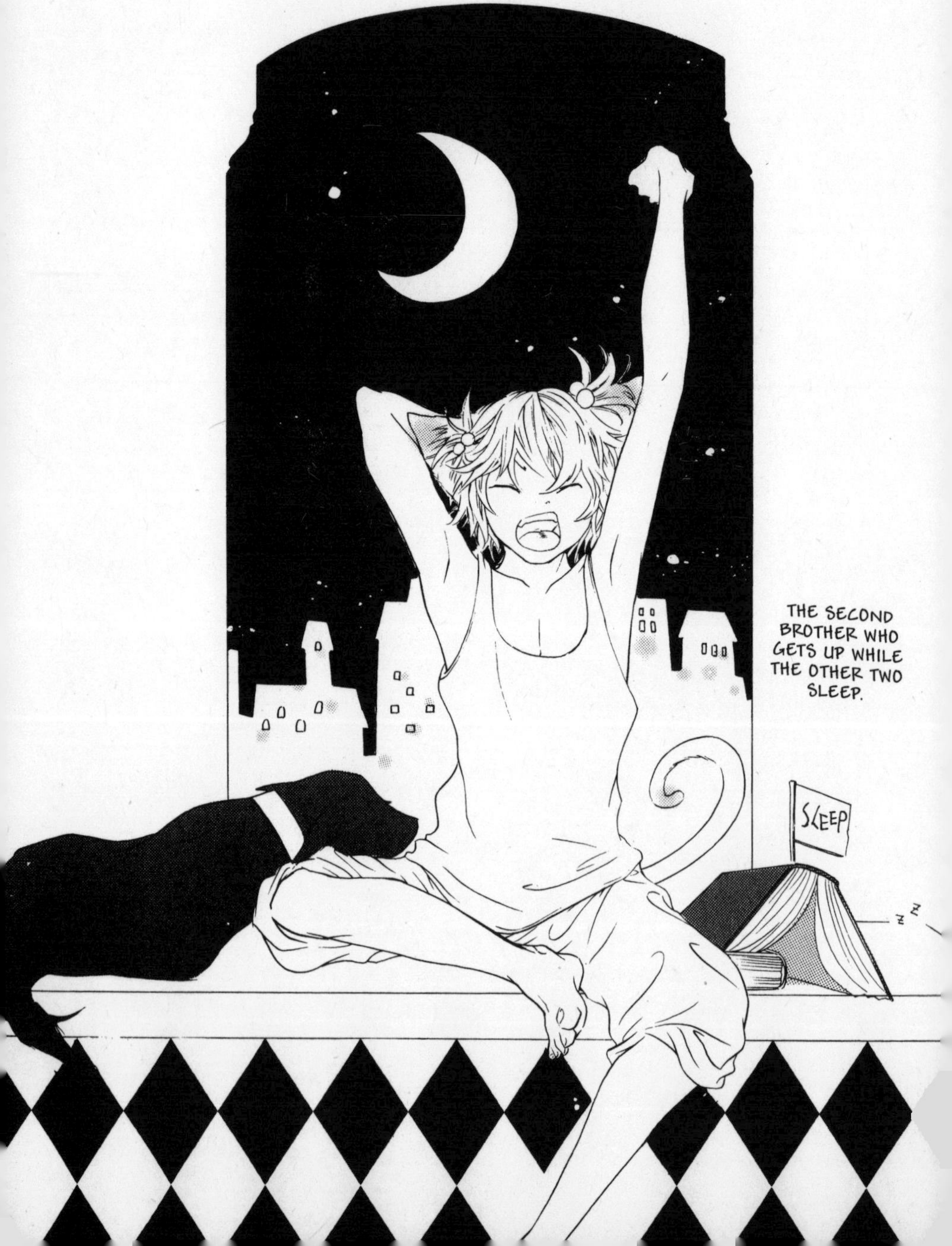
THE SECOND BROTHER WHO GETS UP WHILE THE OTHER TWO SLEEP.
SLEEP

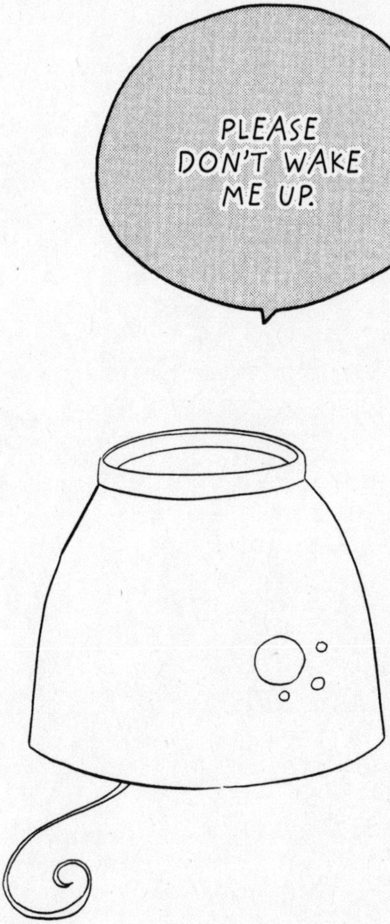
PLEASE DON'T WAKE ME UP.

The end of **one fine day**!!

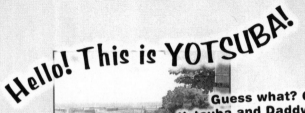

Hello! This is YOTSUBA!

Guess what? Guess what? Yotsuba and Daddy just moved here from waaaay over there!

And Yotsuba met these nice people next door and made new friends to play with!

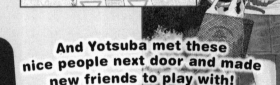

The pretty one took Yotsuba on a bike ride!
(Whoooa! There was a big hill!)

And Ena's a good drawer!
(Almost as good as Yotsuba!)

And their mom always gives Yotsuba ice cream!
(Yummy!)

And...
And...
OHHHH!

ENJOY EVERYTHING.

YOU SHOULD COME PLAY WITH YOTSUBA TOO!

Join Yotsuba as she delights in the
things many of us take for granted in
this Eisner-nominated series.

VOLUMES 1-8
AVAILABLE NOW!

Visit our website at www.yenpress.com.

Yotsuba&! © Kiyohiko Azuma / YOTUBA SUTAZIO

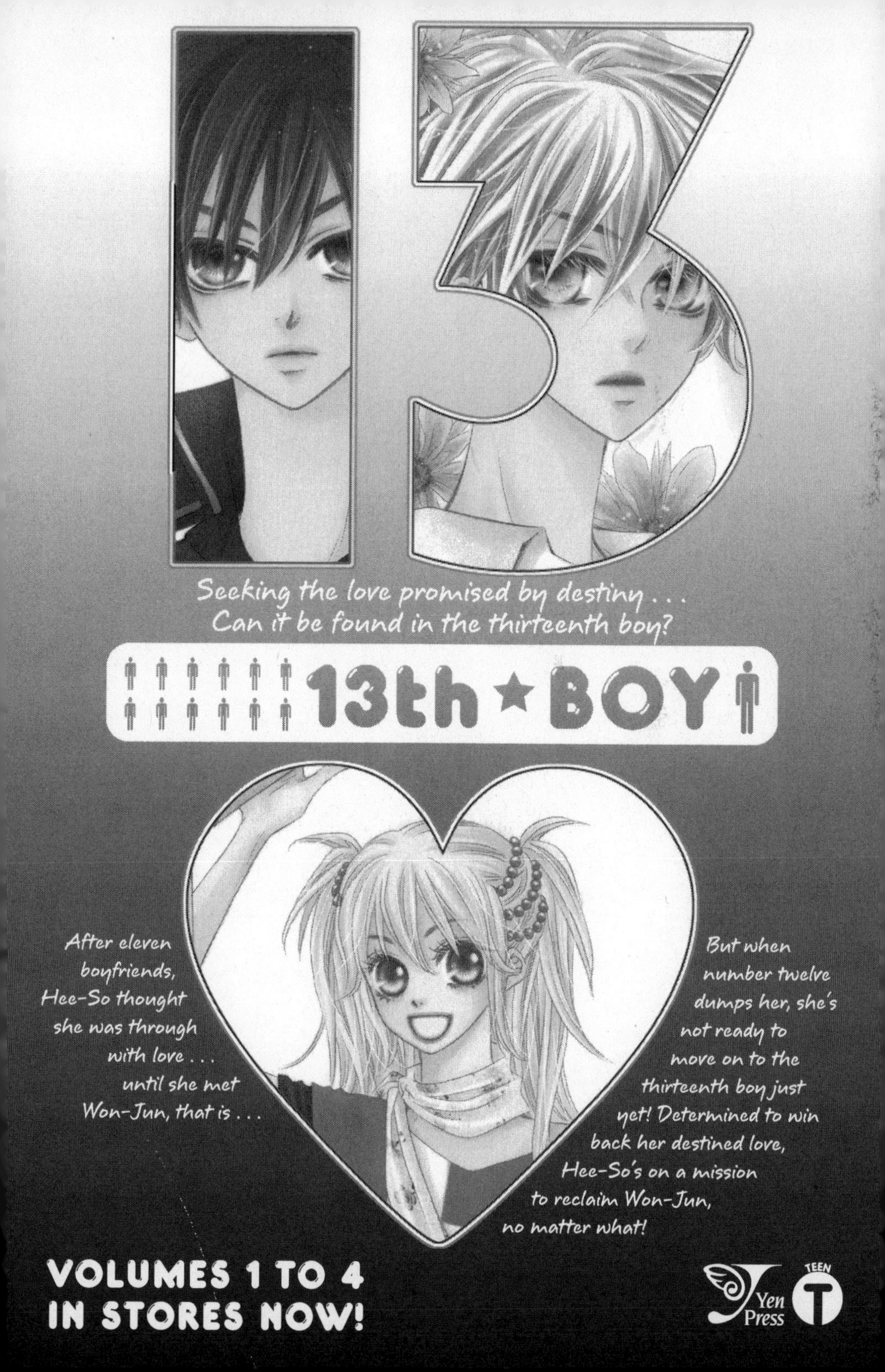
13
Seeking the love promised by destiny . . .
Can it be found in the thirteenth boy?
13th ★ BOY
After eleven boyfriends, Hee-So thought she was through with love . . . until she met Won-Jun, that is . . .
But when number twelve dumps her, she's not ready to move on to the thirteenth boy just yet! Determined to win back her destined love, Hee-So's on a mission to reclaim Won-Jun, no matter what!
VOLUMES 1 TO 4
IN STORES NOW!
Yen Press
TEEN
T

Wonderfully illustrated modern day crossover fantasy, available at your local bookstore or comic shop!

Apart from the fact her eyes turn red when the moon rises, Myung-Ee is your average, albeit boy-crazy, 5th grader. After picking a fight with her classmate Yu-Da Lee, she discovers a startling secret: the two of them are "earth rabbits" being hunted by the "fox tribe" of the moon!

Five years pass and Myung-Ee transfers to a new school in search of pretty boys. There, she unexpectedly reunites with Yu-Da. The problem is he doesn't remember a thing about her or their shared past!

Moon Boy 월요일 소년 1~8

Lee YoungYou

Yen Press
www.yenpress.com

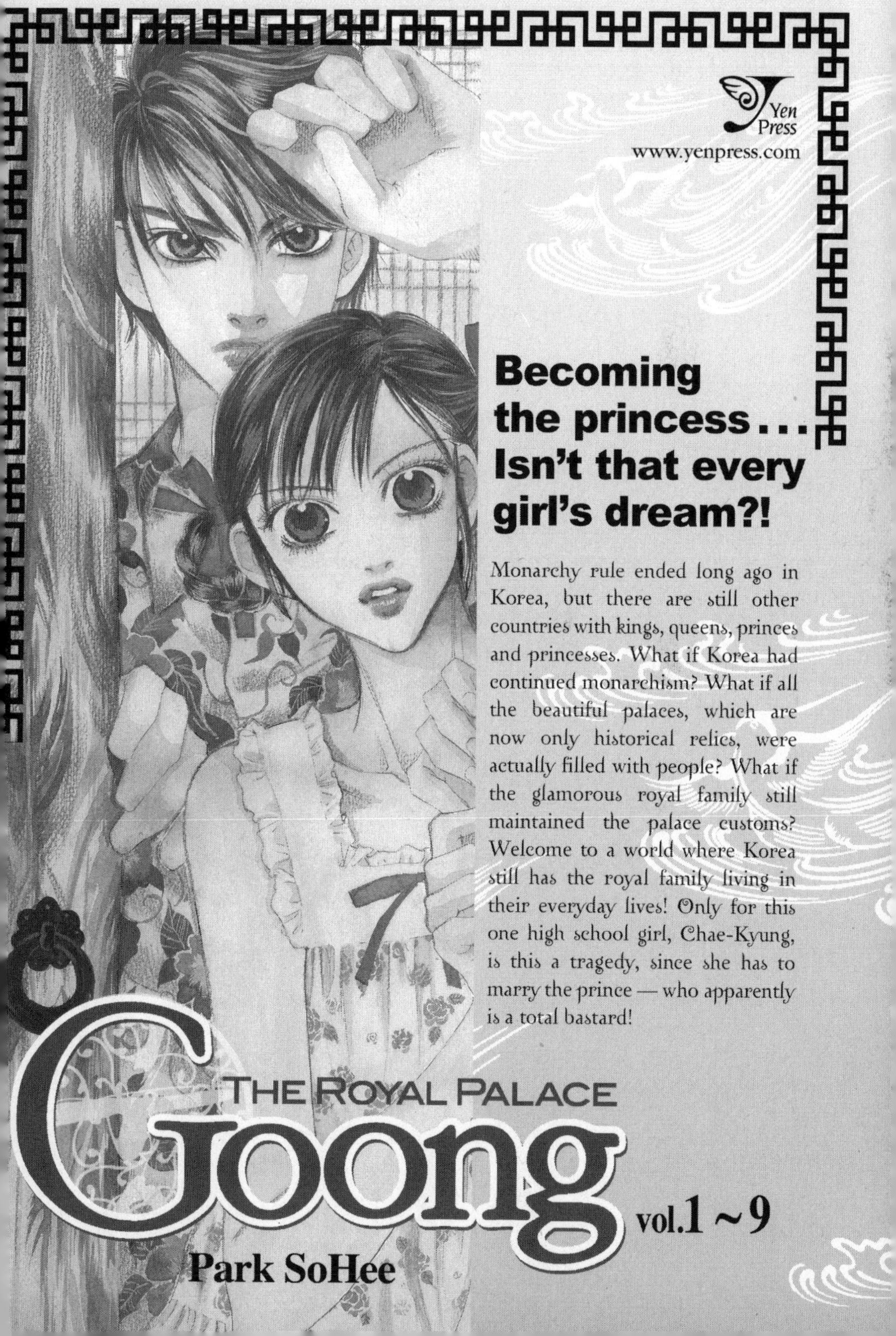
Yen Press
www.yenpress.com
Becoming the princess... Isn't that every girl's dream?!
Monarchy rule ended long ago in Korea, but there are still other countries with kings, queens, princes and princesses. What if Korea had continued monarchism? What if all the beautiful palaces, which are now only historical relics, were actually filled with people? What if the glamorous royal family still maintained the palace customs? Welcome to a world where Korea still has the royal family living in their everyday lives! Only for this one high school girl, Chae-Kyung, is this a tragedy, since she has to marry the prince — who apparently is a total bastard!
THE ROYAL PALACE
Goong
vol.1 ~ 9
Park SoHee

www.yenpress.com

THE HIGHLY ANTICIPATED NEW TITLE FROM THE CREATORS OF <DEMON DIARY>!

Dong-Young is a royal daughter of heaven, betrothed to the King of Hell. Determined to escape her fate, she runs away before the wedding. The four Guardians of Heaven are ordered to find the angel princess while she's hiding out on planet Earth - disguised as a boy! Will she be able to escape from her faith?! This is a cute gender-bending tale, a romantic comedy/fantasy book about an angel, the King of Hell, and four super-powered chaperones...

AVAILABLE AT BOOKSTORES NEAR YOU!

Angel Diary 1~12

Kara · Lee YunHee

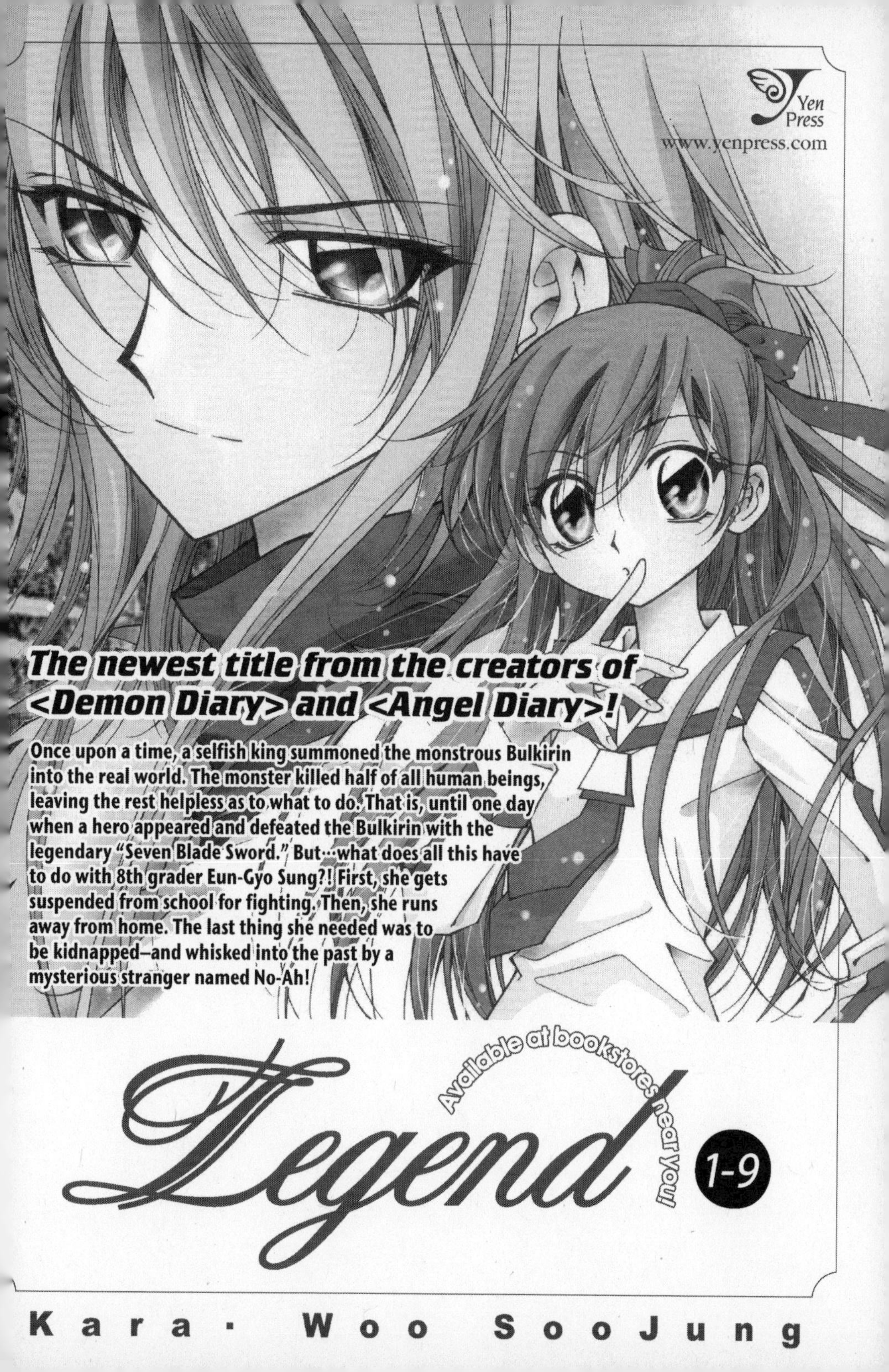
Yen Press
www.yenpress.com
The newest title from the creators of <Demon Diary> and <Angel Diary>!
Once upon a time, a selfish king summoned the monstrous Bulkirin into the real world. The monster killed half of all human beings, leaving the rest helpless as to what to do. That is, until one day when a hero appeared and defeated the Bulkirin with the legendary "Seven Blade Sword." But…what does all this have to do with 8th grader Eun-Gyo Sung?! First, she gets suspended from school for fighting. Then, she runs away from home. The last thing she needed was to be kidnapped–and whisked into the past by a mysterious stranger named No-Ah!
Legend
Available at bookstores near you!
1-9
Kara · Woo SooJung

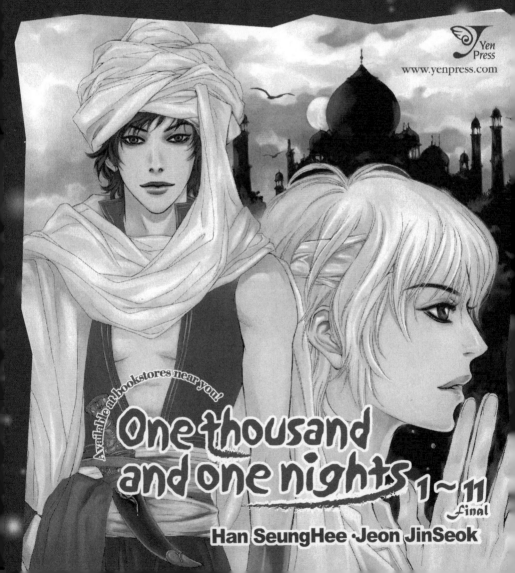

A totally new Arabian nights, where Scheherazade is a guy!

Everyone knows the story of Scheherazade and her wonderful tales from the Arabian Nights. For one thousand and one nights, the stories that she created entertained the mad Sultan and eventually saved her life. In this version, Scheherazade is a guy who disguises himself as a woman to save his sister from the mad Sultan. When he puts his life on the line, what kind of strange and unique stories will he tell? This new twist on one of the greatest classical tales might just keep you awake for another ONE THOUSAND AND ONE NIGHTS!

Yen Press

www.yenpress.com

Available at bookstores near you!

One thousand and one nights 1~11 final

Han SeungHee · Jeon JinSeok

ONE FINE DAY ③

SIRIAL

Translation: JuYoun Lee

Lettering: Abigail Blackman

ONE FINE DAY Vol. 3 © 2008 by Sirial, DAEWON C.I. Inc. All rights reserved. First published in Korea in 2008 by DAEWON C.I. Inc. English translation rights in USA, Canada, UK and Commonwealth arranged by Daewon C.I. Inc. through TOPAZ Agency Inc.

English translation © 2010 Yen Press, LLC

Yen Press
1290 Avenue of the Americas
New York, NY 10104

Visit us at yenpress.com
facebook.com/yenpress
twitter.com/yenpress
yenpress.tumblr.com
instagram.com/yenpress

First Yen Press Edition: September 2010

Yen Press is an imprint of Yen Press, LLC.
The Yen Press name and logo are trademarks of Yen Press, LLC.

ISBN: 978-0-316-09761-1

10 9 8 7 6 5 4 3 2

OPM

Printed in the United States of America